Microsoft®

Windows® Embedded CE 6.0 Fundamentals

D1359978

Stanislav Pavlov
Pavel Belevsky

PUBLISHED BY
Microsoft Press
A Division of Microsoft Corporation
One Microsoft Way
Redmond, Washington 98052-6399

Library of Congress Control Number: 2008931433

Printed and bound in the United States of America.

1 2 3 4 5 6 7 8 9   QWT   3 2 1 0 9 8

Distributed in Canada by H.B. Fenn and Company Ltd.

A CIP catalogue record for this book is available from the British Library.

Microsoft Press books are available through booksellers and distributors worldwide. For further information about international editions, contact your local Microsoft Corporation office or contact Microsoft Press International directly at fax (425) 936-7329. Visit our Web site at www.microsoft.com/mspress. Send comments to mspinput@microsoft.com.

Acquisitions Editor: Ben Ryan
Editorial Production: Biblioso Corporation
Technical Reviewer: Stas Pavlov and the Windows Embedded CE development team
Project Sponsor: Sondra Webber
Cover: Tom Draper Design

Body Part No. X14-95993

Dedication

Dedicated to Taras V. Demyankov,
without whom I would not have become the kind of person and the specialist that I am,
and without whom this book would have never been possible.
He was really looking forward to this book appearing,
but unfortunately he did not live to see that day.

Contents at a Glance

Table of Contents

Chapter 1
Introduction

This book addresses technical aspects of building operating system (OS) images for embedded applications and contains a wide spectrum of practical information. A developer can use this book as an everyday reference. It is our hope that this book will help the reader to build successful solutions by using the Microsoft Windows Embedded CE platform. This book is intended for everyone who develops or plans the development of embedded devices based on Windows Embedded CE. If you are just learning about the Windows Embedded CE operating system, this book can serve as a starting point for further learning. If you are already familiar with Windows Embedded CE, this book provides advice and recommendations for developing devices.

About This Book

The book consists of 10 chapters, a reference list, and resources, as follows.

Chapter 1: Introduction

This chapter provides a first look at Windows Embedded CE 6.0 R2, as well as its capabilities and development tools. The chapter provides an overview of the operating system, where and how it can be used, and a brief description of other available embedded operating systems from Microsoft.

Chapter 2: Operating System and Application Development Tools

The Windows Embedded CE 6.0 R2 operating system includes an easy-to-use suite of developer tools that enables you to configure and build an image of the operating system, develop drivers, and create applications. The chapter discusses the process of installing the development environment and covers the available tools and their capabilities.

Chapter 3: Operating System Architecture

This chapter provides a detailed look into the architecture of the Windows Embedded CE 6.0 R2 operating system, including kernel architecture, virtual memory, processes, interrupts, and scheduler. Windows Embedded CE 6.0 is a real-time, componentized, multithreading operating system that supports preemptive multitasking and runs on multiple processor architectures, including ARM, Microprocessor without Interlocked Pipeline Stages (MIPS), x86, and SH4. The Windows Embedded CE operating system operates in the virtual address space of 4 gigabytes (GB). The system kernel uses the upper 2 GB of virtual memory in the OS, while the user process uses the lower 2 GB of virtual memory.

Chapter 4: Build System

This chapter addresses the Windows Embedded CE 6.0 R2 unified build system for OS images. The Windows Embedded CE tools use a unified build system. An operating system can be built by using the Microsoft Visual Studio 2005 integrated environment or by using the command line. The build tools are composed of batch files and console utilities. The build process is controlled by the preconfigured environment variables and the parameters that are passed when a program call is made. Environment variables are initialized during the first stage by using the command files (the PBInitEnv.bat file is called, from which a call is then made to the Wince.bat file by supplying it with all necessary parameters). Blddemo.bat is the main command file of the build system. It represents a point of entry into the system because it launches other files and build utilities that can launch other command files and build utilities.

Chapter 5: Board Support Package (BSP)

This chapter discusses various aspects of the BSPe, such as the architecture, the structure of package directories, and the common platform code. The BSP enables a developer to build a run-time image for a specific hardware platform. To build an operating system image for a hardware platform, it necessary to have the corresponding BSP. Usually, BSP development is the most labor-intensive part of building a device. BSP development requires that the developer know the hardware architecture as well as the operating system architecture. All interaction between the operating system and the device is implemented in the BSP. Therefore, the quality of the BSP determines the resulting quality of the device.

Chapter 6: Driver Architecture

This chapter covers the architecture of drivers for Windows Embedded CE 6.0 R2, including classification according to various criteria, implementation architecture, native and stream drivers, loading drivers, and driver development. A driver represents code that provides the operating system with an interface to a physical or a virtual device. The operating system expects a driver to implement a predetermined interface, which creates an abstraction of a specific hardware or virtual device implementation. Under Windows Embedded CE, in most cases, a set of functions and control codes (IOTCLs) represents this interface that the driver code implements. The driver infrastructure makes it possible for a certain component of the operating system to enable other components of the operating system and applications to use an integrated interface with the hardware, regardless of its implementation.

Chapter 7: Starting the Operating System

Understanding the processes that occur at system startup is important for building Windows Embedded CE–based devices. By looking at the process of system initialization, you can more clearly understand the role of each component included in the system kernel, as well as the role of the code supplied by Microsoft and the one developed by the BSP manufacturer.

Chapter 8: Building Devices

The process of building devices on the Windows Embedded CE platform can be divided into the following several stages:

- Device planning.
    - Defining the device requirements.
    - Choosing and/or planning the development of the hardware platform.
    - Selecting the base template of the operating system design.
- Developing the hardware platform (optional).
- Developing and updating the BSP for a selected hardware platform (optional).
    - Launching Windows Embedded CE on a target hardware platform.
    - Updating and developing the drivers.
- Operating system design.
    - Configuring a run-time image.
    - Application development.
    - Building a staging version of the OS image.
    - Building a Software Development Kit (SDK) set to provide outside developers with an opportunity for development under this device.
    - Building the final version of the image for the release.
- Image testing.
- Planning for image deployment and the process of image deployment.

Chapter 9: Application Development

This chapter covers the differences between native (unmanaged) and managed code, choosing when to create an OS design subproject or a separately developed project, how to prepare for application development, making device connections, and application debugging approaches.

Device applications for Windows Embedded CE can be developed by using the native code and managed code. You can develop native code applications either as subprojects of the operating system design, or as separate projects. While developing projects in the native code separately from the operating system design, you must first build a design of the operating system for which you will be developing applications. After that, you can create an SDK and install it on a development workstation. You can develop applications that use managed code only as separate projects. However, as opposed to native code applications, managed code applications do not require an SDK to be installed. Instead, they rely on the device's run-time environment.

Chapter 10: Testing Operating System Images

The process of testing operating system images for target devices is an integral part of the device-development process. A thorough and regular testing during the development stage reduces the overall cost of the device maintenance during its life span. Testing and verification also enable developers to find potential problems and resolve them.

Microsoft's toolset offers a wide selection of advanced testing tools included in the Windows Embedded CE Test Kit (CETK).

Glossary

The glossary contains a listing of terms used in the book and their explanation.

References

This section contains the literature sources that were referred to or otherwise used for writing the book.

Resources

A list of useful resources, such as:

- Web sites.
- Newsgroups.
- Developer forums.
- Books.

Embedded Systems

Each day, computer technologies are becoming more and more integrated with our lives. Most of us cannot imagine being without a cell phone or an MP3 player. No one is surprised to see an automated teller machine (ATM) on the street or at a subway station. People's homes often contain cable and satellite receivers. A growing number of amateur photographers prefer digital cameras. What do all these devices have in common? The answer is quite simple—they all have a microprocessor. Often times, these microprocessors are very powerful. Not long ago, most computer users would have dreamed about having the processing capabilities available to us now. Yet, in order to utilize a modern processor and to make sure it performs its assigned functions, you need to have an operating system and an application.

At the initial stage of the embedded device market 10 years ago, the producer had no other choice but to create a new, specialized operating system for each new device that was tightly integrated with software responsible for the execution of certain functions. This approach, in addition to being time-consuming, required the efforts of a large team of highly skilled programmers. All of this, in turn, resulted in high development costs and high product costs, which sharply limited the number of potential consumers. Despite this, demand for various intelligent devices noticeably increased. The emergence of specialized operating systems designed for a broad spectrum of solutions helped in addressing the resource and time requirements of the development. Now, developers can focus on creating applications and implementing new features for consumers.

In 1996, Microsoft Corporation introduced its first Microsoft Windows CE 1.0 operating system for non-personal-computer embedded devices. Microsoft wanted to create an operating system suitable for a wide range of tasks and provide developers with the opportunity to use already existing knowledge in the development of programs for computers running Windows, through the use of a common programming interface for all systems. In this way, the task of creating a single platform for embedded devices was resolved. Developers who have experience in writing software for desktop computers could build applications for embedded devices. This development also fulfilled an important requirement for the platform, which is the ability to implement all the latest achievements in information technology, such as Internet technologies, wireless communications, and digital audio and video recording. All this has led to a further reduction in costs and development time, and thus enabled developers to create mass-produced, high-tech devices.

Today, Microsoft offers manufacturers and developers of embedded devices a line of operating systems. This line includes several classic operating systems that have licensing restrictions to be used only with embedded and non-personal-computer devices; two operating systems designed for general use; an operating system targeting a certain market; as well as versions of server operating systems for creating specialized network servers. Specifically, Microsoft includes:

- **Windows Embedded CE** is designed for mobile devices, terminals, cell phones and IP phones, multimedia devices, TV/video consoles, industrial automation equipment, and other devices that require a minimum size, integration of multiple microprocessor architectures, and support for real-time operations.

- **Windows XP Embedded** is designed to be used in ATMs, gaming devices, heavy-duty TV/video consoles, cash registers, point-of-sale devices, and information kiosks—Areas that require high productivity, data security, the use of standard computer equipment, and minimal expenses for developing and using software applications.

- **Windows Embedded for Point of Service (WEPOS)** is designed for the service industry. It is based on the Windows XP Embedded technology, and it enables original equipment manufacturers (OEMs) to deploy from standard distribution media.

- **A line of embedded server solutions** from Microsoft is a logical conclusion of the broader line of embedded operating systems. It enables developers to build infrastructure solutions based on the Windows Embedded platform.

Aside from the operating systems mentioned above, it is necessary to also mention the Microsoft Windows Mobile operating system, which is designed for the manufacturers of pocket PCs and smart phones. It is based on the CE operating system and contains additional wireless technologies and specialized software.

Windows Embedded CE History

The history of Windows Embedded CE began in 1996, when Microsoft released its first operating system (CE 1.0) for non-personal-computer devices, which was originally positioned for the pocket PC market. In 1997, the system (2.0 CE) became componentized and was designed for a wide range of devices and more processor types. Following that, there were two more minor releases (2.11 and 2.12), which expanded and enlarged the functionality of the operating system. Version CE 3.0, released in 2000, contains support for real-time operation and advanced multimedia technologies such as DirectDraw, DirectShow, and Windows Media Player.

The next version (CE 4.0) came out in 2001. It contained support for advanced technologies such as Direct3D, Universal Disc File System (UDFS), Simple Object Access Protocol (SOAP), advanced power management, and SQL Server CE database. Minor releases 4.1 and 4.2 provided developers with expanded accessibility functionality by adding support for viewing files, Bluetooth profiles, and IPv6, as well as support for Voice over Internet Protocol (VoIP) telephony, transaction-safe FAT (TFAT), and .NET Compact Framework 1.0.

In 2005, Microsoft released the next version of the system (CE 5.0), which provided developers with support for new technologies, such as Universal Serial Bus (USB) 2.0, Secure Digital Input/Output (SDIO), Windows Media 9, and Microsoft Internet Explorer 6, as well as a unified build system, release-quality drivers, and a BSP with a dedicated general development infrastructure of BSP and OEM adaptation layer (OAL) available to the developer. In response to the demands of today's embedded devices market, Microsoft released a Network Multimedia Feature Pack in 2006.

With Windows Embedded CE version 6.0, released in the fall of 2006, the system architecture has undergone substantial changes. Now every process has 2 GB of virtual memory (previously 32 MB), and the number of possible simultaneously running processes increased to 32,000 (previously 32). In previous versions, parts of the system kernel were implemented as a set of separate processes, whereas in Windows Embedded 6.0, they are combined into one kernel. System processes have become dynamic-link libraries (DLLs) that are loaded into kernel space. This increases the performance of the operating system, reduces overhead for system application programming interface (API) calls, and unifies the kernel interface. Now a developer can load drivers into kernel space and also be able to create drivers that load in a special user process.

In November 2007, Microsoft released the Windows Embedded CE 6.0 R2 upgrade, which adds new components and BSP packages to the CE 6.0 operating system.

Windows Embedded CE Solutions

Many developers come across different versions of Windows Mobile created on pocket computers based on Windows CE, and that may create a stereotype that CE was intended exclusively for mobile devices. In reality, there are already Windows CE–based solutions available for various applications, from car-based computers, consumer electronics, and telecommunication equipment to industrial automation systems and robotics equipment. The entire spectrum of available applications was initially designed in the system's architecture. As opposed to many other operating systems, from the beginning, Windows Embedded CE was created without being tied to a specific processor architecture or hardware implementation. The only limitation was that it used a 32-bit processor. Today, Windows Embedded CE 6.0 supports four processor architectures (ARM, MIPS, SH4, and x86) and a considerable number of their implementations offered by different processor manufacturers.

Windows Embedded CE provides developers with flexibility to choose from more than 600 components that can be used to create operating system images that include only the functionality that is necessary for a given device. The operating system offers application developers a set of APIs based on standard Win32 API as well as additional APIs specifically for embedded devices. Because Windows Embedded CE supports only part of the Win32 API and has certain specifics that have to do with the embedded nature of the operating system, applications written for the desktop versions of the Windows operating system may require additional adaptation and modification in order to be functional on embedded devices. Either way, launching programs on a device requires recompiling.

Similar to the desktop versions of Windows, Windows Embedded CE uses a standard format of the executable file—Portable Executable (PE), which enables the developer to use the majority of standard utilities that support PE format, such as Dependency Walker or DumpBin.

Windows Embedded CE 6.0 offers the developer a wide range of opportunities and supports a large selection of technologies, such as:

- Rapid systems and application development.

  - ARM emulator and design templates for various types of devices.

  - AYGShell API, which ensures compatibility with Windows Mobile applications.

  - .NET Compact Framework 2.0 and 3.5, including the headless device version, Active Template Library (ATL), Microsoft Foundation Classes (MFC), Windows Template Library (WTL), Standard Template Library (STL), ActiveSync, Exchange Server client, intermediate Global Positioning System (GPS) driver, Speech API 5.0, Windows Messenger, Pocket Outlook Object Model (POOM), Extensible Markup Language (XML), and Microsoft SQL Server Compact 3.5.

  - Simple Network Management Protocol (SNMP).

  - 3.9 million lines of source code, 100 percent of the source kernel code.

  - Production Quality OAL (PQOAL), a set of libraries and source code for creating the OAL.

  - BLCOMMON, a set of libraries and source code for creating a boot loader.

  - Production-quality drivers and BSPs included with the shipped product.

  - Reference implementations of drivers and technologies.

  - Support for several languages and building devices with several language interfaces.

- Network and wireless technologies.

  - Transmission Control Protocol/Internet Protocol (TCP/IP), IPv4, IPv6, Network Driver Interface Specification (NDIS) 5.1, Winsock 2.2, Internet Protocol security (IPsec) v4.

  - Personal area network (PAN), local area network (LAN), wide area network (WAN), Bluetooth, 802.11.

  - SOAP, OBject EXchange (OBEX), Lightweight Directory Access Protocol (LDAP) client, Remote Desktop Protocol (RDP).

  - VoIP, real-time communications (RTC), Session Initiation Protocol (SIP).

  - Radio Interface Layer (RIL), support for Short Message Service (SMS), Wireless Application Protocol (WAP), support for Subscriber Identity Module (SIM) cards.

  - Remote API (RAPI) and RAPI2, Point-to-Point Protocol over Ethernet (PPPoE), Telephony Application Programming Interface (TAPI), virtual private network (VPN).

- Server-side technologies.

  - Telnet, File Transfer Protocol (FTP), server message block (SMB), Common Internet File System (CIFS), Microsoft Message Queuing (MSMQ), Remote Access Service (RAS), Point-to-Point Tunneling Protocol (PPTP), Universal Plug and Play (UPnP).

  - Web server with support for Active Server Pages (ASP).

  - Parental control.

  - Print server, Web proxy.

- Multimedia.

  - DirectDraw, DirectShow, Direct3D.

  - Windows Media Player, Windows Media Audio (WMA), MP3.

  - Internet Explorer.

  - DVD Video API.

  - Digital Rights Management.

- Storage and file systems.

  - File Allocation Table (FAT), TFAT, Extended File Allocation Table (exFAT), binary ROM image file system (BinFS), Object Store.

  - CD File System (CDFS)/UDFS.

  - File System Driver (FSD) Manager, cache manager.

  - CEDB, EDB database.

With its wide selection of technologies and support for a variety of independent third-party software, Windows Embedded CE enables developers to create a broad range of devices, including:

- Personal mobile devices.

- Tablet PCs.

- Smart phones.

- IP Phones.

- Digital cameras.

- Personal multimedia devices.

- Thin clients.

- Gateways.

- TV/video plug-in devices.

- Industrial controllers.

- Medical equipment.

- Printers.

- Scanners.

- Gaming devices.

The development tools for Windows Embedded CE 6.0 are integrated with Visual Studio 2005. They are supplied as an addition to this advanced development suite. Integration with Visual Studio makes it possible to use a single environment for application and system development. Along with the new development tools, the tool suite also includes a new ARM device emulator integrated with Platform Builder, which simplifies configuration tasks and the process of developing and testing of operating system images. The entire capability of the Visual Studio source-code editor is now available to CE 6.0 developers, including syntax highlighting and Microsoft IntelliSense technology. New graphic editors are available, including registry editor and OS image editor. Windows Embedded CE 6.0 uses the improved Visual Studio 2005 compiler, which has better compatibility with C++; includes improved libraries; support for CRT, ATL, and MFC; and more advanced run-time safety checks. The new version of CE also includes postmortem debugging. This presents additional opportunities for diagnosing potential problems and optimizing the efficiency of the system. The software package includes a utility that determines the appropriate run-time license and supports export of reports into HTML. This improves coordination and tracking while working with a project.

Developer Workstation Requirements

- Microsoft Windows 2000 Professional with Service Pack 4 or Windows XP Professional with Service Pack 2.

- Minimum 933 MHz processor (2 GHz is recommended).

- Minimum 512 MB RAM (1 GB is recommended).

- 18 GB of free disk space for installation.

- 1 GB of free disk space on system disk.

- DVD-ROM drive.

A trial version of Windows Embedded CE can be obtained from a local distributor of embedded Microsoft systems; it can also be ordered or downloaded from the Microsoft Web site.

Windows Embedded CE installation instructions are included in the setup CD supplied with the software. You can also use step-by-step installation instructions in Chapter 2, "Operating System and Application Development Tools."

Chapter 2
Operating System and Application Development Tools

Microsoft Windows Embedded CE includes a set of tools to assist with the design and configuration of operating system (OS) images, as well as the development of drivers, services, and applications. Platform Builder for Windows Embedded CE 6.0 is a plug-in for Microsoft Visual Studio 2005. Windows Embedded CE includes a version of Visual Studio 2005 Professional and the Platform Builder toolset. During Platform Builder installation, Platform Builder's Help is integrated with Visual Studio's Help.

Using the popular Visual Studio development suite as a base for the Windows Embedded CE 6.0 development toolset makes it possible to substantially increase the ease of image development under Windows Embedded CE. Visual Studio includes helpful features such as Microsoft IntelliSense auto-complete, syntax highlighting, the graphic registry editor, the system image viewer, and many others. In addition to the development tools, Platform Builder also includes numerous command-prompt utilities that assist with certain tasks during the development of plug-in devices. In subsequent chapters, I cover the core toolset and some of the additional utilities in more detail.

Installing Visual Studio 2005

Because Windows Embedded CE development tools are an addition to Visual Studio 2005, setup should begin with the installation of Visual Studio 2005. After you insert the distribution DVD into the DVD drive with the Auto-Play option enabled, the Visual Studio 2005 installation screen appears, as shown in Figure 2–1.

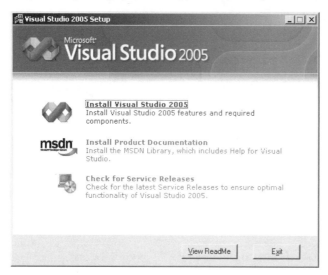

FIGURE 2–1 Visual Studio 2005 installation screen

The only available option is Install Visual Studio 2005. After you click this option, the Welcome to the Microsoft Visual Studio 2005 Installation wizard screen appears, as shown in Figure 2–2.

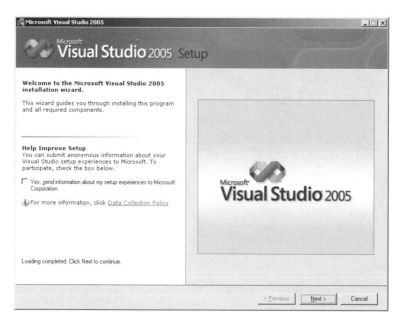

FIGURE 2–2 Welcome to the Microsoft Visual Studio 2005 Installation wizard screen

Click Next and read the terms and conditions. If you agree, select I accept the terms of the license agreement and enter the license key, as shown in Figure 2–3.

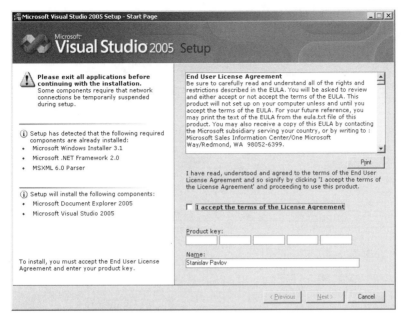

FIGURE 2–3 License key entry screen

The Microsoft Visual Studio 2005 Setup wizard prompts you to select the installation type: Default, Full, or Custom. Choose Default, as shown in Figure 2–4.

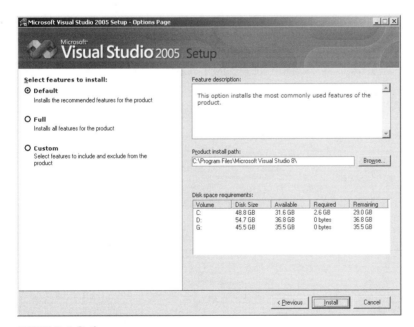

FIGURE 2–4 Options page

Click the Install button and wait for the setup routine to finish, as shown in Figure 2–5.

FIGURE 2–5 Setup routine progress

After the installation completes, a screen appears indicating that the Visual Studio setup completed, as shown in Figure 2–6. Click Finish.

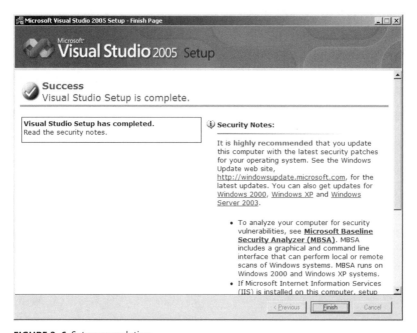

FIGURE 2–6 Setup completion

After a while, a Setup Menu screen appears with links to all setup options enabled, as shown in Figure 2–7.

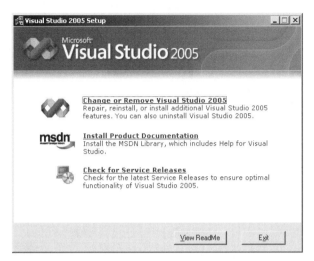

FIGURE 2–7 Setup options

You must install the product documentation. Click Install Product Documentation. After you click this option, a Welcome to the Setup wizard for MSDN Library screen appears, as shown in Figure 2–8.

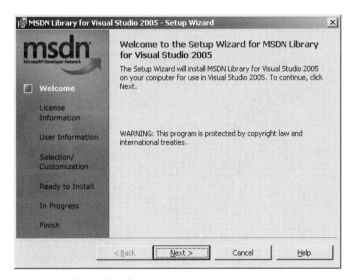

FIGURE 2–8 Setup wizard

Click Next. The license agreement screen appears, as shown in Figure 2–9.

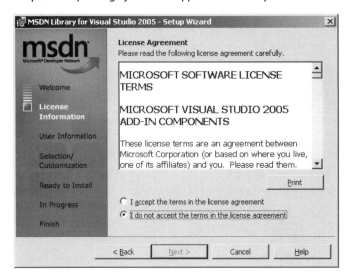

FIGURE 2–9 License agreement screen

Read the license agreement. If you agree, select I accept the terms in the license agreement and click Next to bring up the Customer Information screen, as shown in Figure 2–10.

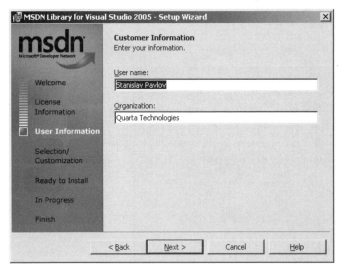

FIGURE 2–10 Customer Information screen

Enter your information and click Next to bring up a selection screen listing three setup types: Full, Custom, and Minimum. Choose the setup option selected by default (Full), as shown in Figure 2–11.

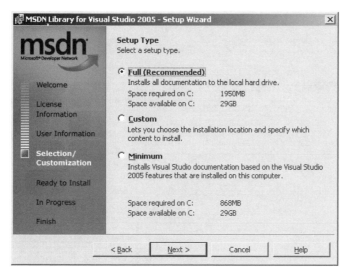

FIGURE 2–11 Setup Type screen

Click Next. A screen prompting a selection of the setup files' location appears, as shown in Figure 2–12.

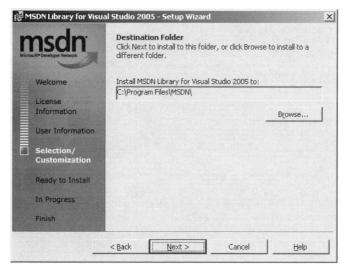

FIGURE 2–12 Destination folder selection

Accept the default location and click Next.

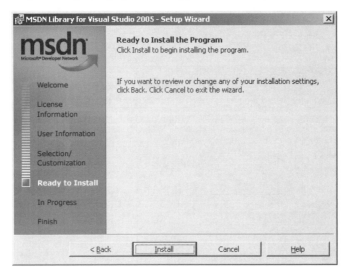

FIGURE 2–13 Ready to Install the Program screen

The Ready to Install the Program screen appears, as shown in Figure 2–13. Click Install and wait until the installation process completes. After setup completes, a screen indicating that installation has been successfully completed appears, as shown in Figure 2–14. Click Finish.

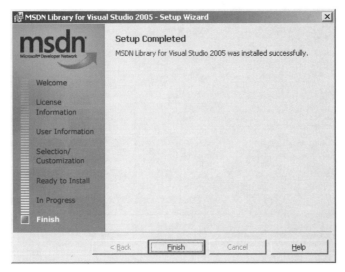

FIGURE 2–14 Setup Completed screen

After a while, a setup welcome screen appears with all setup options enabled. Click Exit. In order to use the enhancements available in Service Pack 1 for .NET Compact Framework 2.0, it is necessary to install an update for Visual Studio 2005. This update can be downloaded directly from: www.microsoft.com/downloads/details.aspx?familyid=7BEFD787-9B5E-40C6-8D10-D3A43E5856B2, or you can search the list of available updates from the Microsoft Web site. Double-click the downloaded NETCFSetupv2.msp file to launch the update process. A setup welcome screen appears, as shown in Figure 2–15.

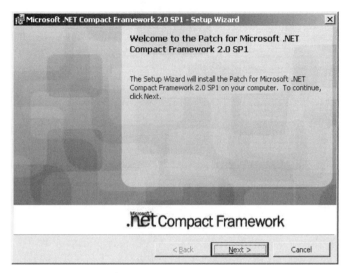

FIGURE 2–15 Patch welcome screen

Click Next. The license agreement screen appears, as shown in Figure 2–16.

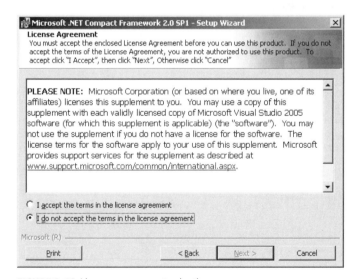

FIGURE 2–16 License agreement selection

Read the license agreement. If you agree, select I accept the terms in the license agreement and click Next. A window appears, as shown in Figure 2–17, indicating that the Setup wizard is ready to begin the installation.

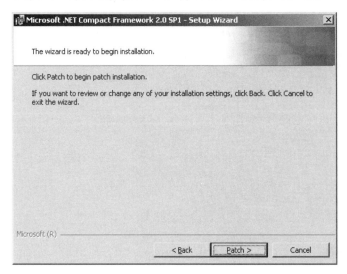

FIGURE 2–17 Ready-to-install screen

Click Patch and wait until setup completes. After setup completes, a screen appears indicating that the installation has finished. Click Finish.

Installing the Platform Builder Toolkit

After you insert the distribution DVD into the DVD drive with the Auto-Play option enabled, the Platform Builder Setup wizard screen appears, as shown in Figure 2–18.

FIGURE 2–18 Platform Builder Setup wizard screen

Click Next. A product key screen appears, as shown in Figure 2–19.

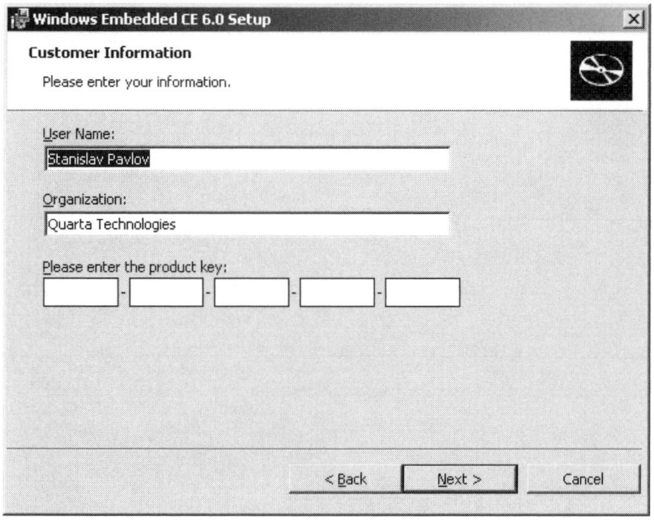

FIGURE 2–19 Customer Information screen

Enter the product key and click Next. The license agreement screen appears, as shown in Figure 2–20.

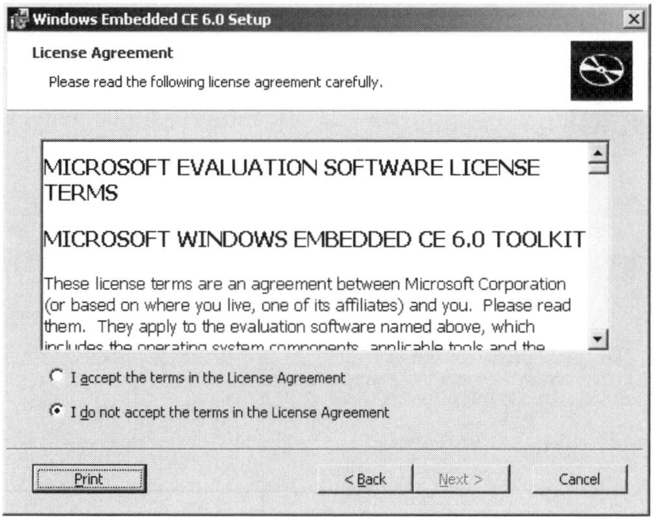

FIGURE 2–20 License agreement screen

Read the license agreement. If you agree, select I accept the terms in the license agreement and click Next. A screen prompting a selection of installation features appears, as shown in Figure 2–21.

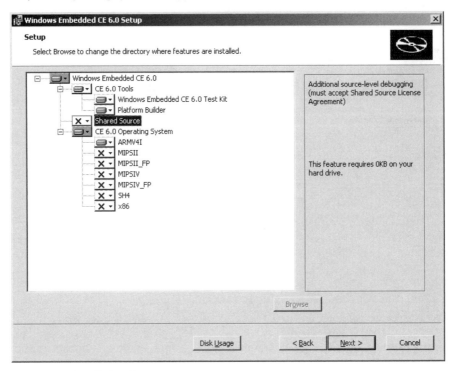

FIGURE 2–21 Installation directory screen

In addition, choose the Shared Source feature and support for x86 platform, and click Next. The license agreement about the Shared Source screen appears, as shown in Figure 2–22.

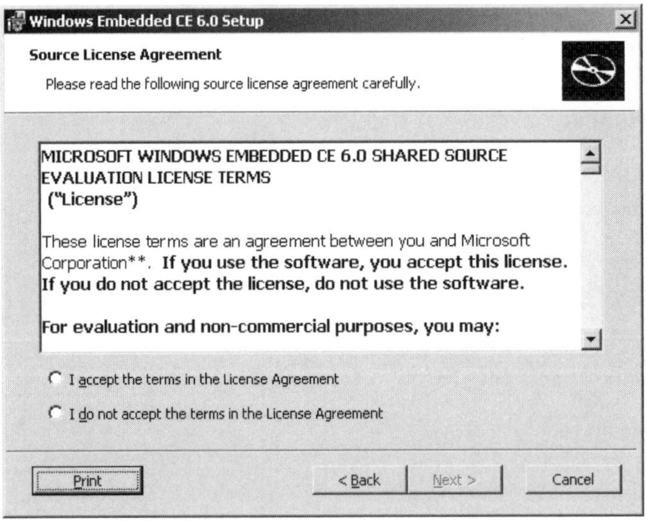

FIGURE 2–22 Shared Source license agreement screen

Read the license agreement. If you agree, select I accept the terms in the license agreement and click Next. A screen appears, as shown in Figure 2–23, indicating that the Setup wizard is ready to begin the installation.

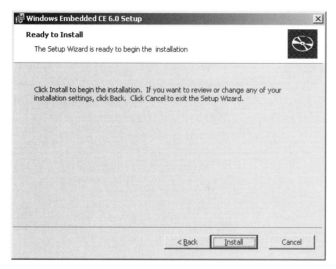

FIGURE 2–23 Ready to Install screen

Click Install and wait until the setup completes. After the setup completes, a screen appears indicating that the installation has finished. Click Finish. The Windows Embedded CE 6.0 toolkit has been installed successfully. Launch the previously installed Visual Studio 2005, which brings up a selection of environment settings, as shown in Figure 2–24.

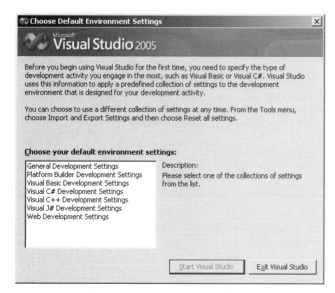

FIGURE 2–24 Default environment settings selection

Select Platform Builder Development Settings and click Start Visual Studio. The current settings will be reset to the default Platform Builder environment settings.

Installing Updates

To ensure that the application developer tools included with Platform Builder are working properly, it is necessary to install Visual Studio 2005 Service Pack 1. This update can be downloaded directly from http://msdn2.microsoft.com/en-us/vstudio/bb265237.aspx, or you can search the list of available updates from the Microsoft Web site. Before you start the installation process, make sure you have 3 GB of available free space on your hard drive. Be prepared to wait. The setup process can take a considerably long time.

Double-click the downloaded file VS80sp1-KB926601-X86-ENU.exe to launch the update process. After a while, a screen appears indicating that extraction is in progress, as shown in Figure 2–25.

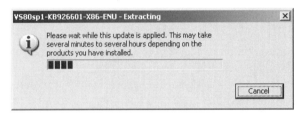

FIGURE 2–25 Extraction progress

After a while, a Preparing to Install window appears. Wait until the installation process has successfully transitioned to the next stage. A window appears, as shown in Figure 2–26, asking you to confirm that you want to install Service Pack 1 for Visual Studio 2005.

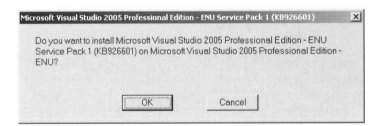

FIGURE 2–26 Confirmation dialog window

Click OK to continue installation. A license agreement screen appears, as shown in Figure 2–27.

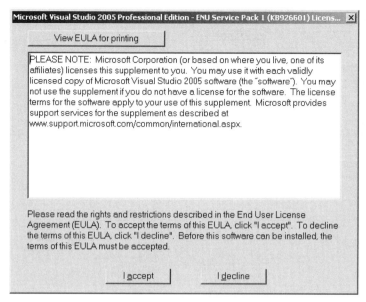

FIGURE 2–27 License agreement

Read the license agreement. If you agree, click I accept. The setup process continues. Wait for the dialog window indicating that setup has been successfully completed, as shown in Figure 2–28.

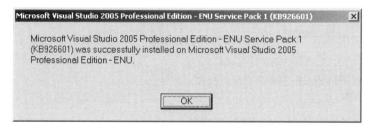

FIGURE 2–28 Installation completion dialog window

Click OK. The Visual Studio 2005 configuration screen appears. Wait until configuration completes. Service Pack 1 for Visual Studio 2005 has been installed.

Now it is necessary to install an update for the development tools for Service Pack 1, which adds a CEDebugX toolkit for multithreaded programming, support for eXDI 2.0 hardware debugging, and support for Remote Tools Framework, which enables you to create customized remote toolkits. Service Pack 1 for Platform Builder for CE 6.0 is available from: www.microsoft.com/downloads/details.aspx?FamilyId=BF0DC0E3-8575-4860-A8E3-290ADF242678

Finish working with Visual Studio 2005 and launch the setup process for Service Pack 1 for Platform Builder for CE 6.0. To launch the installation process, double-click the setup file,

Windows Embedded CE 6.0 Platform Builder Service Pack 1.msi. After a while, the first Setup wizard screen appears, as shown in Figure 2–29.

FIGURE 2–29 Welcome screen

Click Next. The license agreement screen appears, as shown in Figure 2–30.

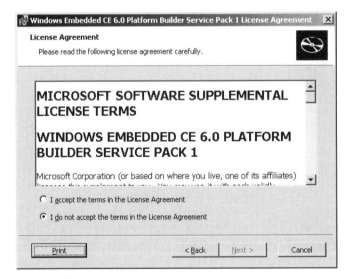

FIGURE 2–30 License agreement screen

Read the license agreement. If you agree, select I accept the terms in the license agreement and click Next. A Ready to Install screen appears, as shown in Figure 2–31.

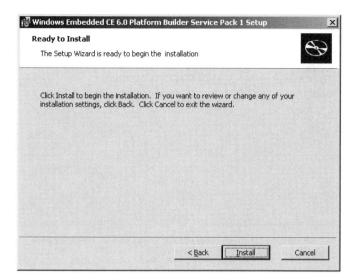

FIGURE 2–31 Ready to Install screen

Click Install to launch the setup process. A screen appears showing the setup progress. Next, the following Setup wizard screen appears, as shown in Figure 2–32.

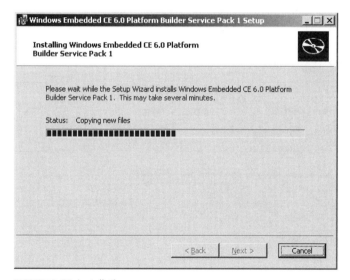

FIGURE 2–32 Installation progress

Wait until setup completes. This may take 10-20 minutes depending on the processor speed. A screen appears indicating that the installation process has been completed, as shown in Figure 2–33.

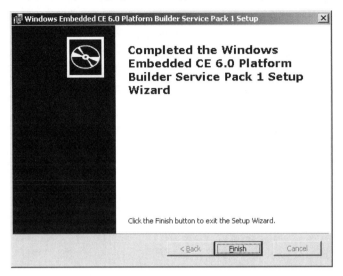

FIGURE 2–33 Installation completion screen

Click Finish. Installation of the Service Pack for Platform Builder for CE 6.0 is now complete.

You must also install the developer toolkit for Windows Embedded CE 6.0 R2. A trial version is available at www.microsoft.com/downloads/details.aspx?FamilyID=f41fc7c1-f0f4-4fd6-9366-b61e0ab59565&DisplayLang=en.

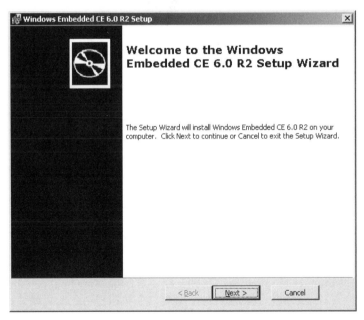

FIGURE 2–34 Setup welcome screen

The installation process is somewhat different if you install from a setup DVD/CD rather than from the Web. The Web installation verifies the currently installed version of the developer toolkit, downloads a special program, and launches the setup routine. With the setup DVD/CD installation, once the disk is inserted into the DVD/CD drive, a browser window opens, prompting you to select an update or launch the Windows Embedded CE R2 setup process, as shown in Figure 2–34.

Click Next. The license agreement screen appears, as shown in Figure 2–35.

FIGURE 2–35 License agreement screen

Read the license agreement. If you agree, select I accept the terms in the license agreement and click Next. A screen appears prompting you to select board support package (BSP) items to install, as shown in Figure 2–36.

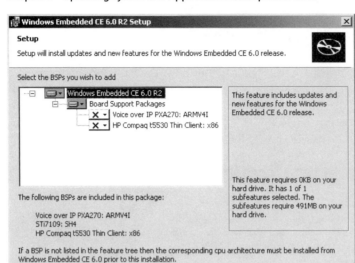

FIGURE 2–36 BSP selection

Choose the BSPs you want to install and click Next. A screen appears indicating that packages are ready to install, as shown in Figure 2–37.

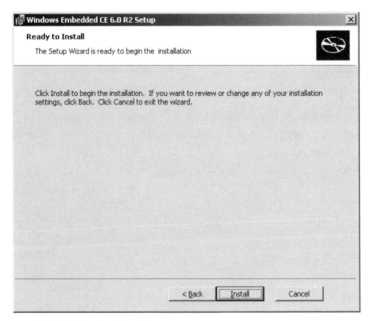

FIGURE 2–37 Ready to Install screen

Click Install to launch the setup process and to bring up a screen showing the setup progress. Wait until setup completes. This may take 20-30 minutes depending on the processor speed. A screen appears indicating that the installation process has been completed, as shown in Figure 2–38.

FIGURE 2–38 Installation completion screen

Click Finish. Installation of Windows Embedded CE 6.0 R2 is now complete. Note that Windows Embedded CE 6.0 R2 contains all upgrades for Windows Embedded CE 6.0 that were released prior to Windows Embedded CE 6.0 R2. After Windows Embedded CE 6.0 R2 has been installed, you need to install all the necessary updates that have been released since Windows Embedded CE 6.0 R2.

Development Tools Interface

Main Views, Windows, and Menus of the Design Interface

After a new OS design project has been created, the main window of Visual Studio 2005 appears, as shown in Figure 2–39.

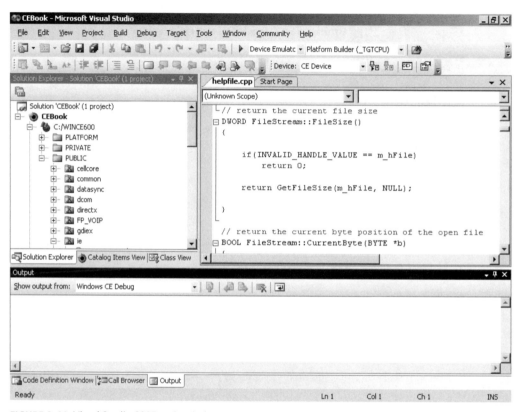

FIGURE 2–39 Visual Studio 2005 main window

The upper portion of the screen contains the menu and a set of toolbars. The selection of toolbars changes depending on the current environment mode: code editing mode, debugging mode, and so on. After Platform Builder for CE 6.0 has been installed, the standard toolbars have all available options enabled, and a new Target toolbar appears, as shown in Figure 2–40 (lower-right-hand corner), which enables you to choose a target device to be loaded, to plug or unplug a device, as well as to open Target Control or Connectivity Options.

FIGURE 2–40 Toolbar options

The left section of the screen contains a workspace with several views. By default, it has the following three views selected: Solution Explorer, Catalog Items View, and Class View. The right section of the screen contains the source-code editor. The bottom section contains various windows, including the Output window (Windows CE Debug and Windows CE Log), Code Definition window, and Call Browser.

The new tools support IntelliSense for the Windows Embedded CE source code and for applications, as well as for configuring system files. Platform Builder also includes a graphical interface for the registry editor and .bin file editor. The graphical registry editor is opened automatically when you double-click the registry configuration file in the design window, as shown in Figure 2–41.

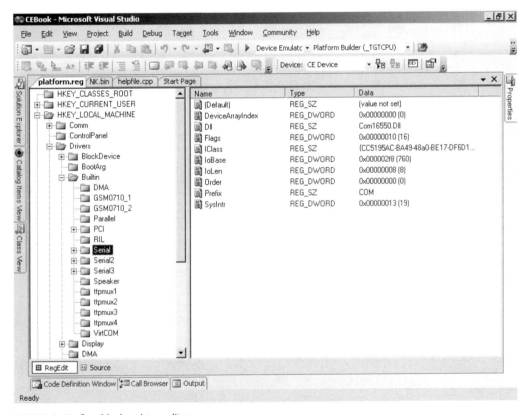

FIGURE 2–41 Graphical registry editor

In order to open a .bin file for viewing or partial editing, choose Open from the File menu. In the menu that appears, choose File to display a standard Windows dialog window for opening files. From there, choose the .bin file and click Open. Figure 2-42 shows the content of the NK.bin file.

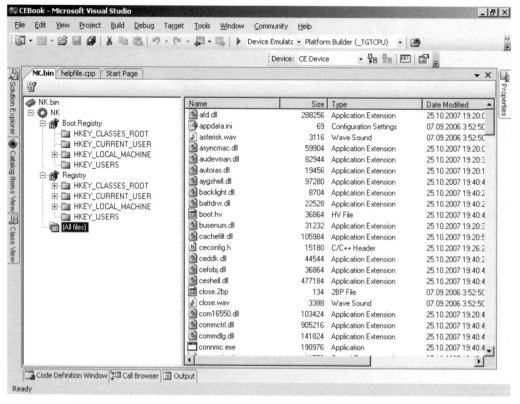

FIGURE 2–42 .Bin file content

If you open the .bin file as a project (Project/Solution from submenu Open), the image can be loaded onto a device and debugged. Now let us take a closer look at each of the views of the main workspace area.

In the Solution Explorer view, you can see a Windows Embedded CE catalog hierarchy, configuration files, OS design subprojects, and Software Development Kit (SDK). The Solution Explorer view also shows the Favorites folder, where you can add links to frequently used parts of the hierarchy of the Windows Embedded CE source code, as shown in Figure 2–43.

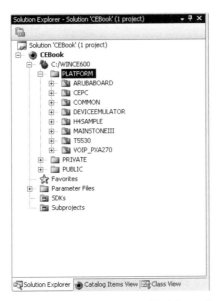

FIGURE 2–43 Windows Embedded CE catalog hierarchy

Once you have selected the node from the Solution Explorer, you can perform the following actions, as shown in Figure 2–44:

- Build BSP, OS components, subprojects, and so on (Build, Rebuild, Sysgen, Build and Sysgen, Rebuild and Clean Sysgen).

- Open Dirs or Sources file (Open), depending on the type of selected node.

- Launch the graphic editor of the Sources or Dirs file (Properties), depending on the type of selected node.

- Open Build Window.

- Exclude from Build.

- Show in Favorites.

- Open the project directory by using Windows Explorer.

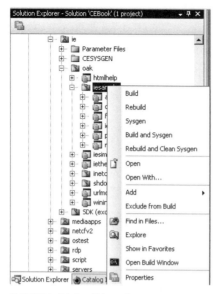

FIGURE 2–44 Possible actions

The Catalog Items View, as shown in Figure 2–45, enables you to add and remove options, modules, and components from the operating system design.

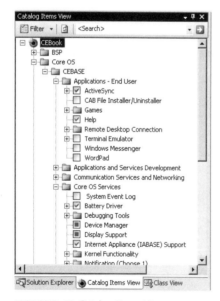

FIGURE 2–45 Catalog Items View

Empty check boxes in the Catalog Items View mean that those options have not been selected. Selected check boxes indicate that the options have been chosen; filled out boxes mean that the options have been automatically added by the system to resolve dependencies.

You can filter a view for User-selected Catalog Items Only, User-selected Catalog Items and Dependencies, and All Catalog Items in Catalog. You can also do a catalog search and launch a view update, as shown in Figure 2–46.

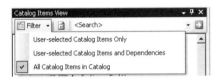

FIGURE 2–46 Filter options

Class View has convenient navigation within the subprojects' source code, as shown in Figure 2–47.

FIGURE 2–47 Class View

Let us take a closer look at the utilities available in the bottom section of the window. The Call Browser enables you to quickly determine what functions are calling a particular function, as shown in Figure 2–48. It also has a search capability.

FIGURE 2–48 Call Browser

The Code Definition window shows the definition of the function code selected in the editor, as shown in Figure 2–49.

```
Code Definition Window - (Subproject1.cpp)                              ▼ ₽ X
    //     This function and its usage is only necessary if you want this code   ▲
    //     to be compatible with Win32 systems prior to the 'RegisterClassEx'
    //     function that was added to Windows 95. It is important to call this function
    //     so that the application will get 'well formed' small icons associated
    //     with it.
  └ //
  ⊟ ATOM MyRegisterClass(HINSTANCE hInstance)
    {
        WNDCLASS wc;

        wc.style = CS_HREDRAW | CS_VREDRAW;
        wc.lpfnWndProc = (WNDPROC) WndProc;
        wc.cbClsExtra = 0;
        wc.cbWndExtra = 0;                                                      ▼
◄                                                                          ►
 📄 Code Definition Window |📋Call Graph |📄 Output
```

FIGURE 2–49 Code Definition Window

You can add additional windows with utilities and views to your design environment. To do that, select them from the View menu of Visual Studio 2005, as shown in Figure 2–50.

Let us look at the options available from the main menu. We shall discuss only those options that are specific to Windows Embedded CE. The Project submenu, as shown in Figure 2–51, enables you to add new and existing subprojects to your OS design. It enables you to set subproject build order, add new and existing SDKs, and access the properties of the objects selected in the Solution Explorer (the last item on the menu that ends in Properties).

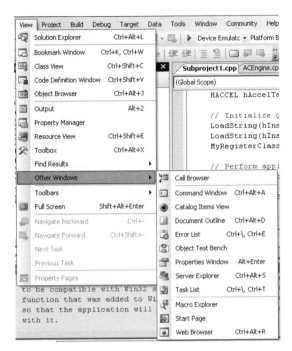

FIGURE 2–50 View menu

FIGURE 2–51 Project submenu

If the Solution Explorer has the root node of the OS design selected, then selecting Properties from the Project submenu brings up the OS design properties, as shown in Figure 2–52.

Common Properties are those that apply to the entire design environment. They have only one setting, and that is to specify the OS build tree where Windows Embedded CE 6.0 is installed. When Configuration Properties is selected, a drop-down list appears where you can choose a configuration type for viewing or editing properties: Active, Debug, Release, or All Configurations.

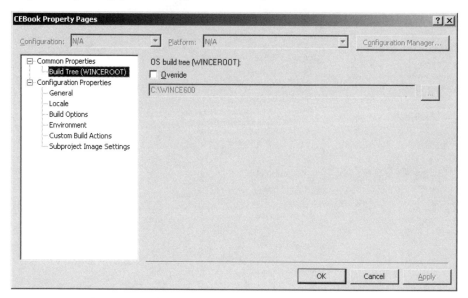

FIGURE 2–52 OS design properties

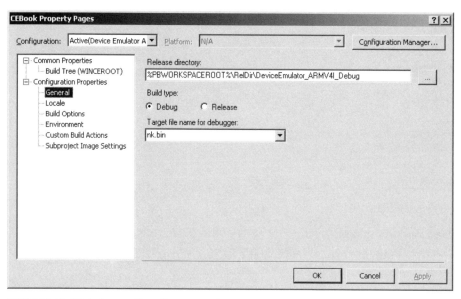

FIGURE 2–53 OS design configuration properties

Now let's look at Configuration Properties. Under General settings, you can set the release directory to which the built modules are copied, the build type (Debug or Release), and the target file name for the image that will be used by the debugger, as shown in Figure 2–53.

The Locale setting enables you to specify the supported locales and codepages. You can set a default locale, check Localize the build, or check Strict localization checking in the build, as shown in Figure 2–54.

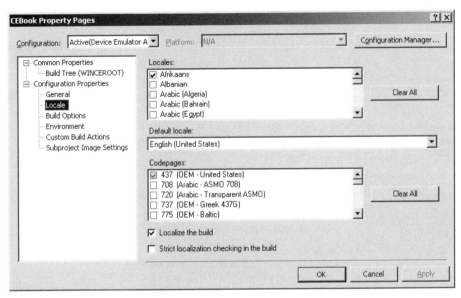

FIGURE 2–54 OS design locale options

Build Options include settings for the variables used most frequently to control the build process, as shown in Figure 2–55.

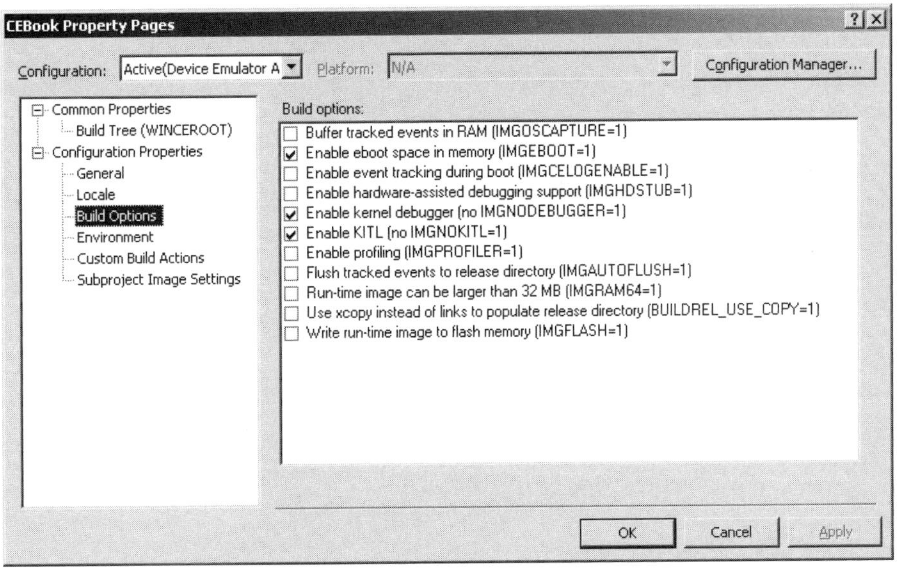

FIGURE 2–55 OS design build options

Table 2–1 provides the variable names and values.

TABLE 2–1 Variable names.

Build Setting	Variable	Value (if selected)
Build tracked events in RAM	IMGOSCAPTURE	Adds the OSCapture.exe module to the image. During the load, the OS module starts writing system events into the random access memory (RAM).
Enable eboot space in memory	IMGEBOOT	Reserves eboot space in memory. Enables the module to preserve the data that can be read by the system during the load.
Enable event tracking during boot	IMGCELOGENABLE	Adds CELog.dll to the image and initializes the system event collection when it loads.
Enable hardware-assisted debugging support	IMGHDSTUB	Enables hardware debugging support.
Enable Kernel Debugger	IMGNODEBUGGER	Includes kernel debugging support in the image.
Enable KITL	IMGNOKITL	Includes support for Kernel Independent Transport Layer (KITL).
Enable profiling	IMGPROFILER	Includes kernel profiling.
Enable ship build	WINCESHIP	OS images built with this flag output no debugging messages.
Flush tracked events to release directory	IMGAUTOFLUSH	Enables flushing of event logging to the release directory.
Run-time image can be larger than 32 MB	IMGRAM64	Enables support for a run-time image larger than 32 megabytes (MB).
Use xcopy instead of links to populate release directory	BUILDREL_USE_COPY	Copies files to the release directory instead of creating hard links.
Write run-time image to flash memory	IMGFLASH	Enables writing of the run-time image to flash memory after download.

The following environment variables enable you to fine-tune build settings by specifying additional environment variables, as shown in Figure 2–56.

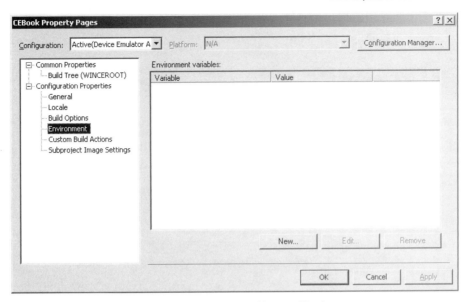

FIGURE 2–56 OS design additional environment variables specification

The following settings enable you to perform custom build actions during certain build stages, as shown in Figure 2–57.

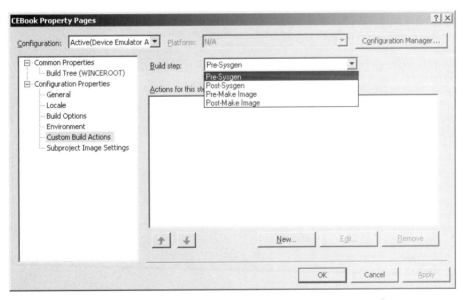

FIGURE 2–57 OS design custom build actions

The last option is Subproject Image Settings for the OS design, as shown in Figure 2–58. Double-clicking a subproject name opens a dialog window where you can choose to exclude a subproject from the build (Exclude from build), exclude it from the image (Exclude from image), and, finally, whether you want to always build and link as debug. No option is selected by default.

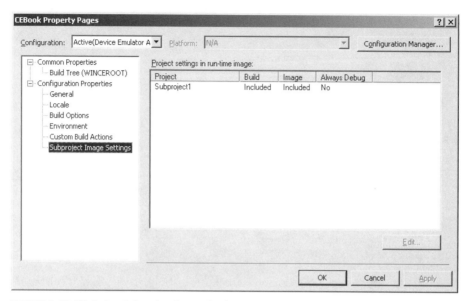

FIGURE 2–58 OS design Subproject Image Settings

Let's proceed to the next menu item, which is Build, as shown in Figure 2–59. This submenu contains actions that pertain to the build of the operating system design, subprojects, and SDK.

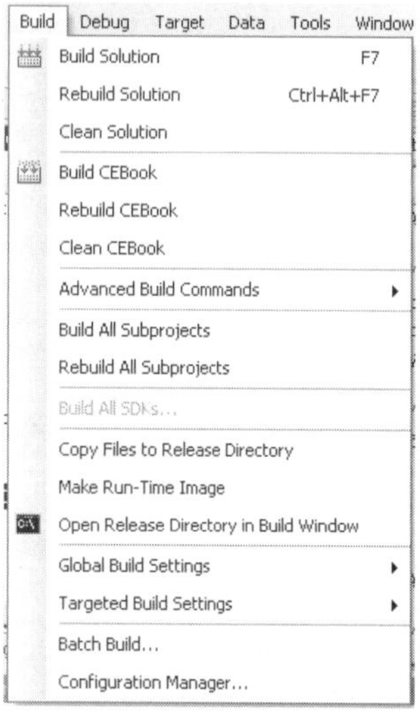

FIGURE 2–59 Build menu

Table 2–2 provides action descriptions for each menu item.

TABLE 2–2 Build menu item descriptions.

Menu Item	Action
Build Solution Build *<OS design name>*	Builds the OS and all projects not excluded from the build. Also creates the run-time image.
Rebuild Solution Rebuild *<OS design name>*	Deletes previously created OS modules. Also builds the OS and all projects not excluded from the build and creates the run-time image.
Clean Solution Clean *<OS design name>*	Deletes previously created OS modules.
Advanced Build Commands	Provides access to advanced commands.
Build All Subprojects	Builds all subprojects.
Rebuild All Subprojects	Deletes previously created binary code, builds all subprojects, and creates the run-time image.
Build All SDKs	Launches building of SDKs included in the current OS design project.
Copy Files to Release Directory	Copies OS files to the release directory.
Make Run-Time Image	Builds the run-time image.
Open Release Directory in Build Window	Opens the command line of the release directory of the current build of the OS design and installs all necessary environment variables for the OS build from the command line.
Global Build Settings	Provides access to the OS build settings when launched from the Build menu.
Targeted Build Settings	Enables you to configure settings for the target BSP and project builds launched from the Solution Explorer view.
Batch Build	Enables you to edit and select several configurations for the build.
Configuration Manager	Enables you to edit and set active configuration for the build.

The Advanced Build Commands submenu provides access to advanced build actions, as shown in Figure 2–60.

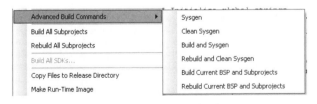

FIGURE 2–60 Advanced Build Commands submenu

Table 2–3 provides action descriptions for the Advanced Build Commands menu actions.

TABLE 2–3 **Advanced Build Commands menu actions.**

Menu Item	Action
Sysgen	Same as Build Solution.
Clean Sysgen	Same as Rebuild Solution.
Build and Sysgen	Builds components from the source code supplied by Microsoft. After that, same as Build Solution. NOT RECOMMENDED.
Rebuild and Clean Sysgen	Removes all previously built OS components. After that, build components from the source code supplied by Microsoft. After that, same as Build Solution. NOT RECOMMENDED.
Build Current BSP and Subprojects	Builds the current BSP and subprojects. To successfully complete the command, you must previously build an OS (by running Sysgen).
Rebuild Current BSP and Subprojects	Deletes the previously created BSP modules and subprojects and rebuilds them.

The Global Build Settings submenu enables you to choose the settings related to the image build by using the Build menu actions, including Advanced Build Commands, as shown in Figure 2–61.

FIGURE 2–61 Global Build Settings submenu

Table 2–4 provides the description of Global Build Settings.

TABLE 2–4 **Description of settings.**

Menu Item	Action
Copy Files to Release Directory After Build	Files are copied to the release directory after build.
Make Run-Time Image After Build	Makes the run-time image from OS modules in the release directory.

The Targeted Build Settings submenu, as shown in Figure 2–62, enables you to choose settings for the BSP, OS components, subprojects, and so on, for the target build launched from the Solution Explorer view.

FIGURE 2–62 Targeted Build Settings submenu

Table 2–5 provides the description of Targeted Build Settings.

TABLE 2–5 **Description of settings.**

Menu Item	Action
Make Run-Time Image After Build	Makes the run-time image from OS modules in the release directory.

If the OS build is launched, most of the Build menu items become unavailable and a new menu item appears (Cancel) that enables you to terminate the current build, as shown in Figure 2–63.

FIGURE 2–63 Menu during build

Let us proceed to the Target menu, as shown in Figure 2–64. It lists actions for working with a device.

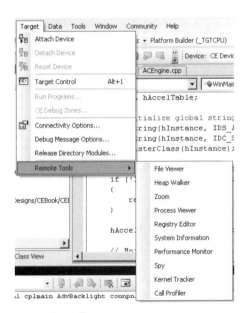

FIGURE 2–64 Target menu

Table 2–6 provides action descriptions for menu items.

TABLE 2–6 Description of settings.

Menu Item	Action
Attach Device	Attach a device. Depending on the settings, download/flash the OS image.
Detach Device	Detach a device.
Reset Device	Reset a device. This action has to be supported by the device.
Target Control	Open the control window of the target device—the client part of CE Shell (CESH). This enables you to receive information about practically all aspects of the device, as well as to launch and stop programs.
Run Programs	Runs a program on the target device.
CE Debug Zones	Establishes debug zones for loaded modules.
Connectivity Options	Brings up a dialog box for connectivity options.
Debug Message Options	Brings up a dialog box for debug message options.
Release Directory Module	Brings up a dialog box for configuring modules that always load from the release directory.
Remote Tools	Remote Tools submenu.
File Viewer	File Viewer utility.
Heap Walker	Heap Walker utility.
Zoom	Utility for taking screen shots with zoom capability.
Process Viewer	Process Viewer utility.
Registry Editor	Registry Editor utility.
System Information	Utility for displaying system information.
Performance Monitor	Utility for monitoring performance.
Spy	Utility for displaying window messages.
Kernel Tracker	Utility for OS execution monitoring, such as threads, synchronization objects, interrupts, and so on.
Call Profiler	Utility for remote call profiling.

Let us take a closer look at each of the menu items, except for the Remote Tools submenu, which we will discuss in more detail later.

- **Attach/Detach/Reset Device** A device can be selected from the Device pane. By default, it is the last device selected in the Connectivity Options dialog box.

- **Target Control** is a view of the control window for the current device to which the design tools are currently attached. To enable this utility, the image needs to include Core OS\CEBASE\Core OS Services\Kernel Functionality\Target Control Support (Shell. exe). The window that appears lists various debugging actions. This is one of the primary debugging utilities. Some of the system information still can be obtained only through this utility.

- **Run Programs** This opens a dialog window that enables you to select a program to launch the device, as shown in Figure 2–65. You will be able to launch programs stored in the image, as well as those in the release directory of the operating system's image.

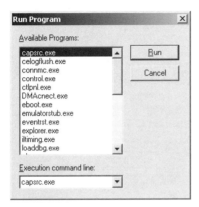

FIGURE 2–65 Run Program window

- **CE Debug Zones** This menu item enables you to view the control window for debug zones. You may select a loaded module and specify which debug zones you want to be active. The debug zones provide an opportunity to receive debugging information without interrupting the operating system/module's operation, as shown in Figure 2–66.

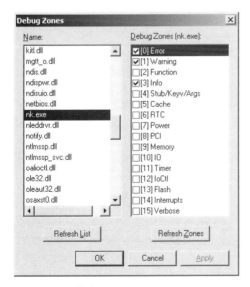

FIGURE 2–66 Debug zones

- **Connectivity Options** This menu item brings up a dialog window that lists options that enable you to connect with a device. This dialog window contains several subwindows for performing various tasks. By default, it opens a window with target device connectivity options, as shown in Figure 2–67.

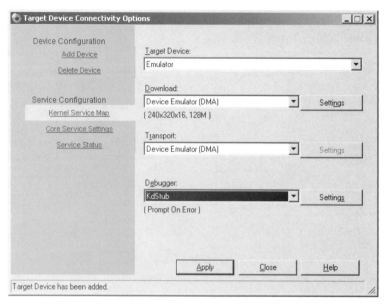

FIGURE 2–67 Connectivity options

When the dialog window appears, it has a Target Device drop-down box with current device settings. If needed, you may choose any other settings or create new ones (use the Add Device option). The Download drop-down box enables you to choose a service that is used for loading the image onto a device. If the selected service enables you to configure its settings, once this service is chosen, the Settings button becomes enabled. Clicking this button brings up a Settings dialog box. The Transport drop-down box enables you to choose the kernel-level transport by which the target device connects to the developer workstation. If the selected transport enables you to configure its settings, once this transport is chosen, the Settings button becomes enabled. Clicking this button brings up a Settings dialog box. From the drop-down Debugger box, you may select the debugger. If the selected debugger enables you to configure additional settings, once that debugger is selected, the Settings option becomes enabled. Selecting this option opens up a Settings dialog window.

The Core Service Settings window, as shown in Figure 2–68, contains information about the image of the operating system associated with the device. It enables you to configure the way the image is loaded onto the device and some of the KITL settings.

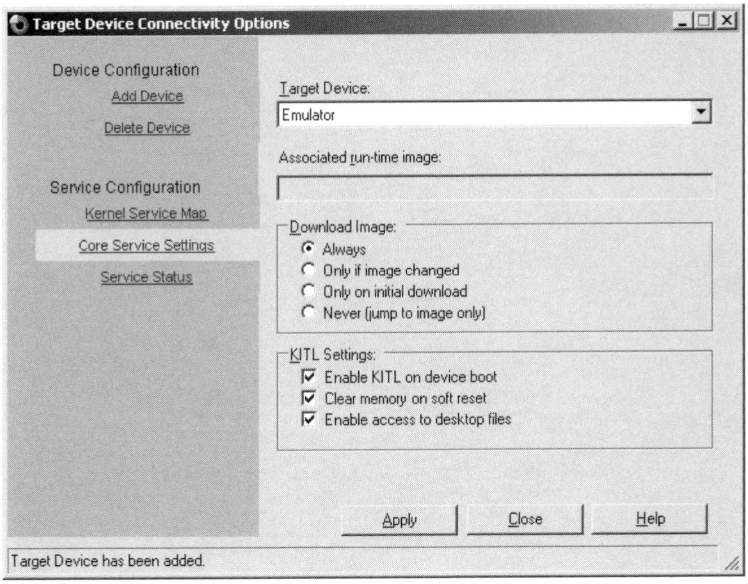

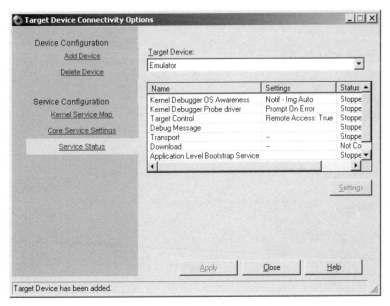

FIGURE 2–68 Core Service Settings window

The Service Status window, as shown in Figure 2–69, provides a view of the current status of the services associated with the load, debugging, transport, and so on.

FIGURE 2–69 Service status

The Add Device window, as shown in Figure 2–70, enables to add you a new configuration to connectivity settings, or, to use Platform Builder's terminology, to add a device.

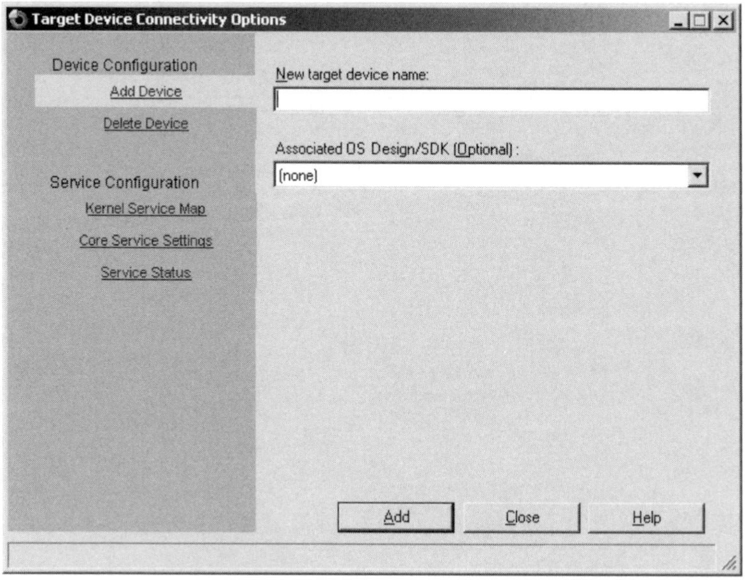

FIGURE 2–70 Add Device window

The Delete Device window enables you to remove a previously created device, as shown in Figure 2–71.

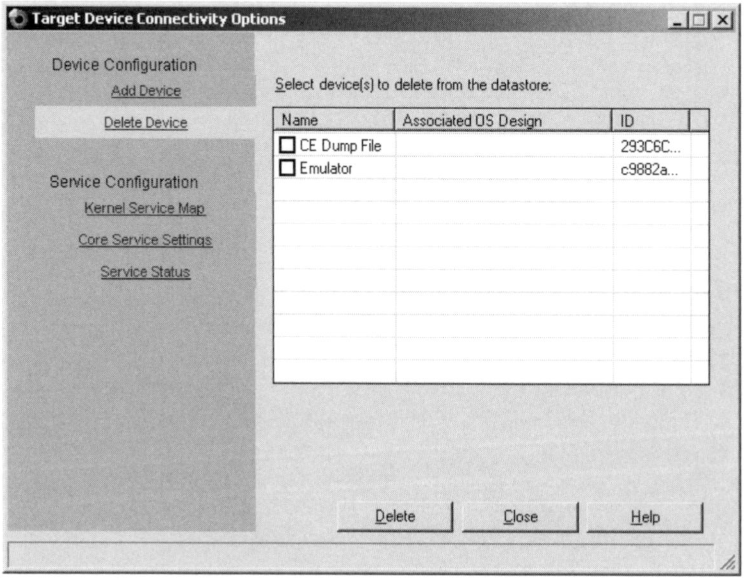

FIGURE 2–71 Delete Device window

The Debug Message Options dialog box enables you to set the format and the output method for debugging messages. The Release Directory Modules dialog box, as shown in Figure 2–72, enables you to tell the debugger what modules must be loaded from the image's release directory. You can debug and rebuild a driver without having to constantly rebuild the system image.

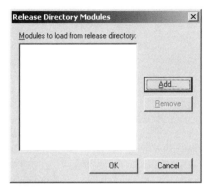

FIGURE 2–72 Release Directory Modules dialog box

Clicking the Add button brings up a list of modules from the release directory. Figure 2–73 shows only a partial list.

FIGURE 2–73 Available modules

Let us proceed to the next menu. The Tools menu contains several CE utilities: Clone BSP; License Run-time Image (not available in the trial version); Run-time License Assessment Tool; and CE Update Check.

The Debug menu is enhanced to include new actions that provide the developer with additional opportunities for debugging, specifically:

- Symbol Search Path.

- Windows CE Debugger Extensions.

- Go To Location.

- Capture Dump File.

FIGURE 2–74 Debug options

The Windows submenu, as shown in Figure 2–74, provides access to various utilities that enable you to collect information about the connected device, including:

- Call Stack.

- Threads.

- Modules.

- Processes.

- Autos.

- Watch.

- Memory submenu.

- Disassembly.

- Registers.

- List Nearest Symbol.

- Advanced Memory.

The Debug menu actions described above become available once the debugger has been connected to the device. In concluding the description of the design interface, it is necessary to point out that at the time of this writing, Windows Embedded CE 6.0 projects were not supported by Team Foundation System.

Remote Utilities

This section covers the following remote utilities for Windows Embedded CE 6.0:

- File Viewer.
- Heap Walker.
- Zoom.
- Process Viewer.
- Registry Editor.
- System Information.
- Performance Monitor.
- Spy.
- Kernel Tracker.
- Call Profiler.

Note that in order for the Zoom and Spy utilities to work correctly, the image must contain the following components: Core OS\CEBASE\Shell and User Interface\Graphics, Windowing and Events\Minimal GWES Configuration, Core OS\CEBASE\Shell and User Interface\Graphics, and Windowing and Events\ Minimal GDI Configuration. The Call Profiler utility requires that the image contain Core OS\CEBASE\International\National Language Support (NLS) or Core OS\CEBASE\International\English (US) National Language Support only with Core OS\ CEBASE\Application and Service Development\C Libraries and Runtimes\ Standard String Functions - ASCII (corestra).

File Viewer

The File Viewer utility enables you to view the contents of the device file system, import files from the device, export files to the device, browse the properties of files and directories, create directories, and rename files and directories stored on the device. To launch this utility, choose Target from the main menu, then select Remote Tools and, in the menu that appears, choose File Viewer. The main program window appears. In the upper section of the screen, there is a dialog box for the target device. If the device has an established active connection with Platform Builder, you may skip all configuration settings and choose Default Device, which uses the default settings of the most recently connected device, as shown in Figure 2–75.

FIGURE 2–75 Windows Embedded CE Remote File Viewer

If it is necessary to add additional settings or to add a new device, you can click Cancel and add new settings to connect to a device. These settings are configured the same way from all remote utilities.

To set the configuration settings, choose Configure Windows CE Platform Manager in the Connection menu. A dialog box appears, as shown in Figure 2–76.

FIGURE 2–76 Configuration dialog box

This dialog box enables the addition of new settings, or, in Platform Builder terminology, to Add Device, Delete, view Properties, or see About information. Clicking the Add Device button adds a new device to the list. You can rename it right away. After the device has been added, you can select it from the list and edit its properties, as shown in Figure 2–77.

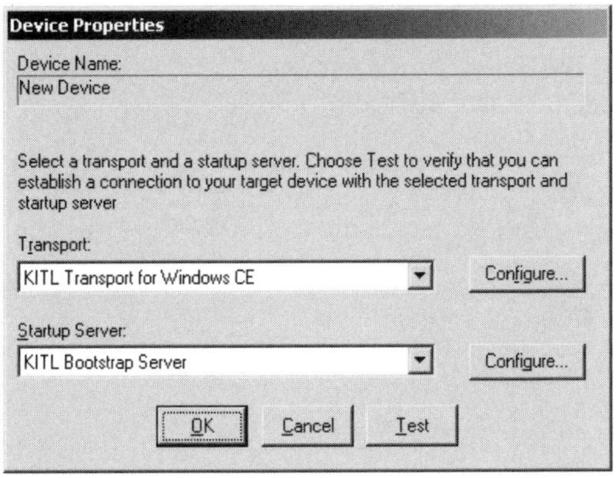

FIGURE 2–77 Device properties

Transport is used for communicating on the application level between the device and the remote utility. The program ships with support for the following transports:

- ActiveSync.

- KITL.

- Transmission Control Protocol/Internet Protocol (TCP/IP).

The use of ActiveSync as a transport mechanism requires that the developer's workstation and the device both support ActiveSync. KITL transport uses the same KITL connection as the Kernel Debugger, and it requires that the device support KITL. TCP/IP transport uses TCP/IP protocol to communicate with the device, and the device has to support the network protocol. If needed, you can additionally configure transport properties by clicking Configure.

The startup server is responsible for copying files needed for Platform Manager to the device, running those files, utilizing the transport, and establishing a connection between the developer workstation and the target device. The program includes the following startup server types:

- ActiveSync Startup.

- CESH Startup.

- KITL Startup.

- Manual Startup.

The ActiveSync startup server uses ActiveSync for copying and launching operations on the target device; CESH and KITL startup servers use Target Control Service (Shell.exe). The Manual startup server brings up a dialog box with a list of files that must be copied to the device as well as the program that needs to be run after copying completes in order to connect to the developer's workstation.

After the necessary transport and the startup server have been selected, you can test the device connection by pressing the Test button. A dialog window appears showing the process of being connected to a device, as shown in Figure 2–78.

FIGURE 2–78 Testing device connection

If connection to the device has been successfully established, a dialog box appears with a Connection to device established message and an OK button, as shown in Figure 2–79.

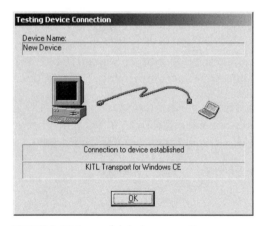

FIGURE 2–79 Successful device connection

To connect to a device, choose Connection, and then choose Add Connection. A dialog box appears, similar to the one that shows up when the program starts. Choose a device and click OK. A dialog box appears showing the progress of being connected to the device. After a successful connection, you can see the catalog hierarchy in the left pane and the currently selected catalog in the right pane, as shown in Figure 2–80.

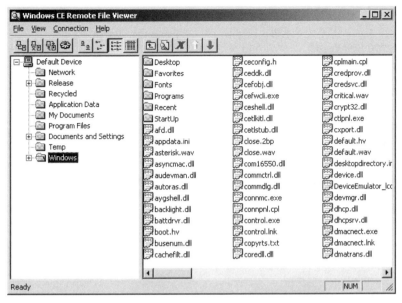

FIGURE 2–80 Windows Embedded CE Remote File Viewer—connected

By using the menu and the toolbox, you may perform the following actions:

- Browse the device file system.

- Import files from the device.

- Export files to the device.

- View properties of files and directories.

- Create directories.

- Rename files and directories in the device.

Heap Walker

The Heap Walker utility enables you to view process heaps, their identifiers, and flags, as well as the structure and the content of each heap. To launch this utility, choose Target from the main menu, then Remote Tools and, in the menu that appears, choose Heap Walker. The main program window appears. In the upper portion of the screen, there is a dialog box for the target device. If the device has an established active connection with Platform Builder, you may skip all configuration settings and choose Default Device, which uses the default settings of the most recently connected device.

To configure additional settings or to add another device, click Cancel and configure the connection settings for the device. These settings are configured in the same way for all remote utilities. They were discussed in more detail in the "File Viewer" section.

To connect to a device, choose Connection, and then choose Connect to Device. A dialog box appears, similar to the one that shows up when the program starts. Choose a device and click OK. A dialog box appears showing the progress of being connected to the device. After the connection has been successfully established, a list appears showing processes and their heaps.

This utility may show three windows: Process_List, Heap_List, and Heap_Dump. After the device has been connected, a window appears showing the process list and the heaps associated with each process, as shown in Figure 2–81.

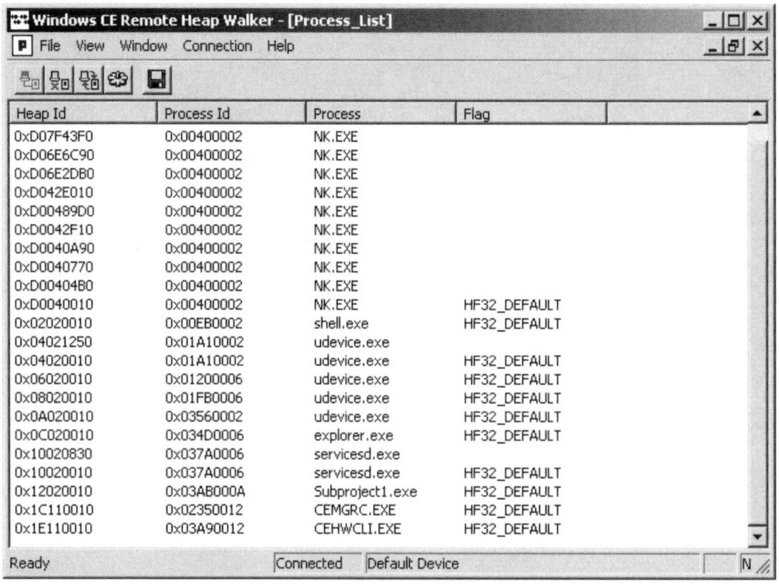
Windows CE Remote Heap Walker - [Process_List]
File View Window Connection Help
Heap Id | Process Id | Process | Flag
0xD07F43F0 0x00400002 NK.EXE
0xD06E6C90 0x00400002 NK.EXE
0xD06E2DB0 0x00400002 NK.EXE
0xD042E010 0x00400002 NK.EXE
0xD00489D0 0x00400002 NK.EXE
0xD0042F10 0x00400002 NK.EXE
0xD0040A90 0x00400002 NK.EXE
0xD0040770 0x00400002 NK.EXE
0xD00404B0 0x00400002 NK.EXE
0xD0040010 0x00400002 NK.EXE HF32_DEFAULT
0x02020010 0x00EB0002 shell.exe HF32_DEFAULT
0x04021250 0x01A10002 udevice.exe
0x04020010 0x01A10002 udevice.exe HF32_DEFAULT
0x06020010 0x01200006 udevice.exe HF32_DEFAULT
0x08020010 0x01FB0006 udevice.exe HF32_DEFAULT
0x0A020010 0x03560002 udevice.exe HF32_DEFAULT
0x0C020010 0x034D0006 explorer.exe HF32_DEFAULT
0x10020830 0x037A0006 servicesd.exe
0x10020010 0x037A0006 servicesd.exe HF32_DEFAULT
0x12020010 0x03AB000A Subproject1.exe HF32_DEFAULT
0x1C110010 0x02350012 CEMGRC.EXE HF32_DEFAULT
0x1E110010 0x03A90012 CEHWCLI.EXE HF32_DEFAULT
Ready
Connected
Default Device
N

FIGURE 2–81 Windows Embedded CE Remote Heap Walker process list

Double-clicking the heap opens a window that lists blocks of the heap memory and includes information about their address, block size, and block flag (fixed or free), as shown in Figure 2–82.

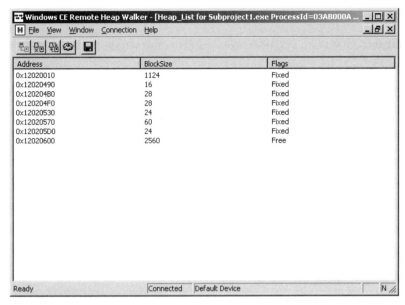

FIGURE 2–82 Windows Embedded CE Remote Heap Walker heap list

Double-clicking a block brings up a window showing the content of the selected heap's memory block, as shown in Figure 2–83.

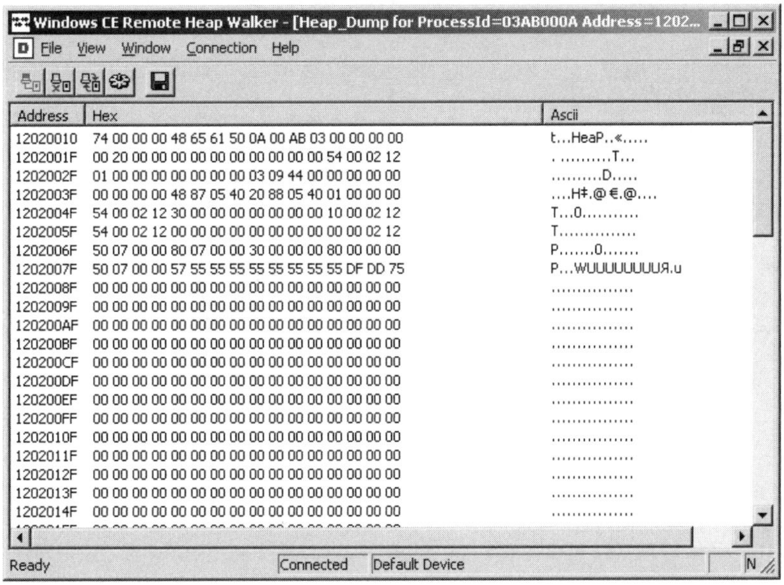

FIGURE 2–83 Windows Embedded CE Remote Heap Walker heap memory block

Zoom

The Zoom utility enables you to capture screen shots of the target device. To launch this utility, choose Target from the main menu, then choose Remote Tools and, in the menu that appears, choose Zoom. The main program window appears. In the upper portion of the screen, there is a dialog box for the target device. If the device has an established active connection with Platform Builder, you may skip all configuration settings and choose Default Device, which uses the default set connected device.

To configure additional settings or to add another device, click Cancel and configure the connection settings for the device. These settings are configured in the same way for all remote utilities. They were discussed in more detail in the "File Viewer" section.

To connect to a device, choose Connection, and then Connect to Device. A dialog box appears, similar to the one that shows up when the program starts. Choose a device and click OK. A dialog box appears showing the progress of being connected to the device. After the connection has been successfully established, a screen shot of the current screen of the target device appears, as shown in Figure 2–84.

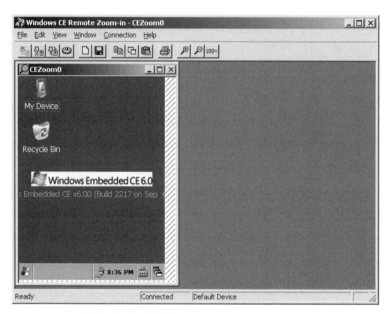

FIGURE 2–84 Windows Embedded CE Remote Zoom-in

By using the menu, you may zoom in on or zoom out on the image (View, and then Zoom In/Zoom Out), open the image of the current device screen in a new window (File, and then New Bitmap), or refresh the image in the current window (Connection, and then Refresh). The resulting image can be copied to the exchange buffer (Edit, and then Copy All/Copy Window), saved as a file (File, and then Save As), or printed out (File, and then Print).

Process Viewer

The Process Viewer utility enables you to gather information about the processes launched in the target device, the process threads, and modules loaded into the processes. To launch this utility, choose Target from the main menu, then choose Remote Tools and, in the menu that appears, choose Process Viewer. The main program window appears. In the upper portion of the screen, there is a dialog box for the target device. If the device has an established active connection with Platform Builder, you may skip all configuration settings and choose Default Device, which uses the default settings of the most recently connected device.

To configure additional settings or to add another device, click the Cancel button and configure the connection settings for the device. These settings are configured in the same way for all remote utilities. They were discussed in more detail in the "File Viewer" section.

To connect to a device, choose Connection, and then Connect to Device. A dialog box appears, similar to the one that shows up when the program starts. Choose a device and click OK. A dialog box appears showing the progress of being connected to the device. After the connection has been successfully established, the information about the processes launched in the device appears, as shown in Figure 2–85.

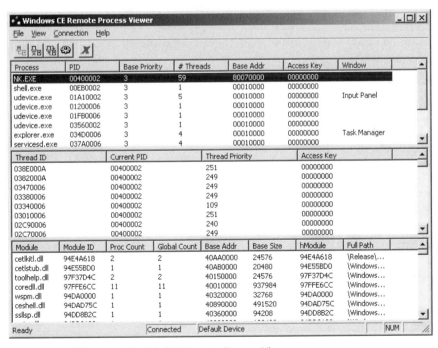

FIGURE 2–85 Windows Embedded CE Remote Process Viewer

When you select a process in the upper section of the screen, the middle section shows information about the process threads; the bottom section shows information about the modules loaded in the processes. Clicking the button with a red cross on the main pane enables you to stop a process. To refresh device information, select Connection and then Refresh from the utility's main menu.

Registry Editor

The Registry Editor utility enables you to view and edit the registry of the target system. To launch this utility, choose Target from the main menu, then choose Remote Tools, and in the menu that appears, choose Registry Editor. The main program window appears. In the upper portion of the screen, there is a dialog box for the device you want to connect to. If the device has an established active connection with Platform Builder, you may skip all configuration settings and choose Default Device, which uses the default settings of the most recently connected device.

To configure additional settings or to add another device, click the Cancel button and configure the connection settings for the device. These settings are configured in the same way for all remote utilities. They were discussed in more detail in the "File Viewer" section.

To connect to a device, choose Connection, and then Add Connection. A dialog box appears, similar to the one that shows up when the program starts. Choose a device and click OK. A dialog box appears showing the progress of being connected to the device. After the connection has been successfully established, the left pane displays a hierarchical tree of the registry of the desktop machine and the target device, and the right pane displays the value of the registry keys chosen in the left pane, as shown in Figure 2–86.

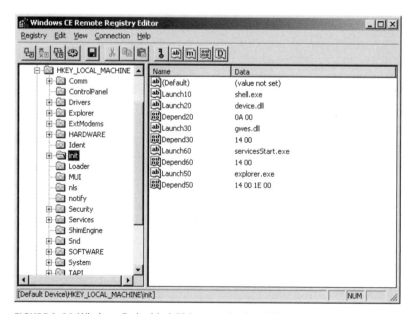

FIGURE 2–86 Windows Embedded CE Remote Registry Editor

This utility is similar to its desktop version of the registry viewer, and it enables you to perform all registry actions, including exporting registry files. The registry actions are accessible from the context menu (right-click mouse menu) and from the main utility's pane. To refresh device information, choose Connection and then choose Refresh from the utility's main menu.

System Information

The System Information utility enables you to browse system information about the device, including memory, device storage, and metrics. To launch this utility, choose Target from the main menu, then choose Remote Tools and, in the menu that appears, choose System Information. The main program window appears. In the upper portion of the screen, there is a dialog box for the device you want to connect to. If the device has an established active connection with Platform Builder, you may skip all configuration settings and additionally choose Default Device, which uses the default settings of the most recently connected device.

To configure additional settings or to add another device, click the Cancel button and configure the connection settings for the device. These settings are configured in the same way for all remote utilities. They were discussed in more detail in the "File Viewer" section.

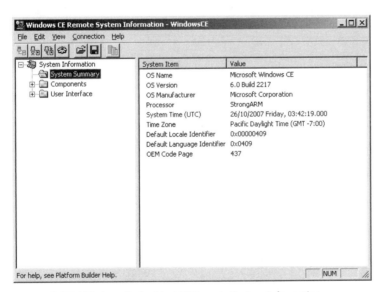

FIGURE 2–87 Windows Embedded CE Remote System Information

To connect to a device, choose Connection, and then Connect to Device. A dialog box appears, similar to the one that shows up when the program starts. Choose a device and click OK. A dialog box appears showing the progress of being connected to the device. After the connection has been successfully established, the left pane displays a hierarchical tree of system information, and the right pane displays information about the items chosen in the left pane, as shown in Figure 2–87.

Performance Monitor

The Performance Monitor utility enables you to track various performance indicators of the target system. To launch this utility, choose Target from the main menu, then Remote Tools and, in the menu that appears, choose Performance Monitor. The main program window appears. In the upper portion of the screen, there is a dialog box for the target device. If the device has an established active connection with Platform Builder, you may skip all configuration settings and choose Default Device, which uses the default settings of the most recently connected device.

To configure additional settings or to add another device, click the Cancel button and configure the connection settings for the device. These settings are configured in the same way for all remote utilities. They were discussed in more detail in the "File Viewer" section.

To connect to a device, choose Connection, and then Connect to Device. A dialog box appears, similar to the one that shows up when the program starts. Choose a device and click OK. A dialog box appears showing the progress of being connected to the device. After the connection has been successfully established, the program starts copying the files that are needed in order to monitor the performance of the target system. After copying and initialization of the remote part of the device are completed, the developer will have access to the interface that is similar to an interface of the desktop version of Performance Monitor, as shown in Figure 2–88.

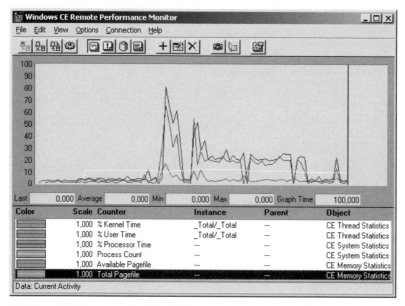

FIGURE 2–88 Windows Embedded CE Remote Performance Monitor

Just like the desktop version, this utility enables you to represent data in several forms, including Chart, Alert, and Report, as well as to write information to a log. Views can be toggled from the main pane (the second group of the four buttons on the right-hand side) or from the main menu (View). You can add counters to each view. To add or remove a counter, you can use the Edit menu and then the first item (Add to Chart, Add to Log, etc.) or the main pane (the first button in the third button group on the left).

Pressing the Add button brings up a dialog box showing a counter selection to add. The dialog boxes are slightly different depending on the selected view (Chat, Alerts, or Report).

The utility can show the current target device information, as well as the information from a log created previously by this utility. Developers may add their own counters to Performance Monitor by creating special extension libraries.

Spy

The Spy utility enables you to browse open windows of the device and their properties. To launch this utility, choose Target from the main menu, then Remote Tools and, in the menu that appears, choose Spy. The main program window appears. In the upper portion of the screen, there is a dialog box for the target device. If the device has an established active connection with Platform Builder, you may skip all configuration settings and choose Default Device, which uses the default settings of the most recently connected device.

To configure additional settings or to add another device, click the Cancel button and configure the connection settings for the device. These settings are configured in the same way for all remote utilities. They were discussed in more detail in the "File Viewer" section.

To connect to a device, choose Connection, and then Connect to Device. A dialog box appears, similar to the one that shows up when the program starts. Choose a device and click OK. A dialog box appears showing the progress of being connected to the device. After the connection has been successfully established, a window appears showing the hierarchical tree of the system windows, as shown in Figure 2–89.

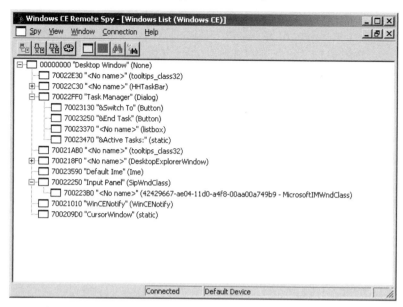

FIGURE 2–89 Windows Embedded CE Remote Spy

Double-clicking a node of the hierarchical view displays a dialog box listing the properties of the corresponding window, as shown in Figure 2–90.

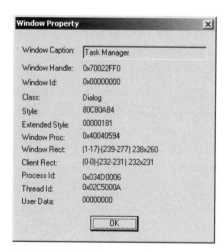

FIGURE 2–90 Window property screen

Kernel Tracker

The Kernel Tracker utility enables you to watch the operations of the system and the applications in real time, including:

- All the processes, threads, and their interaction.

- System events and the threads that represent them.

- System interrupts (the image should include support for profiling).

- System information.

Kernel Tracker also enables you to view the execution of the system and the application in the target device dynamically from within. It provides effective solutions to the problems a developer may be faced with including thread interaction analysis in a multithreaded application and finding the root causes of the slow performance of a driver.

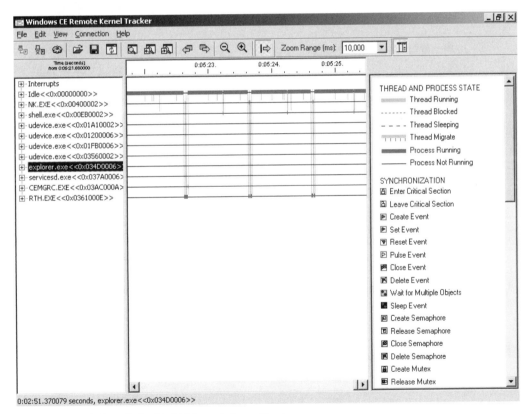

FIGURE 2–91 Windows Embedded CE Remote Kernel Tracker

To launch this utility, choose Target from the main menu, then Remote Tools and, in the menu that appears, choose Kernel Tracker. The main program window appears. In the upper portion of the screen, there is a dialog box for the target device. If the device has an established active connection with Platform Builder, you may skip all configuration settings and choose Default Device, which uses the default settings of the most recently connected device.

To configure additional settings or to add another device, click the Cancel button and configure the connection settings for the device. These settings are configured in the same way for all remote utilities. They were discussed in more detail under the File Viewer utility.

To connect to a device, choose Connection, and then Connect to Device. A dialog box appears, similar to the one that shows up when the program starts. Choose a device and click OK. A dialog box appears showing the progress of being connected to the device. After the connection has been successfully established, the program will start copying the files needed for monitoring the target system. After copying and initialization of the remote section of the device are completed, a window with three vertical views appears. The left pane displays the process tree, threads, and interrupts; the central pane displays system details; and the right pane displays the symbols' explanation. The main application pane enables you to access the main utility controls, as shown in Figure 2–91.

In the left pane, the tree can be expanded in order to view what process threads have been started. The central pane displays a detailed view of the system, as shown in Figure 2–92.

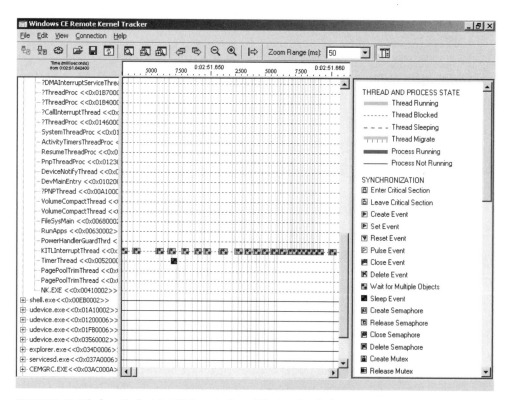

FIGURE 2–92 Windows Embedded CE Remote Kernel Tracker detailed system view

By using the main pane of the application, you may set the zoom level (Zoom Range (ms)), with a maximum of 1 millisecond (ms) and a minimum of 10,000 milliseconds. The square boxes in the system details window represent various system events tracked by the utility. If you hover the cursor over a square, you will be able to see detailed information about the selected event. By using the menu (View, and then Event Filter), you can filter system events available for viewing.

FIGURE 2–93 Thread pane context menu

Find Event...	Ctrl+F
Find Next Event	Ctrl+Right
Find Previous Event	Ctrl+Left
Zoom In	Ctrl+Up
Zoom Out	Ctrl+Down
Next Running Thread	Right
Previous Running Thread	Left
Set Time Marker 1 at Cursor	
Set Time Marker 2 at Cursor	

FIGURE 2–94 System details pane context menu

The context menus in a thread pane, as shown in Figure 2–93, and in a system details pane, as shown in Figure 2–94, enable you to perform additional actions to analyze the system processes, as well as to find and resolve problems. The utility saves the session data for subsequent analysis, for which the user is prompted at the end.

Call Profiler

The Call Profiler utility enables you to track the time it takes to run parts of the application code and therefore to locate problems in the code that impact the application performance as a whole in a negative way. To ensure that this utility is capable of collecting data, the application code needs to receive additional instructions that will send Call Profiler the information about code operation. In order to perform this build, it is necessary to set additional parameters for the application build:

- WINCECALLCAP=1, for CallCAP profiling.
- WINCEFASTCAP=1, for FastCAP profiling.

This can be done in the Command Prompt window of the design interface or in the Sources file. As we mentioned earlier, the profiler subsystem supports two types of profiling, FastCAP and CallCAP. FastCAP inserts a service code before calling each function and right after the return from the application function. CallCAP inserts a service code right after a function is called and before the return from the function. FastCAP functionality is not supported for x86 processors.

To launch this utility, choose Target from the main menu, then Remote Tools and, in the menu that appears, choose Call Profiler. The main program window appears. In the upper portion of the screen, there is a dialog box for the target device. If the device has an established active connection with Platform Builder, you may skip all configuration settings and choose Default Device, which uses the default settings of the most recently connected device.

To configure additional settings or to add another device, click the Cancel button and configure the connection settings for the device. These settings are configured in the same way for all remote utilities. They were discussed in more detail in the "File Viewer" section.

To connect to a device, choose Connection, and then Connect to Device. A dialog box appears, similar to the one that shows up when the program starts. Choose a device and click OK. A dialog box appears showing the progress of being connected to the device. Next, a dialog box for launching the Call Profiler appears, as shown in Figure 2–95.

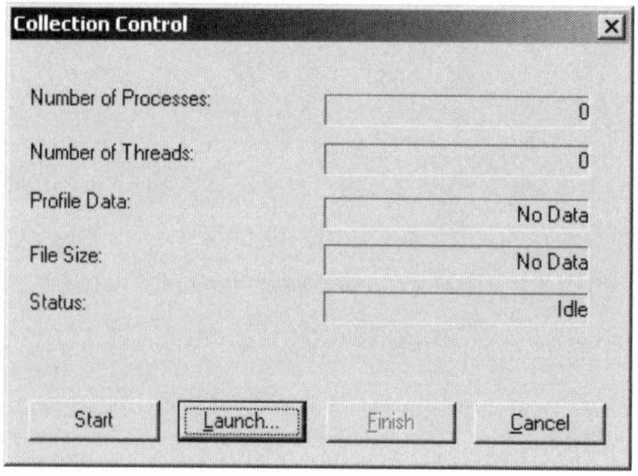

FIGURE 2–95 Collection Control dialog box

Click the Start button to start collecting data. After that, you will be able to launch programs on the device and perform all necessary actions. After the test scenarios have been run, click the Finish button to stop collecting data and to view it in a graph. A second option is to launch the application on the device by pressing the Launch button and entering the application name, as shown in Figure 2–96.

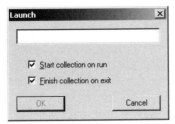

FIGURE 2–96 Launch program for profiling

Collected information can be available in various views. It enables you to analyze the application performance, as shown in Figure 2–97.

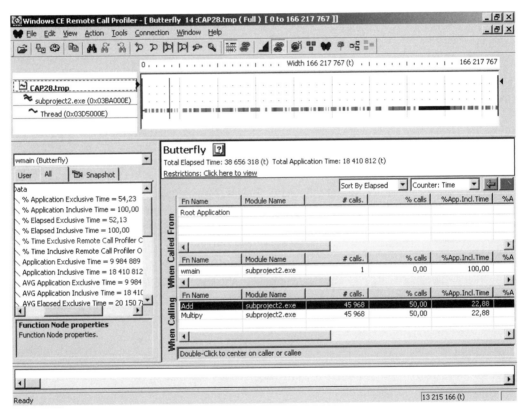

FIGURE 2–97 Analysis of collected data in Call Profiler

Note that the Call Profiler utility is not intended for profiling the system code.

Table 2–7 shows other utilities included in the toolkit.

TABLE 2-7 Other utilities.

Utility	Purpose
CEAppCompat.exe	Checks the compatibility of libraries and applications of earlier version of CE with the new version of the operating system.
BinCompress.exe	Prepares compressed files for the x86 BIOS loading utility.
BinMod.exe	Extracts and replaces files in the image. Only for files from the FILES section.
CEBackup.exe	Backs up and restores system libraries supplied with Platform Builder (.lib files from the Public directory tree).
CreateMUI.bat	Creates Multilingual User Interface (MUI) files for a given language.
CvrtBin.exe	Converts ROM files (.bin) into true binary format or into the Motorola format.
DumpBin.exe	Collects information from 32-bit Common Object File Format (COFF) files (.exe, .DLL), such as imported and exported functions.
KbdGen.exe	Generates keyboard layout files for Windows Embedded CE using DLL files of the Windows XP keyboard layout as a base.
ReadLog.exe	Converts the log file CELog into a text format or a format readable by the Kernel Tracker utility.
StampBin.exe	Enables you to view and modify data in the ROMPID and ROMHDR regions of the binary image (BIN).
Sysgen_capture.bat	Generates Sources files for Public projects that the developer wishes to transfer to his or her own code tree; for example, a driver that can be transferred to the developer's own BSP for subsequent modification.
ViewBin.exe	Views information about the system's image (.bin).
CabWiz.exe	Creates .cab files for installing programs on the device.
Wceldcmd.exe	Used to install .cab files to a specified location. Supports standalone devices.
Unldcmd.exe	Used for uninstalling created .cab files. Supports standalone devices.

Chapter 3
Operating System Architecture

Microsoft Windows Embedded CE 6.0 is a real-time, componentized, multithreaded operating system (OS) that supports preemptive multitasking and runs on multiple processor architectures, including ARM, Microprocessor without Interlocked Pipeline Stages (MIPS), x86, and SH4. Windows Embedded CE 6.0 operates in the virtual address space of 4 gigabytes (GB). The system kernel uses the upper 2 GB of virtual memory, while the active user process uses the lower 2 GB. Windows Embedded CE 6.0 supports up to 32,000 user processes, with the actual number of processes limited by the system resources. User processes include special processes that make the application programming interface (API) available for user applications. Such applications are named user-mode servers. These include Udevice.exe (User Mode Driver Host, a process that loads user-mode drivers) and Servicesd.exe (a process that loads services such as Hypertext Transfer Protocol (HTTP), File Transfer Protocol (FTP), Universal Plug and Play (UPnP), and so on). The system shell makes the main interface available to the user. If the system shell makes an additional API available, it is also a user-mode server.

The core of the operating system is the Nk.exe process, into which dynamic libraries responsible for various types of system functionality are loaded. You can also load system libraries and drivers into the kernel. Kernel libraries that make the API available for user applications are named kernel-mode servers.

The system API is available to applications through the coredll.dll library, which is linked to all executable modules of the operating system. The kernel modules are linked to a special version of coredll.dll for the kernel named k.coredll.dll. If a module is linked to coredll.dll and is loaded into the kernel, then all coredll.dll calls are automatically rerouted to k.coredll.dll.

In addition to the system API, the operating system offers an application API that is similar to the desktop Win32 API. A developer can access applied functionality through various application libraries, such as Wininet.dll, Winsock.dll, Msxml.dll, and Winhttp.dll. The system architecture includes the following components, as shown in Figure 3–1.

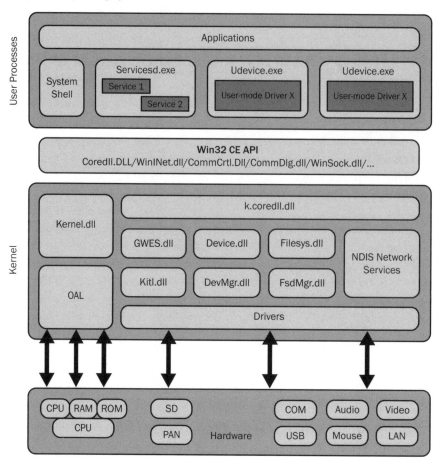

FIGURE 3–1 System architecture

Operating System Kernel Architecture

Let us take a closer look at the structure of the system kernel. A system kernel can be graphically represented as shown in Figure 3–2.

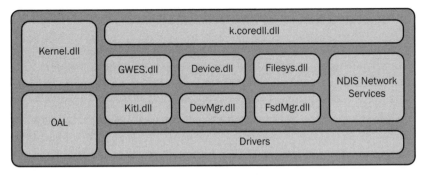

FIGURE 3–2 System kernel

The Nk.exe process is built from a static OEM adaptation layer (OAL) library, which is linked to the kernel.dll library file. Therefore, in Windows Embedded CE 6.0, the interface between the OAL and the system kernel is predetermined as much as possible. Table 3–1 outlines the main kernel-mode system servers and their functionality.

TABLE 3–1 Kernel-mode system servers.

Kernel-Mode Server	Functionality
kernel.dll	This is the system kernel. It provides basic functionality such as memory management, process loading, scheduler, and process and thread management.
kitl.dll	Implements Kernel Independent Transport Layer (KITL).
filesys.dll	File system, object store, registry, CEDB database, and system initialization.
fsdmgr.dll	File system manager, file system filter manager, and media manager.
device.dll	Together with devmgr.dll, it provides the Device Manager functionality.
devmgr.dll	Loads and manages drivers; loads input/output (I/O) resource manager.
gwes.dll	Responsible for the Graphics, Windowing, and Events Subsystem (GWES). Supports windows, dialog boxes, controls, menu, and other resources related to the user interface. Controls window manager and window messaging manager, including keyboard messages, mouse messages, touch screen messages, and so on.
k.coredll.dll	A version of coredll.dll for the system kernel.

In addition to the system libraries, you can also load kernel-mode drivers into the kernel.

Operating System and Hardware Interaction

The Windows Embedded CE 6.0 kernel interacts with hardware through the OAL, which conceals specific implementation of the processor and its periphery from the kernel implementation for the processor type shipped with the developer tools. It also performs hardware initialization. The operating system interacts with hardware by using drivers. A combination of the OAL, drivers, and configuration files for a specific hardware platform is named a board support package (BSP). The development suite includes samples of BSP implementations for reference platforms. Usually, a new BSP development starts by cloning the existing BSP sample that most closely matches the development BSP.

As mentioned before, drivers can be loaded into the kernel space. Such drivers are named kernel-mode drivers. Drivers that are loaded into a specialized user process, Udevice.exe (or User Mode Driver Host), are named user-mode drivers. Kernel-mode drivers offer higher productivity. Systems that use user-mode drivers are more fault-tolerant. The infrastructure of system drivers is designed in such a way that if certain requirements are met, you can develop drivers that function in both user mode and kernel mode.

Operating System Virtual Memory Architecture

The Windows Embedded CE 6.0 operating system is built based on virtual memory, which provides the operating system with a flexible and effective way of managing the limited resources of physical memory. The architecture of virtual memory is a mapping of virtual memory addresses to physical addresses. The architecture of virtual memory implies that virtual memory is mapped to physical memory, and not vice versa. Generally speaking, it is impossible to determine a corresponding virtual address if you know the physical address. Besides, sometimes it is common for multiple virtual addresses to be mapped to the same physical address. For example, the binary code of a dynamic-link library (DLL) can be loaded once into physical memory, yet be used by various processes.

Windows Embedded CE 6.0 is a 32-bit operating system. The 32-bit architecture provides 4 gigabytes (GB) of address space. Windows Embedded CE 6.0 operates in a flat 4-GB address space where the system kernel uses the upper 2 GB and the active user process uses the lower 2 GB. Virtual memory is allocated by page. The size of a virtual memory page in CE 6.0 equals 4 kilobytes (KB) and is determined by the architecture of the supported processor types. A virtual memory page represents a contiguous sequence of bytes, which corresponds to a contiguous physical memory page. The memory management unit (MMU) of the processor is responsible for working with virtual memory and for translating virtual addresses into physical addresses. Information about virtual-to-physical memory mapping is stored in the page table. The page table stores information about virtual-to-physical memory page mapping as well as additional page properties such as write access, availability for execution, access denial, and so on. When the system accesses the memory address, the processor checks page tables in order to find the physical page that the system is addressing. If the physical page is not found, a page fault occurs. A page fault also occurs if the requested access to the address does not match the page, such as during attempts to write to a page that is marked as read-only.

There are three states of virtual memory in CE 6.0:

- **Free** when memory is not allocated or used by the system.

- **Reserved** when memory is reserved but has not yet been mapped to the physical addresses.

- **Committed** when memory is reserved by the system and its mapping to physical addresses has been set.

Windows Embedded CE 6.0 commits virtual pages by request, which means that the process of committing a page is postponed for as long as possible. For example, when Windows Embedded CE allocates a stack or a heap, virtual memory is reserved, not committed. When an active application thread tries to access a reserved address, a page fault occurs, the active thread execution is suspended, the kernel processes the page fault, a necessary number of pages are committed, and code tables are corrected, after which the active threads resume operations. Page fault processing happens entirely inside the kernel and is thus hidden. Therefore, the process of addressing the memory (in this case, a stack memory or a heap memory) is completely transparent to the application.

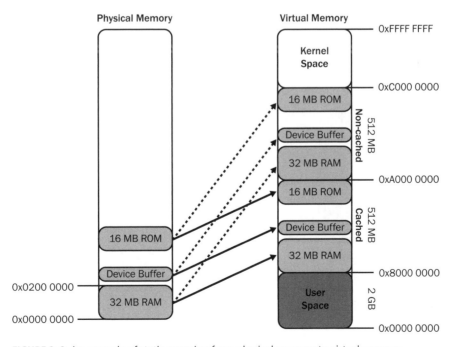

FIGURE 3–3 An example of static mapping from physical memory to virtual memory

A key element of the virtual memory architecture is the ability to map virtual addresses to physical addresses. Windows Embedded CE provides two virtual-to-physical mapping types, static and dynamic. The processor (for MIPS and SH4) or the manufacturer in an OAL (for x86 and ARM) in a special structure named OEMAddressTable determines static mapping. An example of static mapping is shown in Figure 3–3.

An important distinction of statically mapped virtual memory is that it is always available (committed), as opposed to dynamically mapped memory. Therefore, the kernel has guaranteed access to statically mapped virtual memory, which is required for low-level kernel initialization and for processing exception errors such as page faults. The necessity of enabling memory access for the kernel produces a requirement that the entire read-only memory (ROM)/random access memory (RAM) of the device can be statically mapped, including the device memory that is used for processing interrupt service routines (ISRs), which are processed in the kernel-exception context.

Windows Embedded CE supports static mapping of two virtual memory regions, each 512 MB in size. The lower 512 MB (0x8000 0000–0x9FFF FFFF) of virtual memory is mapped to physical memory with caching, and the upper 512 MB (0xA000 0000–0xB999 9999) of virtual memory does not use caching. Static mapping of the virtual memory is a good demonstration of the virtual memory architecture having two different virtual memory addresses with different access properties mapped to the same physical memory. Accessing virtual memory in region 0x8000 0000–0x9FFF FFFF does not necessarily result in accessing physical memory, because the value can be read from the cache. Accessing virtual memory in region 0xA000 0000–0xB999 9999 always results in accessing physical memory. This distinction is important to keep in mind while developing drivers.

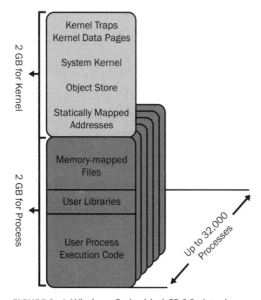

FIGURE 3–4 Windows Embedded CE 6.0 virtual memory space map

Dynamic mapping of the virtual memory occurs as part of the system and application operations by calling functions such as VirtualAlloc, VirtualAllocEx, VirtualCopy, VirtualCopyEx, VirtualAllocCopyEx, and so on. Despite the fact that the system uses 4-KB virtual memory pages, the system API of Windows Embedded CE 6.0 enables you to allocate virtual memory only with a 64-KB alignment (16 pages) that commits (maps) virtual memory by request or by calling designated functions directly by using page-by-page alignment. Figure 3–4 shows a Windows Embedded CE 6.0 virtual memory space map.

The kernel address space takes up the upper 2 GB and is identical for all system processes. The user space takes up the lower 2 GB and is unique for each process. The system kernel maps the address space of each designated process into this address space each time there is a switch between processes. At any given time, there is only one current process that has its own address space; it cannot access the address space of another process or obtain access to the kernel memory space. The system kernel has access to the entire address space and can obtain access to any permitted memory address.

Let us now look at a more detailed map of virtual memory of the operating system by examining the virtual memory allocation in kernel virtual address space, as shown in Figure 3–5.

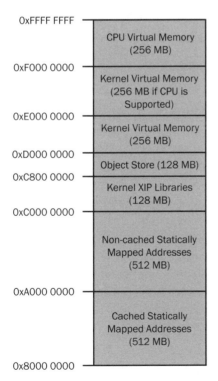

FIGURE 3–5 Kernel virtual address space map

Table 3–2 provides a detailed description of kernel virtual memory allocation.

TABLE 3–2 Kernel virtual memory allocation.

Memory Region	Size	Description
0x80000000–0x9FFFFFFF	512 MB	Statically mapped virtual addresses accessed with caching.
0xA0000000–0xBFFF FFFF	512 MB	Statically mapped virtual addresses accessed without caching.
0xC0000000–0xC7FF FFFF	128 MB	Mapping of execute in place (XIP) DLLs loaded by the kernel, servers, and kernel drivers. XIP entails running without copying into the RAM and fix-up addresses.
0xC8000000–0xCFFFFFFF	128 MB	Object store for RAM file system, CEDB databases, and registry.
0xD0000000–0xDFFFFFFF	256 MB	Virtual memory of the kernel used for all OS kernel modules.
0xE0000000–0xEFFFFFFF	256 MB	Virtual memory of the kernel, if supported by the processor.
0xF0000000–0xFFFFFFFF	256 MB	Captures system calls and includes kernel data pages.

Let us now proceed to the discussion of virtual memory allocation in user address space, as shown in Figure 3–6.

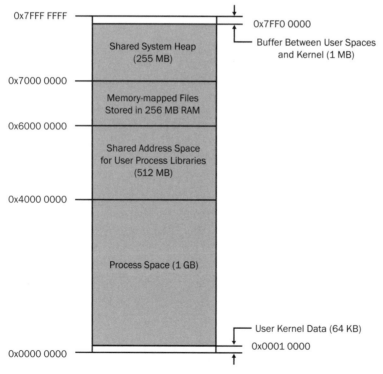

FIGURE 3–6 Kernel virtual address space map

Table 3–3 provides a detailed description of user virtual memory distribution.

TABLE 3–3 User virtual memory distribution.

Memory Region	Size	Description
0x00000000–0x00010000	64 KB	User kernel data. The user process has read-only access.
0x00010000–0x3FFFFFFF	1 GB–64 KB	Contains process space executable code, virtual memory, heap, and stack. Virtual memory allocation starts immediately after executable code and proceeds from the bottom up.
0x40000000–0x5FFFFFFF	512 MB	Contains DLLs, code, and data with memory allocation proceeding from the bottom up. Libraries that are loaded into various processes are loaded by using the same address. At the same time, code pages refer to the same physical pages, and data pages refer to different physical pages for various processes.
0x60000000–0x6FFFFFFF	256 MB	The regions of memory-mapped files that are stored in the memory. Unnamed memory-mapped files are stored at fixed addresses for backward compatibility.
0x70000000–0x7FEFFFFF	255 MB	Shared heap between the kernel and processes. The kernel, servers, and drivers may allocate memory to this region and write to the allocated memory. The user process can only read from this region. It enables the user process to receive data from the kernel without making a system kernel call.
0x7FF00000–0x7FFFFFFF	1 MB	Cannot be viewed for protection purposes; acts as a buffer between user space and kernel space.

Memory Management

The processes of dynamic allocation, which consists of committing and freeing virtual memory directly by using a designated API (VirtualXxxx), provide an opportunity to utilize the maximum capability of the virtual memory architecture. However, the use of those functions implies that you have knowledge of the structure and virtual memory architecture of Windows Embedded CE 6.0 and, possibly, of the processor physical architecture.

Table 3–4 describes the main API for working with virtual memory and its purpose.

TABLE 3–4 Functions for virtual memory API.

Function	Purpose
VirtualSetAttributesEx	Enables you to modify memory attributes on a page level. Accessible only in kernel mode.
VirtualProtectEx	Sets access protection for the page region in the address space of a specified process.
VirtualQueryEx	Provides information about the page region in the address space of a specified process.
VirtualAlloc	Commits the page region in the address space of a process in which it is called.
VirtualFree	Frees or decommits the page region in the address space of a process in which it is called.
VirtualProtect	Sets access protection for the page region in the address space of a process in which it is called.
VirtualQuery	Provides information about the page region in the address space of a process in which it is called.
VirtualAllocEx	Commits the page region in the address space of a specified process; the allocated memory is initialized to zeroes.
VirtualFreeEx	Releases and/or decommits the page region in the address space of a specified process.
VirtualCopyEx	Dynamic mapping of the virtual address to the physical address; a new entry is created in the page table. The resulting mapping is turned off by calling VirtualFree.
VirtualAllocCopyEx	Works as a consecutive execution of the VirtualAllocEx function and then the VirtualCopyEx function. The resulting mapping is turned off by calling VirtualFreeEx. Accessible only in kernel mode.

The application development process often does not require that you interact directly with virtual memory; however, you must have the ability to dynamically allocate a large number of memory regions of variable size (usually, a lot less than 64 KB) with granularity of at least 1 byte. To solve this problem, the operating system provides applications with a heap created through direct interaction with virtual memory. A heap provides a developer with an ability to allocate memory blocks of variable size with granularity of 1 byte without having to commit virtual memory.

Windows Embedded CE 6.0 implements a heap as follows:

- It is a sequence of unmovable blocks.

- When searching for free memory, the first suitable block is allocated.

- If the first block of the needed size is not found and the heap has no restrictions on maximum size, additional memory is allocated for the heap.

- When additional memory is allocated, a heap is not guaranteed contiguity of its resulting address space.

- Free heap blocks are combined forward according to a list with each memory allocation and deallocation cycle.

- A search for blocks for new memory allocation always starts from the last allocated or deallocated block.

- Each time there is a request for more than 16 KB of memory, a separate heap is created.

Because unmovable blocks are used, virtual memory pages (4 KB) are deallocated by the heap only when all of its blocks are deallocated. An application can allocate and deallocate memory from a heap arbitrarily. However, considering the sequential structure of the heap and the algorithm of searching for unallocated blocks, that are being used, there is a possibility of heap fragmentation. Heap fragmentation may result in the increase of time that it takes to search for unallocated blocks and, in an extreme case, despite the presence of unallocated memory space, it would be impossible to allocate memory from a heap without having additional memory.

This type of heap implementation works best with smaller memory blocks of the same size or of sizes that are as similar as possible, by using the "first one to be allocated, last one to be deallocated" rule , which provides the most efficient use of the block combining algorithm.

When the operating system creates the process, it automatically creates and reserves (but does not commit) a process heap with 64 KB of memory. The initial heap size is 64 KB, with 60 KB of virtual memory reserved and 4 KB left at the end of the region for additional protection against heap overflow.

A heap that is created automatically when the process is loaded is named a local heap. A developer can create any number of private heaps for use in his or her application. If a heap is created by the kernel process, it may be a shared heap. A shared heap, is available to the kernel for reading and writing, whereas user processes can only have read access to it. Windows Embedded CE 6.0 includes a new type of heap, and that is a remote heap which is a heap that one process (server) creates in another process (client). A process that creates a remote heap has full access to it, whereas the client process has read access and an optional write access.

When a heap is created, the developer may specify the initial and the maximum size of the heap. If a maximum size of the heap is specified, the heap is created with a certain size, so that automatic size growth does not happen.

The main API for working with heaps is described in Table 3–5.

TABLE 3–5 Heap API functions.

Function	Purpose
CeRemoteHeapCreate	Creates a remote heap in a specified process and determines the client process rights to the heap.
CeRemoteHeapMapPointer	Maps a pointer to the memory received from a remote heap in one process to a pointer that is available to another process from a pair.
HeapAlloc	Allocates memory from a given heap.
HeapCompact	Compacts unallocated heap blocks that are close together and stops committing large unallocated blocks of virtual memory.
HeapDestroy	Destroys a specified heap.
HeapFree	Deallocates memory that was allocated from a specified heap.
HeapReAlloc	Reallocates memory from a specified heap.
HeapSize	Returns a memory block size allocated from a specific heap.
HeapValidate	Validates service information about the heap.
LocalAlloc	Allocates memory from a process heap (local heap).
LocalFree	Frees up memory that was allocated from a local heap.
LocalReAlloc	Reallocates memory from a local heap.
LocalSize	Returns a memory block size allocated from a local heap.
GetProcessHeap	Returns a handle to a local heap of the process in which it is called.
CeHeapCreate	Allocates a heap with specified memory allocator and memory deallocator functions.

A stack is the simplest type of memory that is available to a developer. It is created, used, and controlled automatically. A stack is used for storing local variables in functions, addresses of function returns, and the state of the processor registers during exception handling.

Under Windows Embedded CE 6.0, a stack is created for each thread in the system. Stack architecture depends on the hardware architecture, although the stack size is usually limited to 64 KB, out of which 8 KB are reserved to control stack overflow[1]. Therefore, by default, the stack size is limited to 56 KB.

If the entire stack object is used, an attempt to allocate memory from it results in an access violation error and the application terminates abruptly.

---

[1] Default linker settings include a control stack overflow option.

By using the /STACK linking parameter, you can change the default stack size; you can also specify the size of a stack directly during the process of creating a thread by using the CreateThread function. When you change the default stack size, it is necessary to consider that all threads in the system will be created by using the specified stack size, which may result in memory availability issues in the systems with limited resources. Stack memory is committed on a per-page basis only if necessary. Memory is committed initially when the scheduler makes a thread available for execution for the first time.

A static data block represents the next type of memory. This block contains strings, buffers, and other static values that the application references throughout its life. Windows Embedded CE 6.0 allocates two sections for static data, one for read/write data and one for read-only data. Because the operating system allocates these areas on a per-page basis, there may be some space left over from the static data up to the next page boundary. It is recommended that no extra space be left at the end of the static block area. It might be better to move a few buffers into a static data area, rather than allocating those buffers dynamically, as long as there is space in the static data area, or to initialize lines statically rather than dynamically. The easiest way to determine the size of static data is by accessing the map file of the linker.

Memory-mapped files represent the next type of memory used in applications. Memory-mapped files are the files that are mapped into the virtual address space. A developer has access to files by simply accessing certain areas of the memory. Changes made directly in memory are mapped accordingly in the file.

The operating system enables you to create named and unnamed memory-mapped files. The named memory-mapped files can be accessed from another process by requesting a file with the same name, thus enabling different processes to interact with each other. The unnamed memory-mapped files also can be used for interprocess communications. In order for another process to access the mapping, it is necessary to use the DuplicateHandle function to make a new handle to the mapping and pass the handle to the other process.

If the file that is being mapped to memory was created based on an actual media device, the operating system handles this file by reading the file data from the media device in memory and back. These types of memory-mapped files are named file-backed. You can create a memory-mapped file that will have no corresponding file in the media device. In this case, the entire file is stored in the operating system memory and not on a disk. Such files are named RAM-backed.

The main API for working with memory-mapped files and its purpose are described in Table 3–6.

TABLE 3–6 Functions for working with memory-mapped files.

Function	Purpose
CreateFile	Creates and opens a file that can be used for memory mapping. Returns a file handle.
CreateFileForMapping	Creates and opens a file that can be used for memory mapping. The kernel creates the file. The handle automatically closes when the process completes. You should not use this function; instead, you should use the regular CreateFile function. Returns a file handle.
CreateFileMapping	Creates a named or unnamed memory-mapped file based on another file or RAM. This function also returns a handle of a memory-mapped file.
MapViewOfFile	Creates a view of a memory-mapped file or its part in the address space and returns the initial address of the view of a memory-mapped file.
FlushViewOfFile	Flushes the view of a memory-mapped file.
UnmapViewOfFile	Unmaps a view of the memory-mapped file.

Processes, Threads, Fibers, and the Scheduler

The Windows Embedded CE base execution unit is a thread. Each thread has its own context (stack, priority, access rights, and so on) and is executed in the process container. Each process contains at least one thread that is the primary thread. Windows Embedded CE has a theoretical limitation of 32,000 processes that the system can simultaneously load. The number of threads is not theoretically limited, but that number is limited by the number of available descriptors. All process threads have a shared address space—the memory allocated by one thread is available to other threads within that process. Also, all process threads have equal rights to access descriptors regardless of the nature of their handle. Access rights to the address space of another process are determined on a thread level.

The scheduler is a kernel component responsible for managing thread execution. The scheduler ensures a predictable order of thread execution by using thread prioritization. When interrupts occur in the scheduling system, the scheduler takes the interrupts into account and reprioritizes threads accordingly. The Windows Embedded CE scheduler implements a process of time-slotted operation that uses multitasking, is based on priority, and has support for a single-level priority inversion.

The multitasking support system of Windows Embedded CE has the following characteristics:

- Time-sliced multitasking.
  - ❑ Usually, a slice of execution time (quantum) is equal to 100 milliseconds (ms).
  - ❑ A quantum can be set by the device manufacturer.
  - ❑ A quantum can be set programmatically for each thread.
- 256 priority levels.
  - ❑ 0–thread executes until completion.
  - ❑ 251–default thread priority.
- Preemptive multitasking.
  - ❑ If several threads of different priority levels are ready for execution, the thread with the highest priority level as of the time of scheduling is made available for execution.
- Round-robin scheduling of threads with the same priority level.
  - ❑ After a thread has completed executing a quantum, if the system had other threads with the same priority level as the first thread, the system suspends execution of the specified thread and makes another thread available for execution. The suspended thread is scheduled for execution after the system runs all threads with the same priority level. That is, the system executes threads with the same priority level cyclically.
  - ❑ If a time slice is set to zero, the system excludes the thread from cyclical execution and instead runs it until it completes or is blocked, as long as there are no higher-priority threads or interrupts.
- One level of priority inversion is supported.
  - ❑ Priority inversion happens when a lower-level-priority thread blocks the execution of a higher-level-priority thread by holding the resource for which the higher-level priority thread waits.
  - ❑ A one-level priority inversion denotes that only one thread's priority is increased, which helps to resolve one-level blocking problems. If a lower-level-priority thread is blocked by a process with an even lower priority level, then one-level priority inversion will not be able to unblock the resource.

Figure 3–7 shows an example of thread execution that demonstrates time-slicing, a cyclical scheduling of threads with the same priority level, and pushing threads with a lower priority level to the background.

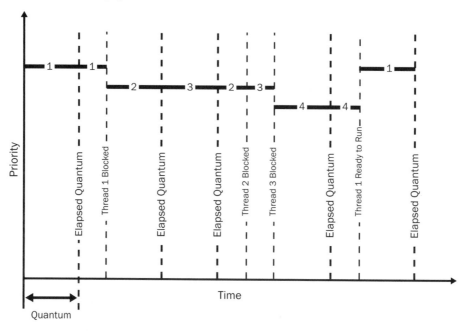

FIGURE 3–7 Windows Embedded CE scheduler thread execution

Let us take a closer look at the process depicted in Figure 3–7. There are four threads. The first thread (1) has the highest priority level, while the fourth thread (4) has the lowest priority level. The second (2) and the third threads (3) have the same priority level, which is higher than that of the fourth thread and lower than the priority of the first thread. At the initial stage, the first thread has the highest priority level of all threads that are ready to be executed. It executes within a quantum (slice) of time, after which the scheduler places it again for execution because the thread continues to have the highest priority level. After a while, in less than one time quantum of execution, the first (1) thread is blocked. Now the second (2) and the third (3) threads can be executed. Because these threads have equal priority, they are scheduled to be executed in a cyclical manner. In our case, first the second (2), then the third (3), then again the second (2) executes until it is blocked and the third one (3) executes until that one is blocked. Now the system has only one thread, the fourth thread (4), that is ready for execution. It is executed in a quantum of time, after which the scheduler once again starts planning its execution because it remains to be a thread with the highest priority level ready for execution. After a while, in less than one time quantum of execution, the first (1) thread is unblocked, so the first thread is ready for execution. Execution of the fourth (4) thread stops, and it is preempted by the first (1) thread, which continues to run.

Figure 3–8 shows a typical scheme of resource blocking that is resolved by priority inversion.

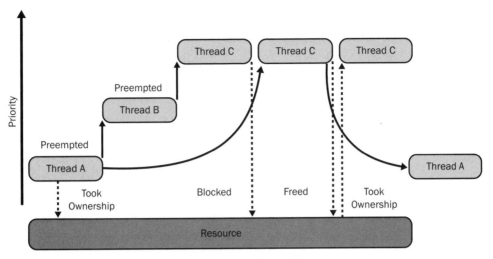

FIGURE 3–8 Resource blocking resolved by priority inversion

Let us take a closer look at the process depicted in Figure 3–8. Thread A acquires a resource, and after a while it is pushed away by a higher-priority thread B, which in its turn is pushed away by thread C, which, after a while, is blocked while waiting for a resource captured by thread A. Because thread A is not the highest-priority thread of the ones that are left, after the high-priority thread C is blocked, it will stop executing and the resource will remain blocked. Therefore, a low-priority thread blocks a higher priority thread as far as the resource is concerned. When a similar situation is detected, the scheduler increases the priority of a lower-priority thread A to the level of a blocked high-priority thread C until a lower-priority thread has freed a resource. After that, the priority level of low-priority thread A is restored, and thread C continues executing.

Windows Embedded CE implements a single-level priority inversion, which means that priority is increased for only one thread. Therefore, if a thread that blocked a higher-priority-level thread is blocked by a lower-priority thread, the single-level priority inversion will not result in unblocking. A fully nested priority inversion may resolve a multilevel mutual blocking; the scheduler will go through all blocked threads and increase the priority if necessary until a higher-priority thread is unblocked. However, this disrupts a predictability of execution and does not provide an opportunity to entirely utilize priority inversion in a system with a real-time support, such as Windows Embedded CE.

A developer is required to write his or her code in such a way that avoids mutual blocking. In real-time systems, a developer must avoid priority inversion because it disrupts the execution thread. To do that, it is necessary to not have race conditions for a resource, which is accomplished by setting the same priority level for all threads that work with one resource.

Let us now look at how APIs work with threads. Table 3–7 shows the main API for working with threads and processes, as well as the functions

TABLE 3-7 Functions for working with threads and processes.

Function	Purpose
CeGetThreadPriority	Returns the priority (0–255) of a thread.
CeGetThreadQuantum	Returns the time slice (quantum) of the thread execution.
CeSetThreadPriority	Sets priority (0–255) of a thread.
CeSetThreadQuantum	Sets the time slice (quantum) of the thread execution.
CreateProcess	Creates a new process and the main thread.
CreateThread	Creates a thread in the address space of a process.
ExitProcess	Finishes the current process and all of its threads.
ExitThread	Finishes the current thread.
GetCurrentProcess	Returns a pseudo-handle of the process in which it was named.
GetCurrentProcessId	Returns the identifier of a process in which it was named; coincides with the pseudo-handle of the process.
GetCurrentThread	Returns the pseudo-handle of the process in which it was named.
GetCurrentThreadId	Returns the identifier of the thread in which it was named; coincides with the pseudo-handle of the process.
GetExitCodeProcess	Returns an exit code for a specified process.
GetExitCodeThread	Returns an exit code for a specified thread.
GetThreadContext	Returns the context for a specified thread.
GetThreadPriority	Returns the priority (248–255) of a specified process.
OpenProcess	Returns a handle for the existing process according to an identifier.
OpenThread	Returns a handle for the existing thread according to an identifier.
ResumeThread	Decreases suspend count by one. Thread execution will continue when the count is equal to zero.
SetThreadContext	Sets context for a specified thread.
SetThreadPriority	Sets priority (248–255) for a specified thread.
Sleep	Suspends execution of the current thread for a specified period of time.
SuspendThread	Suspends thread execution and increases suspend count by one.
TerminateProcess	Terminates a specified process and all of its threads.
TerminateThread	Terminates a specified thread.
TlsAlloc	Receives an index for making an entry in a thread local storage (TLS).
TlsFree	Frees an index of a local thread storage thus making it reusable.
TlsGetValue	Receives a value from local thread storage according to an index.
TlsSetValue	Sets a value in local thread storage according to an index.

In addition to the threads whose execution is scheduled by the system scheduler, there are execution units that are manually scheduled for execution by an application. These units are named fibers. Fibers have the following characteristics in Windows Embedded CE:

- A fiber is executed in a context of a thread that launches it.

- Each thread may execute several fibers.

- In order to manage fibers, the thread itself needs to be converted to a fiber by calling the ConvertThreadToFiber function.

- A fiber is executed when its thread is executed.

- Fibers are not preempted. The thread switches fiber execution directly.

The main API for working with fibers and its purpose are listed in Table 3–8.

TABLE 3–8 Functions for working with fibers.

Function	Purpose
ConvertThreadToFiber	Converts a current thread to a fiber.
CreateFiber	Creates a fiber and sets its stack and the starting address. Does not launch a fiber execution.
DeleteFiber	Deletes a current fiber.
GetCurrentFiber	Returns the current fiber's address.
GetFiberData	Returns data transferred to a fiber by ConvertThreadToFiber and CreateFiber functions.
SwitchToFiber	Launches execution of a specified fiber.

Synchronization Objects

Synchronization routines that ensure a coordinated execution of threads and a safe access to resources are an integral part of a multithreaded execution system. Windows Embedded CE has the following synchronization objects:

- Critical sections.

- Mutexes.

- Semaphores.

- Events.

- Point-to-point message queue.

In addition to these objects, you can also use a thread's handlers and interlocked functions.

Each type of synchronization object has its own name space. An object with an empty string ('') is also considered a named object.

Synchronization objects can be in a signaled or a non-signaled state. A thread requests a synchronization object and is blocked if an object is in a non-signaled state. After an object switches to a signaled state, the thread continues execution.

Table 3–9 provides a list of functions that enable you to block a thread execution until a certain synchronization object has changed to a signaled state.

TABLE 3–9 Function list for blocking threads.

Function	Purpose
WaitForSingleObject	Blocks a thread execution while waiting until a specified synchronization object has switched to a signal state.
WaitForMultipleObjects	Blocks a thread execution while waiting until one of the specified synchronization objects has switched to a signal state.

Let us begin looking at synchronization by examining interlocked functions. Interlocked functions provide synchronized access to a shared variable. The objective of the function is to prevent a preemptive movement of a thread during its execution. Interlocked functions and their purpose, provided by Windows Embedded CE, are listed in Table 3–10.

TABLE 3–10 Interlocked functions and their purpose.

Function	Purpose
InterlockedIncrement	Atomically increments the value of a specified 32-bit variable by one.
InterlockedDecrement	Atomically decrements the value of a specified 32-bit variable by one.
InterlockedExchange	Atomically exchanges the values of two 32-bit variables.
InterlockedTestExchange	Provides a conditional testing and sets the value of a 32-bit variable.
InterlockedCompareExchange	Provides a conditional atomic comparison and sets the value of a 32-bit variable.
InterlockedExchangeAdd	Atomically changes the value of a 32-bit variable to a specified value.
InterlockedCompareExchange-Pointer	Provides a conditional atomic comparison and sets the value of a pointer.
InterlockedExchangePointer	Atomically sets the value of a pointer.

A thread handle can act as a synchronization object. A thread is in a signaled state when it's executing, and it's in a non-signaled state when it's not executing.

A critical section is designed to protect the code area that accesses a shared resource that must not be concurrently accessed by more than one thread of execution. A critical section is a special data structure that an application must allocate and initialize before using it. To protect a code area, a thread calls a critical section (by using the EnterCriticalSection function) and is blocked[2] until the critical section becomes available. When exiting a code area that needs to be protected, the thread frees the critical section (by using the LeaveCriticalSection function).

Critical section functions must have a pointer to the critical section data structure, which limits the range of a critical section to the visibility range of a corresponding variable that contains a specialized structure, that is, the range of the process or the library.

Entering a critical section does not result in turning to the kernel and creating a kernel-based object, as long as there are no blocks. Therefore, using critical sections is a very effective solution when there are only a few blocks.

The main API for working with critical sections and its purpose are provided in Table 3–11.

TABLE 3–11 **Functions for working with critical sections.**

Function	Purpose
InitializeCriticalSection	Initializes a critical section.
EnterCriticalSection	Blocks a thread execution while waiting for access to a critical section. The function is returned when the thread that makes the call becomes the owner of the critical section.
TryEnterCriticalSection	Tries to enter a critical section without blocking execution. If the call is successful, the thread becomes the owner of the critical section.
LeaveCriticalSection	Leaves a specified critical section.
DeleteCriticalSection	Deallocates all resources of a critical section that is owned by any thread.

A mutex is designed to provide mutually exclusive access to a resource. A mutex is in a signaled state when it is not owned by any thread. When it is owned by a thread, it is switched to a non-signaled state. At any point in time, only one thread can own a mutex. As opposed to a critical section, a mutex is a pure-kernel object, and therefore, when accessed by another process, regardless of blocking, the kernel is called, which results in considerable overhead.

A mutex can be named or unnamed. Named mutexes provide synchronization among different processes. Mutex synchronization is achieved by using standard WaitForSingleObject/WaitForMultipleObject functions. After a mutex operation finishes, its handle must be freed by calling a standard CloseHandle function.

---

2 Also available is TryEnterCriticalSection, which enables you to try to obtain a critical section without blocking execution.

The main API for working with mutexes and its purpose are listed in Table 3–12.

TABLE 3–12 Functions for working with mutexes.

Function	Purpose
CreateMutex	Creates a named or unnamed mutex object.
ReleaseMutex	Releases a specified mutex object.

A semaphore is designed to limit the number of threads that are simultaneously using a resource. When a semaphore is initialized, the system specifies the initial number and the maximum number of threads that can simultaneously use a resource. Each time a process takes ownership of a semaphore, the counter is decremented by one. Each time a process frees a semaphore, the counter is incremented by one.

The counter value may be no less than zero and no more than the maximum value specified upon semaphore creation. A semaphore is in a signaled state when the count is greater than zero, and it's in a non-signaled state when it is equal to zero. A semaphore can be named or unnamed. Named semaphores provide the ability to perform synchronization among different processes.

Semaphore synchronization is achieved by using standard WaitForSingleObject and WaitForMultipleObject functions. After a semaphore operation terminates, its handle must be freed by calling a standard CloseHandle function.

The main API for working with semaphores and its purpose are listed in Table 3–13.

TABLE 3–13 Functions for working with semaphores.

Function	Purpose
CreateSemaphore	Creates a named or unnamed semaphore object.
ReleaseSemaphore	Releases a specified semaphore by incrementing the counter by a certain value.

The system uses events for informing that certain events have occurred at a certain moment in time. A thread may await a certain event to perform certain actions. An event is in a signaled state when it is set, and it's in a non-signaled state when it is not set (reset). Based on how resetting is done, events are classified into those with automatic resets and manual resets. Events with an automatic reset are switched into a non-signaled state by the kernel as soon as one thread that is awaiting an event has been freed. Events with a manual reset must be reset manually by calling a special function.

An event can be named or unnamed. Named events provide synchronization among different processes. Event synchronization is achieved by using standard WaitForSingleObject and

WaitForMultipleObject functions. After an event operation finishes, its handle must be freed by calling a standard CloseHandle function.

The main API for working with events and its purpose are listed in Table 3–14.

TABLE 3–14 Functions for working with events.

Function	Purpose
CreateEvent	Creates a named or unnamed event object.
SetEvent	Turns the event object into a signal state.
ResetEvent	Turns off the signal state of the event.
PulseEvent	Turns the event object into a signal state after a certain number of threads have been unblocked. It turns off the signal state of the event object.

Let us take a closer look at the way the API interacts with various event types. When switching a manual reset event to a signaled state by using the SetEvent function, the event remains in a signaled state until it is manually reset by the ResetEvent function. During this reset, all threads awaiting the event are unblocked, along with the threads that start waiting for the event after it is manually set and before it is manually reset. When the PulseEvent function is used with a manual reset event, the event is switched to a signaled state, all threads awaiting the event are unblocked, and the event is switched to a non-signaled state.

When an automatic reset event is set to a signaled state by calling the SetEvent function, only one thread awaiting execution is unblocked. Then, the kernel switches the event to a non-signaled state. An event remains in a signaled state until one thread is unblocked. Then, the event switches to a non-signaled state, while the rest of the threads awaiting the event remain blocked. When using the PulseEvent function with an automatic reset event, the event switches to a signaled state. If there are threads awaiting the event, one thread is unblocked. Then, the event switches to a non-signaled state even if no threads have been unblocked.

A point-to-point message queue is designed for synchronization when it is necessary to transmit additional information. It uses minimum resources and is designed for maximum efficiency. It is used by the power-management subsystem and Plug and Play. A point-to-point message queue can be named or unnamed. Named point-to-point message queues provide synchronization among different processes. Point-to-point message queue synchronization is achieved by using standard WaitForSingleObject and WaitForMultipleObject functions. After a point-to-point message queue operation finishes, its handle must be freed by calling a standard CloseHandle function.

The main API for working with PPP event queues is listed in Table 3–15.

TABLE 3–15 Functions for working with point-to-point message queues.

Function	Purpose
CreateMsgQueue	Creates and opens a user message queue.
CloseMsgQueue	Closes an open message queue.
GetMsgQueueInfo	Returns information about a message queue.
ReadMsgQueue	Reads one message from the message queue.
ReadMsgQueueEx	Reads one message from the message queue and, optionally, returns security context of the message sender.
WriteMsgQueue	Writes one message into a message queue.
OpenMsgQueue	Opens an existing message queue according to a handle.

Interrupt Architecture

Practically all peripheral devices use interrupts to inform the operating system that certain actions need to be taken to provide services for those devices. A device driver must process an interrupt in order to provide a necessary service to a peripheral device.

A physical interrupt request (IRQ) is a hardware line by which a device sends an interrupt signal to a microprocessor. A system interrupt (SYSINTR) is a mapping of the IRQ for which an OAL is responsible.

Some peripheral devices do not generate microprocessor interrupts. In those cases, a device controller processes interrupts.

Under Windows Embedded CE, interrupt processing is divided into two parts: interrupt service routine (ISR) and interrupt service thread (IST).

Each IRQ is associated with an ISR. Several interrupt sources can be associated with one ISR. If an interrupt is rising, the kernel calls a corresponding ISR routine for that interrupt. When the ISR execution completes, the routine returns a logical identifier of SYSINTR. The kernel checks the logical identifier of an interrupt and sets an event that is associated with it. The scheduler plans the execution of the IST that is waiting for the event, as shown in Figure 3–9.

The main task of the ISR is to determine the system identifier of the interrupt (logical interrupt) request and mask it. The ISR can also perform other time-critical tasks. However, it is necessary to minimize the time of ISR operation, because during its operation at least those IRQs that have equal priority level and those with lower priority are not served. An ISR can be statically linked to the kernel or it can be installed by calling the kernel. In both cases, the ISR should have no external dependencies, either explicit or implicit. System kernel architecture supports nested interrupt processing by providing the ability to process higher-priority IRQs that arrive while the ISR runs. A developer must implement the necessary hardware support for his or her device and for his or her ISR routines.

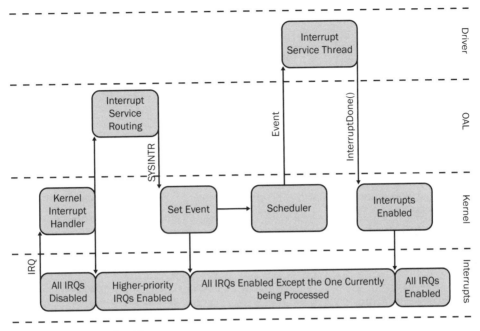

FIGURE 3–9 Interrupt handling

If the processor architecture supports multiple hardware IRQs, then the developer must register the ISR routine in the OAL for each IRQ. For processors with one IRQ, such as ARM, the kernel calls one predetermined procedure that must be implemented in the OAL, and the developer can register separate installable ISRs in the kernel.

The kernel loads the installable ISRs dynamically while executing the LoadIntChainHandler function. The use of the installable ISR (IISR) implies that the kernel has registered the ISR for a designated IRQ, which initiates calling a chain of installable ISRs (NKCallIntChain) and returns a logical identifier of the SYSINTR to the kernel. Processors with one IRQ, such as ARM, require that initiating a call to a chain of interrupts be performed by a predetermined function that processes interrupts (OEMInterruptHandler).

When calling the NKCallIntChain function, the kernel calls the ISRs that were registered by calling LoadIntChainHandler on a first-in, first-out (FIFO) basis. If the IISR procedure that has been called does not process a specified interrupt, it returns SYSINTR_CHAIN, and the kernel proceeds to call the next IISR procedure. If the IISR procedure that has been called is able to process a specified interrupt it returns a non-SYSINTR_CHAIN identifier, and the kernel returns a specified identifier; the rest of the ISRs are not called.

The IST performs the bulk of processing. The IST is a regular system thread that has a high enough priority for handling the tasks of processing a specific interrupt for a specific device. An IST is usually a part of the driver. An IST must perform at least the following actions:

1. It creates a standard event (by using the CreateEvent function).

2. It registers the event in the kernel for a certain logical identifier of SYSINTRs (by using the InterruptInitialize function).

3. It waits for an event associated with the interrupt (by using the WaitForSingleObject function).

4. It notifies the kernel at the end of processing that the interrupt is done (by using the InterruptDone function).

If a driver uses the installable ISR, then it can load the IISR (by using the LoadIntChainHandler function); configure it (by using the KernelLibIoControl function), and, when the driver is finished, unload IISR (by using the FreeIntChainHandler function). When the FreeIntChainHandler function is called, the IISR code is not named when processing a corresponding IRQ, but it remains in the memory. When the LoadIntChainHandler is called the next time, the same IISR procedure uses the previously loaded code. Windows Embedded CE 6.0 includes a configurable IISR procedure that has a common purpose (Generic Installable ISR– GIISR). Its source code is located in the \Public\Common\Oak\Drivers\GIISR directory.

Chapter 4
Build System

The Microsoft Windows Embedded CE development toolset uses a unified build system. A developer can build an operating system (OS) from the Visual Studio 2005 integrated environment or from a command-line interface. Visual Studio 2005 menu items launch the necessary batch files. The build tools suite is composed of a set of batch files (batch files) and console utilities. Designated environment variables and the parameters that are passed during calls to the build system control the build process. Batch files initiate environment variables during the initial stage by calling PBInitEnv.bat, which then calls Wince.bat with the necessary parameters. The file blddemo.bat is the main batch file that controls the overall build system. It in turn launches other batch files and build utilities, which can then launch further batch files or utilities of their own, as needed.

The batch files used by the build system have documentation in the internal comments and in Help, which makes it possible to trace the entire chain of calls to batch files and utilities. The Nmake (Nmake.exe) utility is ultimately used for compiling and linking. It uses all the necessary tools for the chosen processor architecture.

The tools suite and the input files for building the system are located in the catalog directory tree, the root of which is determined by the environment variable _WINCEROOT (by default, it is the WINCE600 directory in the disk's root). The subdirectory structure is designed in such a way that the hardware-dependent part (Platform catalog) is separated from the hardware-independent part (Public and Private catalogs) of the operating system. The functionality of an OS image can be either set through Platform Builder's user interface (UI), or more directly by setting environment variables within the build window.

In order to select a necessary functionality of the OS image, it is necessary to set environment variables of the image, which appear as SYSGEN_XXX. The usual method for setting environment variables of the build is to select items of the Platform Builder catalog. Additional environment variables can be specified in the OS design settings, as well as directly from a command-line window by using the main build batch file, blddemo.bat.

The information about building separate components and the OS image is contained in various configuration files. The Dirs files, Sources files, and Nmake configuration files are used for building modules, whereas .bib, .reg, .dat, and .db files are used for building a binary run-time image. The roles of these files are discussed later in this chapter.

The end result of a build process is a monolithic run-time image that can be loaded onto an emulator or a target device for subsequent debugging.

Directory Tree of the Build System

An operating system is built from a directory tree (catalog hierarchy). Table 4–1 lists standard subdirectories of the root directory and descriptions.

TABLE 4–1 Standard subdirectories.

Directory	Description
SDK	Contains compilers and link utilities for supported platforms (x86, ARM, SH4, Microprocessor without Interlocked Pipeline Stages [MIPS]). Additional utilities for building a system image are located in the %_ WINCEROOT%\PUBLIC\COMMON\ OAK\BIN\I386 folder.
OSDESIGNS	By default, this directory contains the OS designs that are in progress. Each subdirectory corresponds to a named design of the operating system. An OS design consists of various modules, such as tools and drivers.
PLATFORM	The specified directory contains the hardware-dependent part of the operating system, such as board support packages (BSPs) and drivers. Subdirectories contain the implementation of OEM adaptation layer (OAL) and drivers for a specific hardware platform. If a custom BSP needs to be created, its implementation is also located in that directory. The Common subdirectory contains the common platform code, including auxiliary libraries for writing the BSP and drivers.
PUBLIC	Contains hardware-independent components of the operating system.
PRIVATE	Contains the source code of the operating system. Windows Embedded CE creates this directory if the Shared Source feature is chosen and the additional license agreement is accepted during the installation. After Platform Builder is installed, the license agreement is located in the following file: \Program Files\Microsoft Platform Builder\6.00\source.rtf.
OTHERS	Contains various components that for a variety of reasons were not included in the above directories, such as: ■ ATL8, which contains libraries, header files, and initial files for debugging ATL applications. ■ DotnetV2, which contains executable .NET files for supported processor architectures. ■ Edb, which contains executable modules for supporting Enhanced Database files. ■ SQLCE20, which contains SQL Compact Edition libraries for each supported processor architecture. ■ VisualStudio, which is a utility for working with devices for Visual Studio.
3RDPARTY	Directory for own components, such as those that were cloned from Public or Private. It is independently created by a developer and, similar to Public, it is automatically scanned for catalog files.

Let us take a closer look at the subdirectories of the Public directory, as shown in Table 4–2.

TABLE 4-2 Subdirectories of the Public directory.

Directory	Purpose
CEBASE	Device templates for thin client, gateway, and so on.
CELLCORE	Components for working in cellular networks.
COMMON	The CATALOG subdirectory contains the Platform Builder catalog. The OAK subdirectory contains common components of the operating system, files that manage the system build process, and auxiliary utilities.
DATASYNC	Components for supporting synchronization of Windows Embedded CE devices with desktop computers.
DCOM	Components to support DCOM.
DIRECTX	Support for DirectX.
GDIEX	Support for GDI+.
IE	Internet Explorer 6.0 and additional modules.
NETCFV2	For including .NET Compact Framework into the image.
OSTEST	Windows Embedded CE Test Kit (CETK).
PBTOOLS	Example of implementing an extension for Performance Monitor.
RDP	Support for Remote Desktop Protocol (RDP).
SCRIPT	Script support for: Microsoft JScript 5.5 and VBScript 5.5.
SERVERS	Servers: HTTP, FTP, UPnP, OBEX, Telnet, and so on.
SHELL	System shells including Standard Shell, Explorer Browser, and CEShell.
SHELLSDK	Application programming interface (API) shells of Pocket PC 2002 and AYGShell API.
SPEECH	Support for Microsoft Speech API (SAPI) 5.0.
SQLCE	For including SQL CE in the image.
VOIP	Support for Voice over IP (VoIP)–based applications and SIP-based services.
WCEAPPSFE	WordPad and Inbox.
WCESHELLFE	Windows Embedded CE shell components.

Most subdirectories in the Public directory contain Cesysgen, OAK, and SDK folders. Cesysgen contains files, including header files, DEF files for generating DLLs, and other files used in the build process, that are filtered based on selected OS functionality. The OAK folder contains libraries and configuration files that are necessary for building a component. The SDK folder contains auxiliary files for building applications that use the functionality of a specified component. The DDK folder contains files that are needed for developing drivers.

Environment Variables of the Build System

As mentioned above, the OS build process is controlled through environment variables. An OS design is defined by what environment variables it sets. Each OS design has an associated PBInitEnv.bat file that is called to configure the build environment for that OS design. PBInitEnv.bat is called either when a new build window is opened through the Build Open Release Directory in the Build Window menu item in Platform Builder, or when an OS build is initiated through the Platform Builder UI. A sample PBInitEnv.bat file is as follows:

```
@echo off
REM Initial environment configuration
set _PB_INSTALL_ROOT=C:\PROGRA~1\MI0D56~1\6.00
set USING_PB_WORKSPACE_ENVIRONMENT=1
set _WINCEROOT=C:\WINCE600
set _FLATRELEASEDIR=C:\WINCE600\OSDesigns\CEBook\CEBook\RelDir\ _
DeviceEmulator_ARMV4I_Debug
set LOCALE=0409
set _PROJECTROOT=C:\WINCE600\OSDesigns\CEBook\CEBook\Wince600\DeviceEmulator_ARMV4I
REM Workspace and configuration variables
set PBWORKSPACE=C:\WINCE600\OSDesigns\CEBook\CEBook\CEBook.pbxml
set PBWORKSPACEROOT=C:\WINCE600\OSDesigns\CEBook\CEBook
set PBCONFIG=Device Emulator ARMV4I Debug
REM Call wince.bat
call C:\WINCE600\public\COMMON\OAK\MISC\wince.bat ARMV4I CEBook DeviceEmulator
REM Make sure all build options are turned off
set IMGNODEBUGGER=
REM Anchored features
set SYSGEN_WCETK=1
REM BSP features
REM Misc settings
set WINCEDEBUG=debug
set PATH=%PATH%;C:\WINDOWS\system32;C:\WINDOWS;C:\Program Files\ _
Microsoft Platform Builder\6.00\cepb\IdeVS
REM Configuration environment variables
REM Build options
set IMGEBOOT=1
REM Project settings
set _USER_SYSGEN_BAT_FILES=C:\WINCE600\OSDesigns\CEBook\CEBook _
\Wince600\DeviceEmulator_ARMV4I\OAK\MISC\CEBook.bat
REM Locale options
set IMGNOLOC=0
set IMGSTRICTLOC=0
```

As the code sample shows, PBInitEnv.bat calls Wince.bat. Wince.bat is where the majority of environment variables are then set. Table 4–3 describes some of the more common environment variables.

TABLE 4–3 **Environment variables.**

Name	Purpose
_WINCEROOT	Build tree root.
_PUBLICROOT	PUBLIC (%_WINCEROOT%\PUBLIC) directory.
_PROJECTROOT	OS design build directory.
_PLATFORMROOT	PLATFORM (%_WINCEROOT%\PLATFORM) directory.
_TGTCPU	Architecture of the processor for which the system is built.
_TGTPLAT	Target hardware platform (BSP).
_TGTPROJ	Name of the operating system design.
_FLATRELEASEDIR	A directory into which all built modules and configuration files are copied for a subsequent build of a binary image of the operating system.
_DEPTREES	Specifies which Public directories are processed during the Pre-sysgen Build and Sysgen stages.
_CL_	The compiler, Cl.exe, uses this variable. If defined, it appends arguments in the command line.
LINK	The linker, Link.exe, uses this variable. If defined, it prepends arguments in the command line.
Variable of SYSGEN_XXX type	Adds a required component to the OS build.
Variable of BSP_XXX and BSP_NOXXX type	Specifies which BSP components need to be included or excluded during the build.
Variable of MGXXX and IMGNOXXX type	System image settings (KITL, Kernel Debugger).
Variable of PRJ_XXX type	Additional project settings.

Image Build Modes

There are three main modes for building an image: Debug, Release, and Ship. In terms of build options, Debug and Release modes are mostly as you would expect for Visual Studio, but they also control some additional settings that are Windows CE specific. In the Visual Studio integrated environment, you can select a build mode in the Configuration Manager window that can be called from the Build menu by choosing the Configuration Manager submenu. You can also set Debug or Ship modes from a build window by setting the environment variables WINCEDEBUG or WINCESHIP, as described in more detail below.

In Debug mode, the Kernel Debugger and a Kernel Independent Transport Layer (KITL) transport mechanism are enabled by default. The debugger outputs verbose information, the OS run-time image has a bigger size, and it is executed relatively slowly. This type of build is not used very often for building an operating system. It is needed only when it is necessary to debug all modules of the operating system or to use debugging zones. It may also be needed for debugging the BSP and drivers. For that mode, the values are: WINCEDEBUG=DEBUG and WINCESHIP=0.

In Release mode, most of the debugging tools are disabled by default. However, because the Windows CE Kernel Debugger is an OS component, it can be added to the run-time image and used. Also note that RETAILMSG macro messages continue to be displayed. For that mode, the values are: WINCEDEBUG=RETAIL and WINCESHIP=0. In Windows Embedded CE 6.0, the Kernel Debugger is a component; therefore, it can be added to the run-time image. If you add kernel support to the image, you can debug subprojects of the operating system, drivers, and so on without entering Debug mode of the operating system's code.

A final run-time image available to the end user is usually built in Ship mode, with the debugging tools completely excluded from the image. Ship mode uses the following settings: IMGNOKITL=1 (KITL is excluded from the image), IMGNODEBUGGER=1 (Kernel Debugger is excluded from the image), WINCEDEBUG=RETAIL, and WINCESHIP=1. An image built in Ship mode does not output debugging information, and it suppresses the output of some of the error messages.

Build Stages

The build process generally consists of five stages, as follows:

1. Pre-sysgen.

2. Sysgen (system generation).

3. Post-sysgen Build.

4. Build Release Directory (Buildrel).

5. Make Run-Time Image (Makeimg).

A typical diagram of building an image (without the Pre-sysgen stage) is shown in Figure 4–1.

The batch file Cebuild.bat manages the Pre-sysgen, Sysgen, and Post-sysgen Build stages; BuildRel.bat builds a flat build directory; and Makeimg.exe builds the final image. Figure 4–2 shows the main calls to the files responsible for the build.

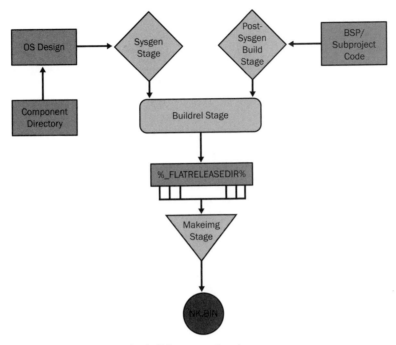

FIGURE 4–1 Build stages for building a run-time image

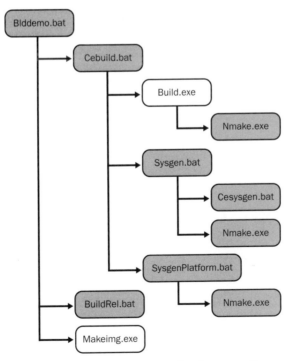

FIGURE 4–2 Calls to files during run-time image creation

Pre-Sysgen Build

During the Pre-sysgen stage, the OS components are compiled from Public and, possibly, Private directories (the list of subdirectories that are being processed is contained in the environment variable _DEPTREES). A complete Pre-sysgen build is never used—components of the operating system come in a preassembled form. You can rebuild a certain component from the command line or from a design interface without having to perform a complete Pre-sysgen build.

If it is necessary to modify an operating system component located in Public or Private directories, it is necessary to clone a component and apply changes to your own copy by possibly moving it to a design directory such as BSP or 3RDPARTY, depending on the purpose of that component.

Sysgen

After Pre-sysgen, we have a full set of components and technologies that the OS provides. Sysgen performs several tasks, including dependency resolution, component filtration, and building OS modules. The built modules include only those technologies and enhancements that were added manually by the developer and automatically during dependency resolution. During the Sysgen stage, the system processes subdirectories listed in the _DEPTREES variable. The build process has to go through this stage at least once. It also has to go through this stage each time an OS component is added or removed (through the component catalog or directly by setting the SYSGEN_XXX variables). The results of the Sysgen stage are stored in the %_PROJECTROOT%\cesysgen directory. Filtered libraries are copied into oak\lib, sdk\lib, and ddk\lib subdirectories; header files and .def files are copied into oak\inc, sdk\inc, and ddk\inc, as shown in Table 4–4. Modules that are built during Sysgen are copied into the oak\target subdirectory. During this stage of a build process, the main tool is the Sysgen.bat file (located in the %_WINCEROOT%\PUBLIC\COMMON\OAK\MISC directory). The functionality is determined by the environment variables by means of launching the batch file %_PROJECTROOT%\OAK\misc\cesysgen.bat.

TABLE 4–4 Filtered and resulting files.

Filtered files	Resulting files
Sdk\Inc*.*	Cesysgen\Sdk\Inc
Oak\Inc*.*	Cesysgen\Oak\Inc
Ddk\Inc*.*	Cesysgen\Ddk\Inc
Oak\Files\Common*.*	Cesysgen\Oak\Files

The filtration of header files and .def files is done by using the Cefilter.exe utility. While processing files, Cefilter.exe is looking for the following comments in the file text, and it performs necessary filtration actions:

```
// @CESYSGEN IF [!]<Component> [[OR | || | AND | &&] [!]Component]
// @CESYSGEN ELSE
// @CEYSSGEN ELSE IF [!]<Component> [[OR | || | AND | &&] [!]Component]
// @CESYSGEN ELSEIF [!]<Component> [[OR | || | AND | &&] [!]Component]
// @CESYSGEN ENDIF
```

If the file is not C/C++, then suitable comment symbols are used, such as a semicolon or pound sign instead of two slashes. In the code sample above, *<Component>* represents variables that are generated from the SYSGEN_XXX type variable during the Sysgen stage. These can be variables that determine modules and appear as *<module_*MODULES_*<submodule>* (for example, DCOM_MODULES_DLLHOST, CE_ MODULES_SHELL, IE_MODULES_WININET), or *<module>_<component>* (e.g., DEVICE_DEVCORE, FILESYS_FSHEAP).

To launch Sysgen from a Visual Studio menu, it is necessary to select Build submenu, and then Build *<Design name>*. Alternatively, you can also launch Sysgen from the command-line build window by running the Blddemo.bat –q command.

The Sysgen stage takes a considerable amount of time to complete. In order to reduce the execution time of the Sysgen stage, in the _DEPTREES variable you can specify only those directories that must go through Sysgen. To do that, it is necessary to create a %_TGTPROJ%.bat batch file in the OS design directory (_PROJECTROOT) with the following contents: set _DEPTREES=*<dir1> <dir2>*... *<dirX>*, where dirX is a subdirectory in the Private or Public directories.

Post-Sysgen Build

During the Post-sysgen build stage, BSP and subprojects that are added to the OS design are built. The build process uses header files that were filtered during the previous stage, .def files, and static libraries. Errors that occur during that stage are usually caused by a lack of the necessary functionality and are resolved by adding the required components (setting environment variables) and subsequently running the Sysgen stage again. BSP developers have an opportunity to perform Sysgen BSP filtration of BSP components depending on the OS functionality they choose (it must be supported by the BSP). To accomplish that, the BSP directory must have a Cesysgen subdirectory that contains a Makefile file. Most BSP packs that provide this functionality simply include the \PUBLIC\COMMON\cesysgen\ CeSysgenPlatform.mak file in their Makefile files.

To launch a build of the BSP and all of the subprojects, from the Visual Studio menu, select Build, Advanced Build Commands, and then select Build Current BSP and Subprojects. Alternatively, from a command line, type Blddemo.bat –qbsp. To build an individual subproject, from the Visual Studio menu select Build from the Subproject context menu.

Alternatively, from a command line, type Build.exe after changing to the Subproject directory, which contains the Dirs or Sources files.

Build Release Directory (Buildrel)

During the Buildrel stage, the files received after Sysgen and Post-sysgen Build stage processing are copied to a flat build directory (_FLATRELEASEDIR), where a run-time image of the operating system is being built. The directory is called flat because all files are copied without file paths. The content of the following directories is copied to the _FLATRELEASEDIR directory.

```
%_PROJECTROOT%\Cesysgen\Oak\Files
%_PROJECTROOT%\Oak\Files
%_PROJECTROOT%\Cesysgen\Oak\Target\%_ TGTCPU%\%WINCEDEBUG% %_PROJECTROOT%\Oak\Target\%_
TGTCPU%\%WINCEDEBUG%
%_PLATFORMROOT%\%_TGTPLAT%\Target\%_ TGTCPU%\%WINCEDEBUG%
%_PLATFORMROOT%\%_TGTPLAT%\Files
%_PLATFORMROOT%\%_TGTPLAT%\cesysgen\Files
```

To enable automatic copying of executable files during a module build, it necessary to set the WINCEREL variable in the Sources configuration file. This ensures that when the initial file of one component (such as the BSP) is changed, you do not have to go through the Buildrel stage again. Despite the ability to copy executable files automatically during the build process, you have to run the Buildrel stage at least once in order to copy all necessary executable and configuration files. When changes are made to configuration files, the Buildrel stage has to be run again.

For NTFS volumes, hard links to files are used instead of file copies by default. When editing hard-linked files, it is important to keep in mind that this modifies the initial files directly. The BUILDREL_USE_COPY environment variable sets the copying method.

Copying can be launched manually. To do that, from the Visual Studio main menu, select Build, and then Copy Files to Release Directory. Alternatively, from the command-line build window, type BuildRel.bat.

Make Run-Time Image (Makeimg)

During the final stage, the content of the flat build directory (_FLATRELEASEDIR) is assembled into a binary run-time image named NK.BIN or NK.NB0. The making of an image is managed by the Makeimg.exe utility. Let us look at the steps that need to be taken during the Makeimg stage to form a monolithic image of the operating system.

First, the Fmerge.exe utility merges the following configuration files and initialization files:

1. The .bib files are merged into a CE.bib file (a configuration file that contains a list of files and parameters for forming a monolithic image).

2. The .reg files are merged into a RegInit.ini file (registry initialization file).

3. The .dat files are merged into an InitObj.dat file (object store initialization file).

4. The .db files are merged into an InitDB.ini file (database initialization file).

After than, the RegInit.ini file is compressed into a binary file named Default.fdf.

The system then localizes executable files and libraries by replacing the resources according to a selected language, as determined by the LOCALE variable. At the end, the Romimage.exe utility creates a binary image of the system from the files specified in Ce.bib. Romimage.exe makes it possible to create a system image in several formats. The main format is a tagged binary image of the system (.bin). A ready .bin file can be converted into an absolute binary format (NBx) or a 32-bit Motorola SRE format by using the CvrtBin.exe utility.

The image-build procedure can be launched manually. In order to do that, from the Visual Studio main menu, select Build and then Make Run-Time Image. Alternatively, from the command line, run Makeimg.exe.

Table 4–5 lists the necessary build stages depending on changes in the OS design.

TABLE 4–5 **Build stages required based on OS design changes.**

	BSP and Subprojects	Image Settings	Adding/Removing Directory Components
Sysgen	-	-	+
Post-sysgen Build	+	Possible	+
Buildrel	Possible	+	+
Makeimg	+	+	+

CONFIGURATION FILES

Binary Image Builder (.Bib)

The .bib files describe the memory structure (ROM/RAM) and specify what files need to be included into the image; they also contain additional configuration parameters related to the memory. A merged .bib file named CE.bib, which the Romimage.exe utility uses for forming a monolithic image, contains the following .bib files:

- BSP files (Config.bib, Platform.bib).

- Files of selected Windows CE components (Common.bib, and so on).

■   OS design files (Project.bib and subproject .bib files).

The .bib files are text files. Their content is divided into the MEMORY, CONFIG, MODULES, and FILES sections.

MEMORY Section

This section is usually located in the Config.bib files, and it determines the allocation of the virtual address space among applications and the system image. Each entry in the MEMORY section that describes a memory region contains the following fields: region name, initial memory address, size, and type. The fields are written as one line and are separated by spaces and/or tabular symbols. Region names have to be unique except for the reserved name, RESERVE, which can be used more than once. Regions that contain RESERVE in their name reserve the memory regions that are not used by the system image.

The types of memory that show how each memory region will be used are listed in Table 4–6.

TABLE 4–6 Memory region types and usage.

Memory Type	Purpose
RAM	Used by the system kernel for the program and file system in the memory. This type of region must be aligned by page boundaries (4 KB).
RAMIMAGE	This type of memory region is marked as read-only. This region stores the system image, which includes the execute in place (XIP)module that is executed locally. On the physical level, this can be a memory region where the system image or flash memory (which is addressed by the processor directly) is loaded. The Romimage.exe utility creates a binary file (.bin) for this region type. This type of region must be aligned by page boundaries (4 KB).
RESERVED	Romimage.exe does not process this type of region. Developers process and use this memory type for information purposes, such as specifying the memory region that is used by the device buffer.
FIXUPVAR	Enables you to set values of the global variables of the kernel during the MAKEIMG stage. The starting address for a variable is always 0, and instead of the size in bytes, it specifies a needed value.

CONFIG Section

This section is usually located in the Config.bib file and is optional. It contains additional parameters for configuring the system image. Listed below are some of the parameters that can be used:

■   **AUTOSIZE (ON|OFF)**   enables you to automatically allocate space that the run-time image does not use for applications. By default, Romimage.exe disables AUTOSIZE.

- **COMPRESS (ON|OFF)** enables compression of the files that are loaded into the memory and are not executed in place (XIP). The compression component has to be present in the system image in order to support file compression functionality. By default, Romimage.exe enables compression.

- **ROMSTART** is a virtual address of the ROM beginning.

- **ROMSIZE** is the size of the ROM in bytes.

- **ROMWIDTH** is the width of the ROM in bits.

    If the ROMSTART, ROMSIZE and ROMWIDTH variables are set, Romimage.exe builds a run-time image in the absolute binary data format (.nb0 or .abx).

- **SRE (ON|OFF)** is used for creating an image in Motorola-S format. This option is disabled by default.

Table 4–7 shows a sample entry in the CONFIG section.

TABLE 4–7 CONFIG section entry.

NK	8C800000	00800000	RAMIMAGE
RAM	8C050000	007B0000	RAM
nk.exe:gpdwVariable	00000000	00000006	FIXUPVAR

MODULES Section

This section contains a list of system image modules that are executed in place without being additionally loaded into the memory and cannot contain more than 2,000 modules. This section may include all executable modules and libraries except for the applications written with managed code, because the latter require that they are additionally loaded into the memory. Each entry in the MODULES section that describes an included module contains the following fields: name, path, region, and attributes. The fields are written on one line and are separated by one or more spaces or tabular symbols.

The Name field denotes the file's name in the image, and it may not coincide with the initial name of the file; paths are not used. A full path to a module in the file system is stored on the developer's machine. The Region field denotes the RAMIMAGE regions specified in the MEMORY section into which the module is added. Table 4–8 shows some possible attribute values, which can be combined.

TABLE 4–8 Attribute values.

Attribute	Purpose
S	System file.
H	Hidden file.
R	Compress the resources. Applies to the MODULES section only.
D	Disables module debugging.
K or Z	Module needs to be prepared for execution in the kernel address space (to map the address).
U	Do not compress the file.
Q	Module needs to be prepared for execution in the user address space and the kernel address space. The line, file.dll $(_FLATRELEASEDIR)\file.dll SHQ is converted into k.file.dll $(_FLATRELEASEDIR)\file.dll SHK and file.dll $(_FLATRELEASEDIR)\file.dll SH.
C	Compress module.
N	Mark module as non-trusted. Applies to the MODULES section only.
P	Do not check CPU type specified in file header. Usually used for resource libraries.
X	Sign module and include signatures to the ROM. Applies to the MODULES section only.
M	Signals that the kernel must not demand page the module. By default, the kernel demand pages modules as needed. This flag is usually set for system services that are called in paging, or which are in out-of-memory (OOM) condition. Applies only to the MODULES section.
U	Keep module uncompressed.

A sample entry in the MODULES section:

```
INIT.EXE  $(_FLATRELEASEDIR)\INIT.EXE NK SH
MYDLL.DLL $(_FLATRELEASEDIR)\MYDLL.DLL NK SHC
```

FILES Section

Files from this section are loaded into the device memory region that is available for applications. As a rule, these files include program data and managed code applications files. The files from this section are compressed by default. Before being loaded in the memory, the compressed files are decompressed. The file entry format is the same as one in the MODULES section.

Object Store Initialization Files (.Dat)

The .dat files are used for initializing a file system in the memory (RAM file system). During the MAKEIMG stage, .data files are merged into the InitObj.dat file. The resulting InitObj.dat file is used by Filesys.dll for creating a directory tree of the file system in the memory. Entries in the DAT files have the following format:

```
root:[-Directory("<directory name>")] [-File("<final_file_name>", "<initial_file>")]
```

where *<directory_name>* is the name of the directory, *<final_file_name>* is the final name of the file that is copied from the \Windows directory, and *<initial_file>* is the name of the initial file in the \Windows directory.

The following content of a .dat file is created the Program Files directory and its My Projects subdirectory and is copied by the MyProg.exe file into the Program Files directory:

```
Root:-Directory("Program Files")
Directory("\Program Files"):-Directory("My Projects")
Directory("\Program Files"):-File("MyProg.exe», "\Windows\MyProg.exe")
```

Registry Initialization Files (.Reg)

Registry files form the initial registry of the operating system. The format of Windows Embedded CE registry files is similar to that of the desktop version of Windows. During the MAKEIMG stage, all registry files in the build directory (_FLATRELEASEDIR) are merged into the RegInit.ini file in the following order:

1. Registry files of components of the operating system (Common.reg, IE.reg, Wceapps. reg, Wceshell.reg).

2. Registry files of subprojects that were added to the OS design.

3. Project.reg is created for each design of the operating system. It enables you to add general configuration settings to the current design and to redefine registry settings of the OS components and subprojects.

4. Platform.reg is usually provided by the BSP manufacturer and includes the initial registry settings for hardware (BSP and device drivers).

Therefore, Project.reg settings can redefine the component settings, whereas Platform.reg settings can redefine the settings for all other files.

Database Initialization Files (.Db)

During the MAKEIMG stage, .db files are merged into an InitDB.ini file and are used for initializing EDB databases that are included in the image. The entry format is described in detail in the supplied .db files.

Component and Module Build

Build.exe utility manages the process of compiling and linking components and modules. Dirs and Sources files are used for telling Build.exe where to build from (Dirs files) and what to build with (Sources files).

Figure 4–3 shows a diagram of the build process managed by Build.exe.

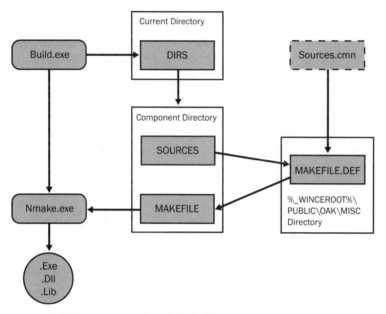

FIGURE 4–3 Components and modules build process

Let us examine the build process in more detail.

Dirs Files

Dirs files tell Build.exe what subdirectories in the current directory that the build needs to take place in, which is similar to launching Build.exe in each of the indicated subdirectories. The structure of a Dirs file is straightforward.

As an example, the following file content is prescribed by Build.exe in order to perform a build in the Oak and SDK subdirectories of the current directory:

```
DIRS=Oak SDK
```

Moving from one subdirectory to another continues until one subdirectory has no Dirs file present; a search for the Sources file is conducted in this directory. If the Sources file is found, Build.exe utility launches Nmake.exe and passes Makefile (located in the same directory as Sources) to Nmake.exe as a parameter.

Makefile Files

The Makefile file contains the rules for Nmake.exe that are necessary for the build. In most cases, the Makefile file contains just one line including the content of Makefile.def file:

```
!INCLUDE $(_MAKEENVROOT)\makefile.def.
```

Makefile.def file contains general rules for compiling and linking of the entire Windows Embedded CE operating system. Aside from the general rules, the file has a directory that includes the content of the SOURCES file of the current directory:

```
!INCLUDE $(MAKEDIR)\sources.
```

Sources Files

The Sources file contains build information for a specific component. The general entry format for the Sources file is as follows:

```
<Variable name> = <Value 1> [<Value 2> … <Value M>] \
<Value M+1> \
…
<Value N>
```

If a variable can have several values, the values are separated by a space. To merge several lines, the backslash symbol is used. Let us look at the variables that are used in the Sources file, as shown in Table 4–9.

TABLE 4–9 Sources file variables.

Variable Name	Windows Embedded CE Shell Components
SOURCES	List of initial files.
TARGETNAME	Name of resulting file without an extension.
TARGETTYPE	Type of resulting file: ■ PROGRAM—application. ■ DYNLINK—dynamic-link library. ■ LIBRARY—static library Depending on the type, the resulting file receives the extension .exe, .dll, or .lib, respectively.
TARGETLIBS	List of static libraries (.lib) and object files (.obj) that are necessary for linking an executable module (.exe) or a dynamic library (.dll). This variable is ignored if a static library is being built.
SOURCELIBS	List of static libraries (.lib) used for linking a static library from several libraries.

Variable Name	Windows Embedded CE Shell Components
RELEASETYPE	Location of the intermediate and final build files: ■ LOCAL—in the subproject directory. ■ OAK—%_PROJECTROOT%\Oak\Target or %_ PROJECTROOT%\Oak\Lib. ■ PLATFORM—%_TARGETPLATROOT%\Target or %_ TARGETPLATROOT%\ Lib.
POSTLINK_PASS_CMD	Command to be executed after linking. As a rule, it is used for copying additional files into the build directory.
PRELINK_PASS_CMD	Command to be executed before linking.

Sources.cmn File

The Sources.cmn file enables you to determine general build settings for several projects. The content of this file is included in Makefile.def by the directory before the content of the Sources file. Sources.cmn must be located in the upper directory that contains the Dirs file.

Build Errors

The presence of a Build.err file in the root directory of the build is an indication that an error exists. The main tool for analyzing errors during the build stage is the Output window in Visual Studio's integrated interface and the Build.log file located in the root directory of the build system (_WINCEROOT).

Sysgen Error

During the Sysgen stage, errors usually occur when the OS design does not have necessary components. This problem is solved by adding a necessary component by using Platform Builder directory and setting certain environment variables. Errors can also occur while editing the content of Public and Private directories directly.

Post-Sysgen Build Error

During this stage, compiling and linking errors occur. Such errors can be caused by a lack of the necessary header files and libraries. Because filtered files are used during this stage, the problem can usually be resolved by adding the necessary components with a subsequent execution of the Sysgen stage.

Buildrel Error

Copying errors occur during the Buildrel stage. Possible causes of errors are the following:

- Insufficient disk space.

- Blocking of the simultaneously used files.

- Files marked as read-only.

Makeimg Error

The most common errors during this stage are the following:

- The absence of a file specified in CE.bib in the flat release directory (_FLATRELEASEDIR).

- Syntax errors in the registry files.

- The image size exceeds the value specified in Config.bib.

Chapter 5
Board Support Package (BSP)

The board support package (BSP) enables a developer to build a run-time image of the Windows Embedded CE operating system for a specific hardware platform. Each hardware platform for which an operating system needs to be built must include its designated BSP. Usually, building a BSP is the most labor-intensive part of creating a device. Building a BSP requires that the developer is familiar with the hardware architecture as well as the architecture of the operating system. All of the interaction of the operating system with the device is implemented in BSP, and therefore, the quality of the BSP determines the resulting quality of the device.

The tools supplied with Platform Builder for CE 6.0 R2 contain several examples of BSP implementation and at least one BSP for each supported processor architecture, as follows:

- ARM.
    - Intel PXA27x Processor Development Kit (MainstoneIII).
    - Texas Instruments SDP2420 Development Board.
    - TI OMAP5912 Aruba Board.
    - Voice over IP PXA270 Development Platform.
    - Device Emulator.
- X86.
    - CEPC.
    - HP Compaq t5530 Thin Client Development Platform.
- MIPS.
    - NEC Solution Gear 2-Vr5500 Development Kit.
- SH4.
    - Renesas US7750R HARP (Aspen) Standard Development Board.
    - STMicroelectronics STi7109 MB442 Development Platform.

The BSP contains the entire hardware-dependent source code that is necessary for creating an abstraction of the operating system that is independent of a specific hardware platform implementation. The main components of a BSP are as follows:

- Boot loader.
- OEM adaptation layer (OAL).
- Drivers.
- Configuration files.

The main tasks of the boot loader are to load a run-time image into the memory and to move to its starting point. The boot loader can receive an OS image from a variety of sources: the network (eboot), COM port (sboot), Universal Serial Bus (USB), flash card, hard disk, and so on. A boot loader is not required for launching an operating system on a device; the Windows Embedded CE 6.0 operating system can function without a boot loader. The presence of a boot loader expedites the process of building a device, and on a production device, it makes it possible to offer additional service functions such as reflash device firmware, diagnostics, and so on.

A BSP includes the following components:

- **OAL**   creates a kernel abstraction that is separate from a specific processor implementation; it includes code for interrupt processing, timers, IOCTL, etc.

- **Drivers**   provide the operating system with an interface to the platform's hardware devices.

- **Configuration files**   contain information needed by the build system in order to build a run-time image with a given BSP.

Where can a device developer obtain a BSP? First of all, hardware manufacturers often include BSPs with their product. Second, as mentioned above, the development tool suite has at least one BSP for each of the supported processor architectures, which can be used directly or as a base for building a custom BSP. Finally, a device developer can use the most suitable BSP that has an available source code as a base to build a custom BSP. In order to do that, the device schematics or similar information must be available.

As mentioned above, the process of building a BSP is the most labor-intensive part of building a device, and thus, it is important to know what resources, libraries, and implementation architecture Microsoft offers for building a BSP.

BSP Directory Structure

During installation, each BSP is deployed as a subdirectory of the Platform directory located in the Windows Embedded CE 6.0 directory tree root. All BSP shipped by Microsoft and third-party BSP are installed there. The BSP that is being developed also needs to be located in that directory.

Let us examine the typical structure of a directory used to build a BSP. Table 5–1 shows the subdirectory names of a BSP and their purpose.

TABLE 5–1 **Standard BSP subdirectories.**

Directory Name	Purpose
CATALOG	Mandatory directory. It contains a catalog file that publishes the BSP in the Platform Builder catalog.
CESYSGEN	Optional directory. It contains the Makefile file that is necessary for involving BSP in the Sysgen stage of building the operating system by making it possible to filter the BSP functionality that is being built, depending on the selected system components.
FILES	Mandatory directory. It contains BSP configuration files, such as Platform.bib, Config.bib, Platform.reg, Platform.db, etc. During the Buildrel stage, the files are copied into a flat release directory (FLATRELEASEDIR). If a BSP is involved in the filtering process, the filtered files are copied into the CESYSGEN\FILES directory then copied into a flat release directory (FLATRELEASEDIR). It means that if any changes were made to the files in this directory and the BSP supports file filtering, then in order for a new filtered version of the files to be sent to FLATRELEASEDIR, it is necessary to perform the Sysgen stage of the BSP..
SRC	Optional directory. It is present in all BSP packages included in Platform Builder. It is a root directory for the source code that implements a BSP. The BSP source code is built during the Post-sysgen Build stage; the build process is controlled by the Dirs and Sources files. The developer has no requirements to meet as far as implementation of the BSP source code tree is concerned.

Table 5–2 provides a listing of names of the main subdirectories of SRC directory and their purpose as it applies to the BSP included in Platform Builder.

TABLE 5–2 **Subdirectories of SRC directory.**

Directory Name	Purpose
BOOTLOADER	Contains boot loader implementation.
BOOTLOADER\EBOOT	Contains boot loader implementation for the network environment.
COMMON	Contains common code for a specific BSP. Usually is a common part of the boot loader and OAL.
DRIVERS	Contains directories that store implementation of the platform drivers.
INC	Contains header files.
OAL\OALLIB	Contains source code for OAL implementation and configuration build files.
OAL\OALEXE	Contains configurations files (Sources, Makefile) for building the OAL.exe executable file from the OAL.lib library. It links the OAL.lib library to the required common libraries as well as other libraries. It may contain the function code and the stub code for the functionality that is not implemented by OAL.
KITL	Contains the source code and configuration files for building KITL.dll

Boot Loader

The boot loader is a standard part of any BSP. A boot loader performs at least the following tasks:

- Hardware initialization.

- Platform initialization related to image loading onto a device.

- Loading of the operating system image into the memory (RAM and/or ROM).

- Start the operating system by jumping to the OS entry point.

A boot loader can implement any additional functionality required during the development, testing, or end-user device operation. The boot loader has no formal implementation requirements that need to be met.

Usually the boot loader is implemented as a component that is separate from the operating system. The boot loader has its own configuration binary image builder (.bib) file located in the Bootloader build directory along with the Sources and Makefile files.

The Platform Builder development toolset includes several auxiliary libraries for implementing a boot loader. Table 5–3 provides the library names and locations.

TABLE 5–3 Boot loader library names and locations.

Name	Location
BLCOMMON	\PLATFORM\COMMON\SRC\COMMON\ BOOT
EBOOT	\PUBLIC\COMMON\OAK\DRIVERS\ETHDBG\EBOOT
BOOTPART	\PUBLIC\COMMON\OAK\DRIVERS\ETHDBG\ BOOTPART
ETHDBG	\PUBLIC\COMMON\OAK\DRIVERS\ETHDBG

The BLCOMMON library provides the infrastructure for implementing the boot loader. The main task of this library is to provide implementation that initially supports Platform Builder tools. The BLCOMMON library implements the majority of a boot loader's common tasks. In order to implement a boot loader for a specific hardware platform, it is necessary to utilize the code of low-level hardware implementation as well as a pre-defined set of functions that the BLCOMMON library calls. The Ethernet boot loader (EBOOT) library contains implementation for working with Dynamic Host Configuration Protocol (DHCP), Trivial File Transfer Protocol (TFTP) and User Datagram Protocol (UDP), which can be used for implementing a boot loader in a network environment. The BOOTPART library contains auxiliary functions for working with partitions and for reading from and writing to flash media. The Ethernet debugging libraries (ETHDBG) provide the functionality of a debugging network (Ethernet) driver for some network cards. Table 5–4 shows the card names and implementation locations.

TABLE 5–4 Interface cards and their locations.

Card Name	Location
3COM 3C90X	\PUBLIC\COMMON\OAK\DRIVERS\ETHDBG\3C90X
AMD Am79C970	\PUBLIC\COMMON\OAK\DRIVERS\ETHDBG\AM79C970
AMD Am79C973	\PUBLIC\COMMON\OAK\DRIVERS\ETHDBG\ AM79C973
Crystal CS8900A	\PUBLIC\COMMON\OAK\DRIVERS\ETHDBG\CS8900
DEC/Intel DC21140	\PUBLIC\COMMON\OAK\DRIVERS\ETHDBG\DEC21140
National Semiconductor DP83815 (MacPhyter)	\PUBLIC\COMMON\OAK\DRIVERS\ETHDBG\DP83815
NE2000-compatible	\PUBLIC\COMMON\OAK\DRIVERS\ETHDBG\NE2000
RealTek RTL8139 and compatibles	\PUBLIC\COMMON\OAK\DRIVERS\ETHDBG\RTL8139

Figure 5–1 shows a simplified diagram for implementing a boot loader.

When the system starts, it passes the control to the address where the point of entry into the Startup() function is located. This function is responsible for a low-level hardware initialization and for calling the C function Main(), which calls the BootloaderMain() function from BLCOMMON. The BootloaderMain() function implements the main execution thread of the boot loader by calling return call functions. The functions that determine the base execution procedure are as follows:

- **OEMDebugInit**   provides initialization of the debugging transport subsystem.

- **OEMPlatformInit**   provides a high-level platform initialization.

- **OEMPreDownload**   initializes services that are needed for loading an image.

- **OEMLaunch**   performs initializations that are necessary after the image has been loaded and jumps to the OS entry point.

In order to provide support for serial port operations, a developer utilizes the following functions:

- OEMInitDebugSerial().

- OEMWriteDebugString().

- OEMWriteDebugByte().

- OEMReadDebugByte().

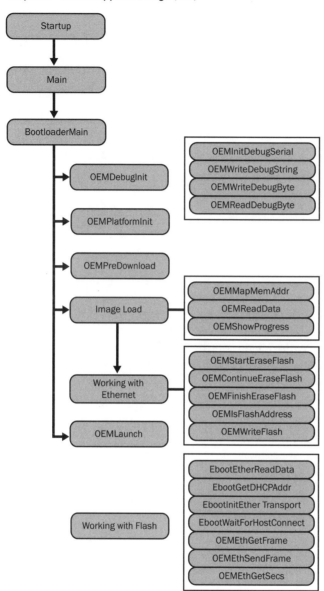

FIGURE 5–1 Boot loader implementation

Usually, the OEMDebugInit() function calls the function OEMInitDebugSerial() for initializing the debugging transport subsystem via a serial port. In order to load the image, the BLCOMMON library calls the function OEMReadData(), which reads the transport protocol data. By implementing the OEMShowProgress() function, a developer can display the progress of the image-load process. The OEMMapMemAddr() function is intended for caching the images designed for flash memory. If a network boot loader is implemented, usually the EBOOT library is used (consisting of functions with the Eboot prefix), which is awaiting the OEMEthGetFrame(), OEMEthSendFrame(), and OEMEthGetSecs() functions to be implemented. These functions usually call the corresponding functions of a matching debugging network driver directly. In order to work with flash memory, a developer must implement the following designated set of functions: OEMStartEraseFlash(), OEMContinueEraseFlash(), OEMFinishEraseFlash(), OEMIsFlashAddress(), and OEMWriteFlash(). A developer may implement only the necessary functions instead of the others by using stubs.

OEM Abstraction Layer

The OAL contains the code that creates an abstraction of the operating system kernel independent of a specific physical platform implementation. This enables the common kernel[1] of Windows Embedded CE to function on several platforms.

The OAL implements the system's starting code, interrupt processing code (ISR, support for installed ISR, a table of interrupt request (IRQ) static mapping in system interrupt (SYSINTR), and so on), power management code (On, Off, and Idle power states), timer code, and various IOCTL control codes (IOCTL_HAL_GET_DEVICE_ID, IOCTL_HAL_GET_UUID, and so on), The OAL provides an interface to the system kernel by implementing a certain set of functions and IOCTL.

At the same time, the system kernel provides the OAL with a set of functions that must be used while implementing the OAL. Therefore, in Windows Embedded CE 6.0, interaction between the kernel and the OAL is unified as much as possible, which is a result of architectural changes in the kernel—the OAL is no longer statically linked to the operating system kernel. Instead, the OAL is built into an executable file, OAL.exe, by being dynamically linked to the kernel library (kernel.dll).

In standard BSP implementations, the OAL layer is built in two stages and is located in the following directories: \SRC\OAL\OALLIB, which contains the platform-specific code that is built into a static library, and \SRC\OAL\OALEXE, which contains the code and the specific build instructions for OAL.exe (it links OAL.lib to other libraries). Furthermore, during the Makeimg stage, OAL.exe is built into a run-time image as NK.exe, which is a traditional name for the OS kernel in Windows CE. During the load of NK.exe by OAL.exe, the system kernel is loaded dynamically (kernel.dll).

As mentioned before, it is necessary to implement a predefined set of functions and IOCTL control codes. Table 5–5 provides a list of some of the functions with their description.

---

[1] One kernel per processor architecture (ARM, MIPS, SH4,x86).

TABLE 5–5 **Predefined functions.**

Name	Purpose
OEMInitDebugSerial	The first Original Equipment Manufacturer (OEM) function called by the kernel. Provides initialization of the debugging input/output (I/O) through a serial port.
OEMWriteDebugByte	Writes a byte into a debug port.
OEMWriteDebugString	Writes a string into a debug port.
OEMReadDebugByte	Reads a byte from a debug port.
OEMInit	This is the second OEM function that the kernel calls. It provides initialization of all of the required hardware, including timer, bus, and I/O; ISR registration except for ARM and Kernel Independent Transport Layer (KITL) initialization. The function is called at an early stage of system initialization, and therefore, during initialization it is necessary to take into account the following environment characteristics: a single-thread execution, system calls are disallowed, there is no blocking, and there is no support for exception handling.
OEMInterruptEnable	Enables an interrupt with a specified identifier. This function is called from the InterruptInitialize and InterruptMask functions.
OEMInterruptDisable	Disables an interrupt with a specified identifier. This function is called from the InterruptDisable and InterruptMask functions.
OEMInterruptDone	Processes the announcement stating that interrupt processing is done. This function is called from the InterruptDone function.
OEMInterruptHandler	Applies only to the ARM architecture. This is an interrupt-handing function that is called with any interrupt on the ARM platform; it returns a SYSINTR identifier and therefore ISR is not registered in OEMInit on the ARM platform. The role of this function is to determine a corresponding source of the interrupt.
OEMInterruptHandlerFIQ	Applies only to the ARM architecture. Support for Fast Interrupt Query has limitations. It is not used in the BSPs included with Windows Embedded CE.
OEMIdle	This function is called only if there are no threads scheduled for execution. It provides an opportunity to switch the processor into a low energy consumption mode.
OEMPowerOff	Switches the processor to the minimum power usage mode or simply turns power off.
OEMIoControl	This function is called from the KernelIoControl function. It implements the IOCTL interface of OAL for the operating system kernel. A device manufacturer may implement additional IOCTL codes to suit its own needs.
OEMSetRealTime	Provides the kernel with an interface to the real-time hardware clock—setting real time.
OEMGetRealTime	Provides the kernel with an interface to the real-time hardware clock—getting real time.
OEMSetAlarmTime	Provides the kernel with an interface to the real-time hardware clock—setting the Alarm.

Table 5–6 shows some of the IOCTL control codes.

TABLE 5–6 IOCTL control codes.

Name	Purpose
IOCTL_HAL_GET_DEVICE_INFO	Device information.
IOCTL_HAL_GET_UUID	Unique device identifier.
IOCTL_HAL_REQUEST_IRQ	IRQ request for a device based on device location (DEVICE_LOCATION).
IOCTL_HAL_REQUEST_SYSINTR	SYSINTR request through IRQ.
IOCLT_HAL_REBOOT	Hot device restart.
IOCTL_HAL_POSTINIT	Called while initializing the operating system before the start of other processes.

Developers can build the OAL by implementing its functionality directly, or they can utilize the common platform code (common libraries). The OAL architecture based on common libraries is named Production Quality OAL (PQOAL). It includes all common libraries, implementation infrastructure, and so on. All BSPs included with Platform Builder have the OAL implemented in the PQOAL architecture.

Common Platform Code

The Platform directory contains another directory named Common that contains the source code of function libraries that Microsoft supplies, which are available to developers while building their own BSP (boot loader, OAL and drivers). These libraries implement most of the required functionality that is common for all BSPs. Common libraries do not contain code that is dependent on a specific platform based on a specific implementation of a microprocessor chip.

The purpose of creating a common code (common libraries) is to provide maximum code reusability and thus to reduce labor and time needed to create a BSP. Common code provides an opportunity to develop a BSP in a modular fashion by using all the necessary components from the included common libraries.

Common platform code consists of a set of libraries that Microsoft includes in the source code. These libraries implement the functionality that is common for all BSP devices of Windows Embedded CE. BSP developers may use these libraries for building or customizing their own BSPs. These libraries were created in order to reduce the complexity of creating custom BSPs by reusing existing code. The common code contains functionality implementation that may be useful while building a boot loader, OAL, and system drivers.

In addition to the libraries, the common code offers an implementation framework for situations such as when OAL code specific to a given hardware platform is implemented through return function calls and for providing data structures implemented in a BSP. This framework greatly simplifies the task of porting BSPs. At the same time, there are no requirements a developer has to meet as far how and in what form common libraries are be used. The developer may use only those libraries that are necessary by implementing the rest of the functionality independently or by cloning the implementation of the required common libraries into a personal BSP directory and making all necessary changes directly in it.

The use of common code enables a developer to substantially reduce the time needed to build a BSP by using a code that was tested by Microsoft and to create a BSP that has the same architecture as the BSPs Microsoft includes with the OS development tools.

The common code located in the \PLATFORM\COMMON\SRC\ directory is organized by the following subdirectories depending on the processor architecture and functionality:

- **ARM**   common code for the ARM processor architecture.
- **COMMON**   common code that is not dependent on the processor architecture.
- **MIPS**   common code for the Microprocessor without Interlocked Pipeline Stages (MIPS) processor architecture.
- **SHX**   common code for the SHX processor architecture.
- **SOC**   common code for various system-on-chip (SOC) systems.
- **X86**   common code for the X86 processor type architecture.

The code located in these directories is built into libraries during the platform build process. These libraries are located in the \PLATFORM\COMMON\LIB\<*PROCESSOR_TYPE*>\<*BUILD_TYPE*>\ folder, where <*PROCESSOR_TYPE*> means ARM, MIPS, SHX or X86, and <*BUILD_TYPE*> means Retail or Debug. BSPs refer to \PLATFORM\ COMMON\LIB\ directory by using the _PLATCOMMONLIB variable.

The \PLATFORM\COMMON\SRC\COMMON\ subdirectory contains the code that is not dependent on processor architecture, and it is organized within the subdirectory according to its functionality:

- **BOOT**   support infrastructure for building a boot loader.
- **CACHE**   used for working with cache and Translation Lookaside Buffer (TLB).
- **CEDDK**   part of CEDDK.
- **ETHDRV**   network drivers that have debugging function for the boot loader.
- **FLASH**   used for working with CFI NOR Flash.
- **ILT**   part of the Interrupt Latency Timing (ILTiming) implementation, which includes the utilities for measuring delays during IRQ processing.
- **INTR**   common code for working with interrupts (IRQ mapping into SYSINTR).

- **IO**   general I/O code.
- **IOCTL**   common hardware-independent IOCTL control codes.
- **KITL**   hardware-independent part of KITL implementation.
- **LOG**   outputs debugging information.
- **OTHER**   various stub functions.
- **PCI**   simplified implementation for working with the Peripheral Component Interconnect (PCI) bus for the boot loader and for initializing the operating system.
- **PERREG**   retains the registry for NOR Flash.
- **POWER**   implements hardware-independent IOCTL codes for managing the power supply.
- **RTC**   implementation of the Real Time Clock functions.
- **TIMER**   a timer implementation.

The following directories contain the code that is dependent on processor architecture:

- \PLATFORM\COMMON\SRC\ARM\
- \PLATFORM\COMMON\SRC\MIPS\
- \PLATFORM\COMMON\SRC\SHX\
- \PLATFORM\COMMON\SRC\X86\

These directories can contain code in the Common subdirectory that functions for the architecture of the respective processor, as well as for specific architecture implementations (for example \MIPS\ MIPS32, \ARM\ARM920T, and \ARM\ARM926).

The \PLATFORM\COMMON\SRC\SOC\ directory includes subdirectories that contain the code related to a chip-specific implementation, along with its periphery and related processor resources. Most of the code related to a processor is located in a corresponding subdirectory of the \PLATFORM\COMMON\SRC\SOC\ directory. The directory name contains the SOC name, then the underscore, then the developer's initials, and then, after another underscore, the implementation version number, such as X86_MS_V1, OMAP2420_MS_V1, PXA27X_MS_V1. Each subdirectory that corresponds to the SOC chip usually contains subdirectories that store implementation of a certain chip–based functionality, such as drivers and I/O including additional OAL initialization.

It is assumed that implementation of libraries located in the subdirectories is not dependent on the platform hardware on a corresponding SOC chip. As already mentioned, developers may use the common platform code in any way they consider suitable. It is necessary, however, to observe a common rule, and that rule is, you should never directly modify the code shipped with the Platform Builder. First, clone the necessary part of the library into your own BSP directory, and then, make changes to the copy of the code.

Kernel Independent Transport Layer (KITL)

KITL separates the implementation of a low-level transport interface from the service protocol that provides a communication mechanism between a developer's workstation and the target device.

Drivers

In addition to the microprocessor, the platform consists of multiple peripheral devices. The operating system may need drivers in order to use to use these devices. The development tools include a large number of drivers, both as part of the platform-independent code and as part of the supplied BSPs. If a shipped driver is not compatible, it is necessary to implement a custom-built driver as part of the BSP (SRC\DRIVERS). To expedite the build process, the most suitable driver shipped with the software is used as a base. Table 5–7 provides a list of directories that contain the majority of drivers included in Windows Embedded CE.

TABLE 5–7 Included drivers.

Directory	Description
\PUBLIC\COMMON\OAK\DRIVERS\	Contains platform-independent drivers such as bus drivers and the model device driver (MDD) parts of layered drivers.
\PLATFROM\COMMON\SRC\SOC\	Contains implementation of drivers for the SOC peripherals.
\PLATFORM\<PLATFORM_NAME>\SRC\DRIVERS	Contains implementation of drivers for a specific platform and the Platform Dependent Driver (PDD) part of layered drivers.

The structure of drivers and their types is covered in more detail in the next chapter.

Configuration Files

An operating system is built from batch files, and the build process is controlled by configuration files. Prior chapters provide a more detailed description of the file entry formats and the purpose of configuration files. Table 5–8 shows a list of BSP configuration files and describes their purpose.

TABLE 5-8 BSP configuration files and their purpose.

File	Description
<PLATFORM_NAME>.BAT	The file is located in the BSP directory root. It contains settings for environment variables related to the BSP build. It is not launched for execution, and it must not contain any commands except for setting variables and, possibly, for conditional file filtering during the Sysgen stage.
CONFIG.BIB	The file is located in the Files directory of the BSP. It contains the main parameters of the ROM/RAM platform, as well as various additional settings, such as settings for OAL variables, and image builds in various formats.
PLATFORM.BIB	The file is located in the Files directory of the BSP. It contains a list of BSP files included in the run-time image of the operating system.
PLATFORM.REG	The file is located in the Files directory of the BSP. It contains initial registry settings for the BSP components, including the drivers.
PLATFORM.DAT	The file is located in the Files directory of the BSP. It contains details about the initialization of the file system into memory required for the BSP. Usually, the file is empty.
PLATFORM.DB	The file is located in the Files directory of the BSP. It contains details about the initialization of the system base required for the BSP. Usually, the file is empty.

Creating a New BSP

Creating a new BSP is the most complicated task while building embedded solutions based on Windows Embedded CE. Usually, you start building a BSP by cloning the most suitable package that is available in the source code. Then, it is necessary to perform the analysis of platform differences and to modify the code of the cloned BSP. This modofication may include customization of drivers or a low-level initialization code. In any event, in order to build a BSP it is necessary to have the hardware diagram or similar information available.

Quite often, BSPs without included source code have the ability to provide additional platform functionality by building new device drivers that are connected through various interfaces. Specialized IOCTL control codes are usually available in this case for obtaining IRQ and SYSINTR, while the platform supports installable interrupt service routines (IISR).

Chapter 6
Driver Architecture

A driver is software that provides the operating system (OS) with an interface to a physical or a virtual device. The operating system expects drivers to implement a predefined interface that creates an abstraction of a specific hardware or a virtual implementation of a device. In Microsoft Windows Embedded CE 6.0, this interface represents a set of functions and input/output control codes (IOCTL) that must be implemented in the driver's code in most cases. The driver infrastructure makes it possible for a designated part of the operating system to provide parts of the operating system and the application software with a unified interface with the system hardware regardless of its implementation.

In order to understand the various drivers that come with Windows Embedded CE, it is necessary to classify them. Depending on the perspective, such as architecture, loading into memory, loaded modules, system load time, and supported device type, the same driver can be classified in different ways. For example, a layered, kernel-mode driver that the Device Manager (device.dll) loads during the system startup provides support for a serial port. Let us formalize our classification:

- Implementation architecture.
    - Layered driver, which consists of the model device driver (MDD) and the platform dependent driver (PDD).
    - Hybrid driver.
    - Monolithic driver.
- Loading module.
    - Device Manager (device.dll)— stream drivers.
    - GWES (gwes.dll)—drivers that are used only by the Graphics, Windowing, and Events Subsystem (GWES).
    - File system (filesys.dll)—drivers of file systems.
- Loading into memory.
    - Into kernel memory—kernel-mode drivers.
    - Into a specialized user process (Udevice.exe)—user-mode drivers.
- System load time.
    - When starting the system.
    - By request.

- Type of supported device.

  - ❏ Serial port.

  - ❏ Video adapter.

  - ❏ Network card.

  - ❏ Touchscreen.

  - ❏ Keyboard.

  - ❏ Mouse.

  - ❏ Human interface device (HID), and so on.

Driver Implementation Architecture

Several different types of driver implementation architecture are available. The most common architecture type in Windows Embedded CE is a layered driver often called an MDD/PDD driver. In this architecture, a driver is built from two parts, the MDD library and the PDD library.

The MDD library implements a functionality that is common for a certain class of device drivers by providing the operating system with a required interface—usually, as a defined set of IOCTL control codes and, possibly, functions. This interface is usually called Device Driver Interface (DDI). The MDD layer also implements an interrupt service thread (IST) and defines the interface for interacting with the PDD layer, which is called Device Driver Service Interface (DDSI). A service interface depends on the driver type and the MDD library implementation.

The PDD library contains a code that works with a specific hardware device implementation by providing the MDD layer with a pre-defined set of functions (DDSI).

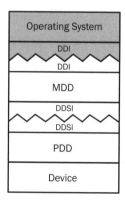

FIGURE 6–1 Layered driver architecture

A two-level model simplifies the development and the process of porting the drivers. All a developer has to do is implement the PDD layer and use the common MDD layer implementation. For each device type that supports this layered architecture, Windows Embedded CE includes an MDD implementation as part of a completely implemented driver. Figure 6–1 illustrates the layered architecture.

The use of a two-level MDD/PDD model implies MDD persistence, where the same MDD is used for all PDDs. When it is necessary to provide the operating system with some unique device functionality that is a logical extension of the MDD/PDD implementation for a given device type, it is possible to clone MDD implementation and to expand the interface between MDD and PDD (DDSI), as well as the interface offered by the MDD layer to the operating system. This hybrid type of driver architecture is shown in Figure 6-2.

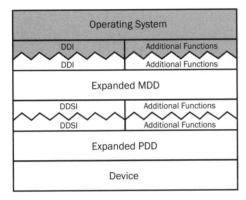

FIGURE 6–2 Hybrid driver architecture

The next available type of driver architecture is the monolithic architecture, which has no intermediate interface. A monolithic driver implements the interface with the operating system (e.g. DDI) and interacts directly with a specific hardware implementation. This type of architecture is usually utilized in the following cases:

- When there is no layered model for a device type.

- Device hardware implements some functionality as the one implemented in the MDD layer.

- It is necessary to provide access to a unique device functionality that does not fit into the architecture of the existing implementation of the MDD layer.

- When using an MDD/PDD model, it is not possible to achieve a required efficiency level.

Building a monolithic driver is the most complex task; however, using this implementation architecture makes it possible to obtain high efficiency and to maximize the hardware use. Figure 6–3 illustrates a monolithic architecture.

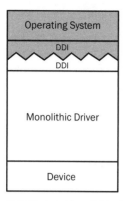

FIGURE 6–3 Monolithic driver architecture

Regardless of the selected implementation architecture, a developer may use as a base the source code included with the development tools. Table 6–1 lists the directories that contain the majority of drivers included with Windows Embedded CE.

TABLE 6–1 Included driver directories.

Directory	Description
\PUBLIC\COMMON\OAK\DRIVERS\	Contains platform-independent drivers, which are usually bus drivers and the MDD parts of layered drivers.
\PLATFROM\COMMON\SRC\SOC\	Contains driver implementation for the system-on-chip (SOC) periphery.
\PLATFORM\<*PLATFORM_NAME*>\SRC\DRIVERS	Contains implementation of drivers for a specific platform and the PDD part of layered drivers.

File System Drivers, Thread Drivers, and Native Drivers

As mentioned earlier, in Windows Embedded CE the following three modules (parts of the kernel) can load drivers:

- Device.dll.

- Gwes.dll.

- FileSys.dll.

The Device Manager (Device.dll) loads the drivers that implement a stream interface. A stream interface is a predetermined set of functions that a driver is supposed to provide to the Device Manager. No restrictions exist in terms of the device types where a stream driver can be implemented. The majority of Windows Embedded CE drivers support a stream interface. Table 6–2 lists stream interface functions with their descriptions (the XXX-prefix that is defined by the developer may not be present).

TABLE 6–2 **Stream interface functions.**

Function	Description
XXX_Init	The Device Manager calls this function while loading the driver. It performs all required initialization.
XXX_PreDeinit	The Device Manager calls this function before calling XXX_Deinit. It marks an instance of the device as invalid and performs all necessary actions to prevent resource contention in a multi-threaded implementation.
XXX_Deinit	The Device Manager calls this function before the driver is offloaded. It performs a necessary procedure of freeing the resources.
XXX_Open	This function is called while calling CreateFile with a device name. It creates a handle for Read/Write/IOControl.
XXX_PreClose	The Device Manager calls this function before calling XXX_Close. It marks the device handle as invalid and performs all necessary actions to prevent resource contention in a multi-thread implementation.
XXX_Close	This function is called when calling CloseHandle with a device handle. It clears the context.
XXX_IOControl	This function is called when calling DeviceIoControl. In many driver types, this is where most of the driver functionality resides.
XXX_Read	This function is called when calling ReadFile. It performs a Read operation. Frequently, it is not implemented.
XXX_Write	This function is called when WriteFile. It performs a Write operation. It is not implemented frequently.
XXX_Seek	This function is called when SetFilePointer. It performs a Move operation. Frequently, it is not implemented.
XXX_PowerUp	The power management system calls this function when the system returns from Suspend mode. It performs the actions that are necessary to return the system from the Suspend state.
XXX_PowerDown	The power management system calls this function when the system goes into Suspend mode. It performs the actions that are necessary to enter a Suspend mode.

Stream drivers are unique in a sense that they can be named and are accessible through functions that interact with the file system. Calling CreateFile with a device name returns a handle that makes it possible to access a driver by using both a standard file API (ReadFile/WriteFile/SetFilePointer) and the so-called worker bee of thread drivers—DeviceIoControl.

The Device Manager registers the following three different file namespaces in the file system for accessing named stream drivers:

- Legacy (DEV1:).

- Device–based (\$device\DEV1).

- Bus–based (\$bus\PCI_0_1_0).

The file system recognizes device calls and reroutes to the Device Manager.

The legacy namespace is used first in CE. A device name is built from the device prefix and its index. The prefix and the index are taken from the registry and the driver-load parameters. An index value can be between zero and nine. Therefore, only 10 devices with the same name or device prefix can be accessible through a legacy namespace.

A device namespace ($device) is similar to a legacy space but the former has no index restriction. A device name is built by adding a device prefix and its index, separated by a back slash (\), to the $device space identifier, preceded by a back slash. A device namespace makes it possible to call more than 10 devices with the same index.

The bus namespace ($bus) provides additional possibilities for working with bus–based device drivers. It is implemented by both the Device Manager and the driver. A device name is built by adding a bus name to the $bus namespace identifier and preceded by a back slash (\), underscore bus number, underscore device number, and underscore function number. The handle that is returned by making a call via a bus name has additional characteristics as opposed to the handles that are obtained by making a call via a legacy space or a driver space, which makes it possible to perform bus architecture-specific operations.

A stream driver does not necessarily have to support a named interface. If a driver does not have to interact with other drivers or applications, then it may not implement the functions that are responsible for the access to a named interface— XXX_Open/XXX_Close.

Figure 6-4 illustrates a stream driver architecture.

The GWES (GWES.dll) module loads the device drivers that are exclusively used by this system, which are all the following drivers related in any way to the user interface: keyboard, video adapter, touch screen, printer, and mouse. These types of drivers are sometimes named native drivers, where each class of devices whose drivers are loaded by GWES has its own interface with GWES.

The file system (FileSys.dll) module loads the file system drivers. File system drivers are implemented as a DLL that implements a predefined set of functions and IOCTL control codes. These functions are called by using a standard set of file system application programming interfaces (APIs) through the files that the file system driver registered.

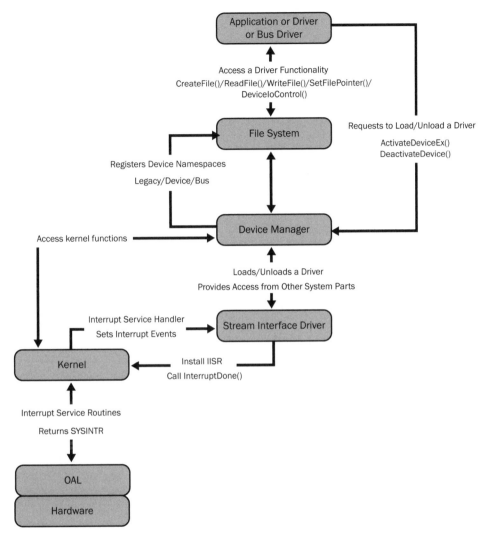

FIGURE 6–4 Stream driver architecture

User-Mode Drivers and Kernel-Mode Drivers

In Windows Embedded CE, drivers can be loaded into either the kernel space (kernel-mode drivers), or into a specialized user-mode drivers host process—Udevice.exe (user-mode drivers). The drivers loaded by the GWES and FileSys subsystems can only be kernel-mode drivers. The drivers loaded by the Device Manager (Device.dll) can be both kernel-mode drivers and user-mode drivers. By default, unless a special flag is set in the registry settings (DEVFLAGS_LOAD_AS_USERPROC(0x10)), a driver is loaded into the kernel space.

As mentioned earlier, drivers provide interfaces to a physical or virtual device. The quality, stability, and security of drivers determine the quality, stability, and security of the entire system. Regardless of a driver's type, it should be robust. A system with only one compromised kernel-level driver becomes fully compromised because a kernel-level driver has full access to user memory, as well as full access to kernel memory. A developer should consider all inputs to driver functions as originating from non-trusted sources. All input should be checked and handled carefully. User-mode drivers do not have full access to kernel and user memory, but through the reflector service discussed below, they have access to kernel memory for operations. A system can be compromised through a low-quality driver, and therefore, all the rules mentioned above are also applicable to user-mode drivers. In addition, the user-mode driver infrastructure provides the possibility to limit access to kernel memory by using registry settings. Developers should keep in mind that access from a user-mode driver to the kernel must be restricted as much as possible.

Kernel-mode drivers have a certain advantage compared to the user-mode drivers in terms of their efficiency, accessibility of internal kernel structures, and API. Kernel-mode drivers can have direct, synchronous access to user buffers because they have direct access to user memory. When loading a driver into the kernel, keep in mind the stability and security requirements discussed earlier. A driver error may result in a kernel error, which results in system failure. In order to reload a driver, it may be necessary to restart the device.

Kernel-mode drivers cannot display the user interface directly. To show the user interface, kernel drivers use an additional kernel capability—support for the UI Proxy device driver. In order to enable this capability in the OS image, it is necessary to add the UI Proxy for kernel-mode drivers (SYSGEN_UIPROXY) component into an OS design. To display the user interface, a kernel-mode driver calls the CeCallUserProc function and passes, as a parameter, the library name that implements the user interface. The internal details of how the kernel-mode driver displays the user interface are as follows:

1. The specified proxy device driver of the user interface is loaded into the Udevice.exe host process.

2. A function specified in the CeCallUserProc function is called, and the specified parameters are passed to this function.

3. The function performs the necessary actions.

4. The result is transformed accordingly and is returned into the kernel-mode driver (output parameters of the CeCallUserProc function).

It is important to point out that the user interface proxy driver is loaded with the first call.

Registry settings determine the drivers that are loaded into the Udevice.exe process. Microsoft attempted to make the kernel-mode drivers and user-mode drivers as compatible as possible. However, loading the drivers into a user process imposes the following certain restrictions upon the driver:

- Kernel structure and kernel memory are not accessible.

- A large part of the kernel API is not available.

- The use of the available part of the kernel API is restricted by registry settings.

- Limited access to user buffers.

Therefore, a universal driver that must have the ability to load into both the user space and the kernel space must be implemented while taking into account the limitations of user-mode drivers.

The use of user-mode drivers can improve the system stability, security, and fault-tolerance. User-mode drivers can be separated from other user-mode drivers by being loaded into different Udevice.exe host processes and by being isolated from the kernel. These drivers have far fewer privileges than the kernel-mode drivers. If a user-mode driver fails, it may be possible to reload it without having to reload the entire system. However, developers should keep in mind the security and stability considerations mentioned earlier. Developing user-mode drivers does not mean that developers can omit security and stability requirements.

Keep in mind that in general kernel-mode drivers are more efficient than user-mode drivers. Moreover, not all types of drivers can be user-mode drivers. All file system drivers, all native (GWES) drivers, and all network drivers can be only kernel-mode drivers.

The support infrastructure for user-mode drivers is called the User-mode Driver Framework. The central part of this framework is the reflector service. This service provides the user-mode drivers with the ability to work in user mode. For each user-mode driver, a reflector service object is created and is responsible for the following functionality:

- It loads and controls the host process.

- It reroutes calls to the driver over to the host process from the operating system.

- It transforms pointer parameters (first-level pointers) of the calling process to the driver address space.

- It provides the user-mode driver with access to some kernel-mode services.

The reflector service object masks the differences between user-mode drivers and kernel-mode drivers from the rest of the system. When utilizing a functionality of a specific driver, an application or another driver does not differentiate between a user-mode driver and a kernel-mode driver. The reflector service object provides a user-mode driver with access to a part of the kernel-level API, including: CreateStaticMapping(); NKDeleteStaticMapping(); VirtualCopy(); FreeIntChainHandler(); InterruptInitialize(); InterruptDisable(); InterruptDone(); InterruptMask(); and LoadIntChainHandler(). At the same time, the reflector service validates input parameters before performing the requested actions in accordance with the registry settings in the driver branch, where IoBase represents the physical address/addresses and IoLen represents the length/lengths. In the case of one contiguous fragment, IoBase and

IoLen are created as a DWORD type. If access is needed to several non-contiguous fragments of physical memory, IoBase and IoLen are created as a multi_sz type, which stores addresses and lengths.

As mentioned earlier, user-mode drivers can be separated from one another by being loaded into different host processes. In order to accomplish that, a special registry key of the following kind needs to be created: HKEY_LOCAL_MACHINE\Drivers\ProcGroup_*XXXX*, where XXXX is the driver group number. The registry key must have the following values:

- **ProcName**   requires Udevice.exe for the user-mode drivers.
- **ProcVolPrefix**   is a prefix that is registered as a volume, such as $udevice, for accessing the drivers via the functions of the file system and DeviceIoControl, such as \$udevice\DEV1.

Furthermore, the ProcGroup type DWORD value needs to be set to the group number of the user-mode driver registry key. Drivers with different group numbers will be loaded into different host processes, while drivers with the same group number will be loaded into one host process.

Note that the Device Manager is responsible for loading user-mode drivers, so all user-mode drivers are stream drivers.

The user-mode driver is loaded as follows:

- The Device Manager receives a request to load the driver.
- The Device Manager validates that this is a user-mode driver.
- The Device Manager creates a reflector service object.
    - ❏ The reflector service object loads the host process for user drivers (udevice.exe) by passing it the volume name specified in registry settings as a parameter.
- The host process for user drivers creates and mounts the specified volume and registers the file system API set.
    - ❏ The request is returned to the reflector service.
- The request is returned to the Device Manager.
- The Device Manager calls XXX_Init.
    - ❏ The reflector service redirects the request to the host process for user-mode drivers.
- The host process processes the request.
- The host process loads the appropriate driver.
- The host process calls the XXX_Init function of the driver.

- The driver returns the device context.

  ❏ The device context is returned to reflector service.

  ❏ The device context is returned to the Device Manager.

- The Device Manager creates a handle and returns it to the initiator that loaded the device driver.

- The driver is loaded and is accessible through a standard file system API set and DevoceloControl.

Figure 6-5 illustrates a user-mode driver loading process.

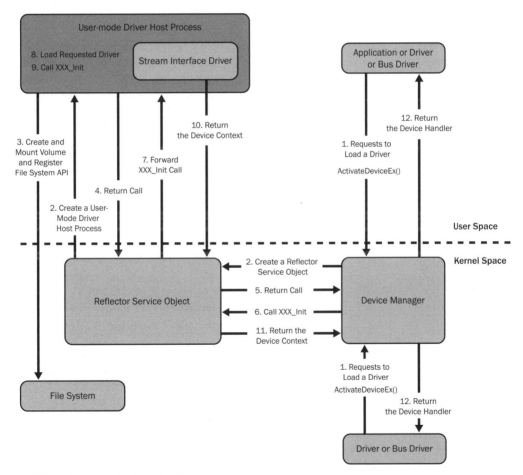

FIGURE 6-5 A user-mode driver loading process

The fixup of the modules located in the MODULES section of binary image builder (.bib) files occurs during the Makeimg stage. Therefore, it is necessary to specify the memory region for address fixup. If a driver is loaded into the kernel address space, then the module needs have the K flag set in the .bib file. If a driver is loaded into the user process, then the K flag does not need to be set. If a load is necessary, both the user space and the kernel space need to have the Q flag set. The drivers located in the FILES section of .bib files can be loaded both into the user space and the kernel space. The address fixup occurs while driver is loaded into memory for execution.

Loading the Drivers

There are three modules that are responsible for loading the drivers: Device Manager (Device.dll), GWES (Gwes.dll), and file system (Filesys.dll). Regardless of the module responsible for loading the drivers, all settings are stored in the registry of the operating system.

The Device Manager is responsible for loading stream drivers. Stream drivers can be loaded by calling a special function named ActivateDeviceEx() that uses a handle of a registry key that contains driver settings as values, or it is done automatically at the system startup.

Table 6–3 provides some of the registry settings that the Device Manager uses for loading stream drivers. Those settings should be placed as values of any appropriate registry key which will be used for a ActivateDeviceEx() call. To specify drivers for automatically loading at the system startup the special keys in registry are used wich will be discussed below.

TABLE 6–3 Registry settings for loading stream drivers.

Value name	Description
Dll	Required. Specifies the driver file name.
Prefix	Optional. Defines the prefix of the stream driver and part of the device name for accessing through the file system. It must match the prefix that is used for implementing driver functions if the 0x0008 flag is not set. This flag means that driver functions were implemented without a prefix (Init, Deinit, Write, and so on).
Order	Optional. It determines the load order of the drivers. It enables you to implement scenarios with drivers being dependent on the load order during the automatic load at system startup. The drivers are loaded in the order specified by this parameter. If the parameter is missing, the drivers will be loaded after with this parameter—usually, according to the registry's numeric order.
Index	Optional. It is part of the device name for accessing through the file system. It is added to the prefix on the right. If the setting is missing, the Device Manager will automatically use the next sequential value for the devices with one prefix.
IClass	Optional. It specifies a class or classes of the device. It is used in the PnP messaging system. Examples: loading a block driver, pointing to the power management system that the driver support power management, etc.
Flags	Optional. It specifies how the driver will be loaded.

Table 6–4 provides some of the values for setting the Flags value.

TABLE 6–4 **Values for setting the Flags value.**

Value	Description
0x00000000	No flags.
0x00000001	The driver is unloaded after the XXX_Init function is called or after the function return.
0x00000002	Driver is loaded by using LoadLibrary instead of LoadDriver.
0x00000004	Driver is not loaded.
0x00000008	Driver is implemented without by using a prefix in the function names (Init, Deinit, Write, etc.).
0x00000010	Loads the driver in user-mode.
0x00000100	Driver is loaded only when there is an exclusive access to IRQ.
0x00001000	Driver is loaded during boot phase one.
0x00010000	Access to the driver is possible only from a privileged application.

There is also a certain set of registry settings, which are accessed through auxiliary functions DDKReg_GetIsrInfo() and DDKReg_GetWindowInfo(), and which are actively used while implementing the drivers supplied with the operating system. Bus drivers can configure these settings, or they can be set manually. Table 6–5 lists the main settings.

TABLE 6–5 **Registry settings for driver implementation.**

Value Name	Description
Irq	Physical IRQ request that the device uses.
Sysintr	System identifier of the interrupt.
IsrDll	Points to the library of the installable ISR.
IsrHandler	Points to the routine function name in the installable ISR.
BusNumber	Number of the bus if the system had more than one bus of the same type.
InterfaceType	The bus type used by the device.
IoBase	A relative address of the I/O window/windows.
IoLen	Length/lengths of the I/O window/windows.
MemBase	Relative address of the memory window/windows.
MemLen	Length/lengths of the memory window/windows.

Let us now look at the automatic loading of stream drivers at the system startup. When the system is started, the Device Manager loads and reads the RootKey value of the registry key HKEY_LOCAL_MACHINE\Drivers. Next, the Device Manager calls ActivateDeviceEx with the

HKEY_LOCAL_MACHINE\<*RootKey*> key where <*RootKey*> is the RootKey value. By default, this value is equal to \Drivers\BuiltIn.

The HKEY_LOCAL_MACHINE\<*RootKey*> key contains the settings for bus enumerator (BusEnum.dll). The bus enumerator driver reads all subkeys of the registry key where it is located, and for each key it calls the ActivateDeviceEx() function. The sequence of calling the ActivateDeviceEx() function for the drivers is determined by the Order value. Drivers with a lower Order value are loaded first. Drivers without the Order settings are loaded after the drivers that have the Order settings—usually, according to the registry's numerical sequence.

Therefore, in order to load a stream driver, at system startup it is necessary to place the registry key with its settings as a subkey of HKEY_LOCAL_MACHINE\<*RootKey*> registry. By default, it is located in HKEY_ LOCAL_MACHINE\ Drivers\BuiltIn.

The GWES (Gwes.dll) loads the keyboard, video adapter, touchscreen, printer, and mouse drivers. The loading of each driver type is determined by its unique registry settings. Let us take a closer look at the load process for some of the native drivers.

The following algorithm is used during the load of the video adapter driver.

At first, GWES looks through a list of values stored in the HKEY_LOCAL_MACHINE\System\ GDI\DisplayCandidates key with the names that contain Candidate*X* where X is a sequential number of a candidate for a video adapter driver; the X value can range from 1 to 32. These values contain a line of code data which points to a registry key in relation to HKEY_LOCAL_ MACHINE. GWES browses through the values sequentially until it finds the key that is present in the system. Next, GWES attempts to load the video adapter driver that is specified in the DisplayDll value of the found registry key. The process of browsing registry key values ends.

If the HKEY_LOCAL_MACHINE\System\GDI\DisplayCandidates key is missing or if there are no registry keys specified in the CandidateX values, GWES loads the driver specified in the value with the name Display from the HKEY_LOCAL_MACHINE\System\GDI\Drivers key. This value must contain the name of the library of the video adapter driver. If the key is missing, GWES will attempt to load the driver with a default file name which is ddi.dll.

Windows Embedded CE supports dual monitors, but the second video adapter driver is not loaded automatically. In order to load the driver of the secondary display, it is necessary to call CreateDC directly by specifying the driver's name and by using the obtained handle for drawing from that point forward, as follows: `HDC hSecondaryDisplay = CreateDC(<Driver_File_Name>, NULL, NULL, NULL)`.

Note that on the secondary display the developer is responsible for rendering the entire display because Windows manager cannot access it.

The PS/2 keyboard driver is loaded by GWES at system startup. The GWES module reads the value that contains the name Status in the HKEY_LOCAL_MACHINE\HARDWARE\

DEVICEMAP\KEYBD key and determines if the keyboard is present and its characteristics. If it does not find it, by default it assumes that the keyboard is present and that it contains the ENTER and ESC keys, as well as alpha-numeric keys and further looks for a value with the name DriverName. It has to contain the name of the keyboard driver. By default, the keyboard driver also contains the mouse drivers,so no separate settings for loading the mouse driver are needed. The HKEY_LOCAL_MACHINE\HARDWARE\DEVICEMAP\MOUSE settings can be used by the mouse driver or other parts of the system, but GWES does not use them for a separate load of the mouse driver.

In order to load a touch screen driver, GWES validates the presence of a value with the name DriverName in the HKEY_LOCAL_MACHINE\HARDWARE\DEVICEMAP\TOUCH registry key and loads the specified library.

The FileSys module loads the file system drivers. File system drivers can be loaded in two different ways. The first method is the automatic load during the system startup, which is typically used for the file systems that do not have a corresponding block driver (HKEY_LOCAL_MACHINE\System\StorageManager\Autoload\<*File_System_Name*> key). The second method is to load during the process of mounting media while a corresponding block driver is being loaded. While loading a block driver, the driver sends a request to mount a media device. The Storage Manager receives this call and requests information about the device profile. After that, it loads a matching driver for that partition. Next, the Storage Manager enumerates the partitions and loads file system drivers based on the partition type.

You can specify file system settings for any mounted media with a given file system. They must be present as values in the registry key HKEY_LOCAL_ MACHINE\System\StorageManager\<*File_System_Name*>, where <*File_System_Name*> is FATFS, UDFS, etc. The registry key settings are HKEY_LOCAL_MACHINE\System\StorageManager\Profiles\<*Device_Profile_Name*>\<*File_System_Name*>, where \<*Device_Profile_Name*> is CDProfile, HDProfile, PCMCIA, SDMMC, etc. override the file system settings stored in the HKEY_LOCAL_MACHINE\System\StorageManager\<*File_System_Name*> key.

Driver Development

A choice of the driver implementation method depends heavily on the device type and additional requirements. For example, a majority of debugging drivers for network cards shipped with the development tools work in poll mode, which is often unacceptable for a regular network driver.

Let us look at a driver implementation that utilizes interrupts. In Windows Embedded CE, the processing of interrupts is divided into two parts: interrupt service routine (ISR) and interrupt service thread (IST). ISR routines are part of the OAL layer. Otherwise, if support is included in the OAL layer, they can be installed during execution (installable ISR routines—IISR). The main tasks of the ISR routine are to determine the source of the interrupt, mask the interrupt, and return the logical system interrupt (SYSINTR) identifier to the system. IST is a worker bee that performs the majority of interrupt processing. It creates an event, registers it in the kernel for a certain logical interrupt, and waits for the event. When the event is created, it performs all the necessary processing based on the event. If a driver uses an installable ISR, then IST loads the installable routine. If a driver has a multi-threaded implementation, then the process of creating and installing an ISR can be executed in one thread, such as the main thread while another thread can wait and process a different event. Driver tasks include the following:

- Determine a system identifier of the interrupt.
    - ❑ Can be specified directly in the driver.
    - ❑ Can be obtained from registry settings by using the DDKReg_GetIsrInfo() function.
    - ❑ Can be obtained by sending the request to the OAL layer by using IRQ – IOCTL_HAL_REQUEST_SYSINTR.
- Create an event (CreateEvent()).
- Register the event in the kernel for a specified system identifier of the interrupt (InterruptInitialize()).
- Wait for an event by using WaitForSingleObject().
- Once the event has been created, process it appropriately.
- After the processing is finished, call InterruptDone().

If a driver uses an installable ISR routine, then it additionally performs the following tasks:

- Determines the settings for the ISR routine (name, entry point, and other parameters).
    - ❑ Can be directly specified in the driver.
    - ❑ Can be obtained from registry settings by using the DDKReg_GetIsrInfo() function.
- Loads an installed IISR procedure for a specific IRQ request (LoadIntChainHandler()).
- Configures the IISR procedure (KernelLibIoControl()).
- After finishing, it calls the FreeintChainHandler() function, which excludes the installed IISR procedure from a chain of installed procedures that are called in the OAL layer while processing a specified interrupt request (IRQ). It keeps the library code loaded in memory.

The installable ISR routine is implemented as a dynamically loaded library. This library must meet the following requirements:

- The entire implementation code must be inside the library; no explicit dependencies should exist.

■ No implicit dependencies can exist (NOMUPS16CODE = 1).

■ The C run-time library cannot be used (NOLIBC = 1).

The development tools are shipped with generic installable service routine (GIISR), which is an installed procedure for processing common interrupts. It is supplied in the source code (\ Public\Common\Oak\Drivers\GIISR\), is applicable for a majority of situations, and reads the registers/ports in order to determine the status of an interrupt. The GIISR procedure can be configured with KernelLibIoControl by setting the following:

■ Register address/port address.

■ Register size/port size.

■ A feature, memory, or input/output (I/O) register or port.

■ A mask.

Working with buffers that are passed from the calling code to drivers is an important part of driver development. Before we start discussing this subject let us provide a few definitions, as shown in Table 6–6, that will be used later on.

TABLE 6–6 Definitions for working with buffers.

Term	Definition
Access Checking	Checks to make sure that the caller process has enough privileges to access the buffer.
Pointer Parameter	A pointer that is passed to an API function as a parameter.
Embedded Pointer	A pointer that is passed to an API function inside a data structure or a buffer.
Secure copy	A local copy of the buffer data that has been passed.
Marshaling or mapping	Usually applies to pointers. Prepares a pointer to be used in another process.
Synchronous Access	Provides access to the buffer during the API call in the caller thread.

When applications need to call some functionality implemented by drivers, usually they need to pass some information to drivers. It is possible for drivers to use shared memory space to pass parameters, such as by using shared heaps or memory mapped files. In most cases, driver functionality is accessable through API calls by using parameters.

This accesibility scenario results in two issues. First, parameters use memory in the user memory process space, while drivers reside in the kernel memory space (for kernel-mode drivers) or in another user process (for user-mode drivers). Second, the caller must have enough rights to access the passed buffer. Therefore, during driver development, you must check access to passed buffers and provide drivers with access to the caller's buffer data. Figure 6–6 illustrate a sample marshaling case.

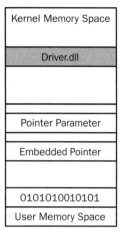

FIGURE 6-6 A sample marshaling case

In this case, App.exe calls a Driver.dll function with two parameters. The first is a pointer pa-rameter, and the second is a structure with an embedded pointer. If the Driver.dll function is called synchronously (from the caller's thread), the App.exe memory space can be accessed directly from the Driver.dll functions during the call. Only synchronous, direct access requires an access check and not marshaling.

There are two options if asynchronous access to the buffers is required: The first is to make a copy of the buffer into the driver memory, and the second is to create an alias to the same physical memory as the buffer that is being passed.

As mentioned earlier, there are several types of marshaling:

- Direct access.
  - ❏ The calling process buffer is directly accessible for the lifetime of the call.
  - ❏ It is possible only with a synchronous access for the kernel-mode drivers.
- Copying.
  - ❏ The buffer being passed is copied to the working buffer of the driver.
  - ❏ A driver is working with a copy. If needed, it is copied back.
- The use of an alias.
  - ❏ Creating a new buffer in the driver that is associated with the same physical memory as the buffer that is being passed.
  - ❏ All buffer changes are automatically accessible in the calling process.

The kernel is independently able to determine the best marshaling method. Depending on whether there is synchronous or asynchronous access to the buffer, a different API set needs to be used for marshaling.

With synchronous access, the kernel automatically converts pointer parameters, and therefore, the developer has to manually map the embedded pointers by calling CeOpenCallerBufer(), which validates access and performs marshaling and at the end calls CeCloseCallerBuffer().

With asynchronous access, the conversion procedure that occurs with synchronous access needs to be supplemented with a preparation of all pointers for asynchronous access by calling the CeAllocAsynchronousBuffer() function, and at the end, calling the CeFreeAsynchronousBuffer() function.

Data marshaling has the following restrictions for user-mode drivers:

- With asynchronous access, the pointer parameter is accessible in Read-Only mode; there is no support for Write mode.

- Despite the capability to perform manual marshaling of built-in pointers, when calling from the kernel to a driver, it is possible to receive pointers that are not accessible from the user-mode drivers.

Thus, it is most efficient to use a flat buffer containing all the data for the user-mode drivers and to not use asynchronous access.

Table 6–7 provides summary information about the system API that should be used for checking access and marshaling a caller's buffers.

TABLE 6–7 **Buffer marshaling API.**

Marshaling	Pointer Parameter	Embedded Pointer
Synchronous Access	No need for additional API calls	CeOpenCallerBufer() CeCloseCallerBuffer()
Asyncronous Access	CeAllocAsynchronousBuffer()	CeOpenCallerBufer() CeAllocAsynchronousBuffer()
	CeFreeAsynchronousBuffer()	CeFreeAsynchronousBuffer() CeCloseCallerBuffer()

The process of passing data to a driver results in additional risks associated with a possibility of modifying the pointers and/or data to which they point during an API execution after being validated by the driver. To prevent these types of attacks, a safe copy method is used which, involves creating a separate copy of the data stored by the driver. When a safe copy is created, the buffer that is being passed is copied into a local buffer of the driver. It is desirable to use it in the following cases:

- For all embedded pointers.

- For all parameters that need to be validated before being used.

Notice that the use of a safe copy reduces efficiency to a certain degree. You can create a safe copy through several ways:

- Manually.

- By using CeOpenCallerBuffer() with the ForceDuplicate parameter set as TRUE for embedded pointers.

- By using CeAllocDuplicateBuffer() for pointer parameters.

Table 6–8 shows the available marshaling API functions.

TABLE 6–8 API for marshaling.

Function	Description
CeOpenCallerBuffer	Validates access and performs marshaling of the pointer. Returns a marshaled pointer. Allocates resources. In order to free resources after the pointer processing is finished, the CeCloseCallerBuffer function must be called.
CeCloseCallerBuffer	Frees up all resources allocated by the CeOpenCallerBuffer function. If necessary, writes back to the buffer that was passed.
CeAllocAsynchronousBuffer	Prepares a buffer that was previously marshaled by the CeOpenCallerBuffer function or automatically by the system, for an asynchronous access. This function must be called synchronously before the return to the calling thread. It allocates resources. In order to free resources after the pointer processing is finished; the CeFreeAsynchronousBuffer function must be called.
CeFreeAsynchronousBuffer	Frees up resources allocated by the CeAllocAsynchronousBuffer function. If necessary, writes back to the buffer that was passed.
CeFlushAsynchronousBuffer	Makes changes in the source buffer in accordance with the changes in the buffer that was changed by the CeAllocAsynchronousBuffer function.
CeAllocDuplicateBuffer	Creates a secure copy of the parameter-pointers.
CeFreeDuplicateBuffer	Frees up resources allocated by the CeAllocDuplicateBuffer function. If necessary, writes back to the buffer that was passed.

Aside from that, Windows Embedded CE 6.0 includes a set of supplemental C++ classes for marshaling (\PUBLIC\COMMON\OAK\INC\MARSHAL.HPP). Table 6–9 provides a listing of classes and their descriptions.

TABLE 6–9 **Additional marshaling classes.**

Class	Description
AsynchronousBuffer_t	Wrapper class for the CeAllocAsynchronousBuffer and CeFreeAsynchronousBuffer functions. Used for marshaled pointers that require an asynchronous access.
DuplicatedBuffer_t	Wrapper class for the CeAllocDuplicateBuffer and CeFreeDuplicateBuffer functions. Used for pointer parameters.
MarshalledBuffer_t	Wrapper class for the CeOpenCallerBuffer, CeCloseCallerBuffer, CeAllocAsynchronousBuffer, and CeFreeAsynchronousBuffer functions. Used for non-marshaled embedded pointers.

Speaking of the development of reliable and stable drivers, keep in mind that it is necessary to insert __try/__except/__finally blocks into the executable code that can cause an exception error, especially for the code that accesses data received from outside.

Debugging is a big part of driver development. Windows Embedded CE development tools provide all needed functionality to debug drivers. Windows Embedded CE provides two possibilities for debugging drivers: the first is standard step-by-step debugging with the possibility to enter kernel-supplied code, and the second is debugging without interruptions by using debug zones. Note that to use the standard kernel debugger, KITL should be implemented for the particular hardware platform and selected transport method.

If you want to have the capability to debug any part of the system, you should build a Debug OS image. If you want to debug an entire driver, then it is enough to build a Retail OS image that includes the kernel debugger, KITL, and the debug version of the driver with all auxiliary debug files. If you want to debug an entire driver and a part of the system, you should include the components in the previous case, as well as the debug version of the required system part with all auxiliary debug files in the image. For detailed information about building an OS image, see Chapter 4, "Build System."

Debug zones are an improved version of the "printf debugging" technique and include the possibility to configure the output at run-time, as well as integrating with Platfrom Builder. Fundamentally, debug zones send conditional output to the debug output. In this way, debug zones can provide you with information about your driver execution without interrupting an execution.

All the supplied system code actively uses debug zones, so you can see not only the output from your driver debug zones but also most of the surrounding system activity. This capability can be helpful to discover and resolve problems during driver development.

To use debug zones in your own code you should do the following:

- Include dbgapi.h in the driver's header file: `#include <DBGAPI.H>`

- Define masks for debug zones, such as:

```
//zone 0
#define ZONEMASK_INIT             (0x00000001<<0)
//zone 1
#define ZONEMASK_ACTIONS          (0x00000001<<1)
//zone 2
#define ZONEMASK_EXCEPTIONS (0x00000001<<2)

//zone 14
#define ZONEMASK_WARNING          (0x00000001<<14)
//zone 15
#define ZONEMASK_ERRORS           (0x00000001<<16)
```

- Define flags to use in conditional debug zones output, such as:

```
//true if zone 0 is enabled
#define ZONE_INIT                 DEBUGZONE (0)
// true if zone 1 is enabled
#define ZONE_ACTIONS      DEBUGZONE (1)
// true if zone 2 is enabled
#define ZONE_EXCEPTIONS   DEBUGZONE (2)

// true if zone 14 is enabled
#define ZONE_WARNING      DEBUGZONE (14)
// true if zone 15 is enabled
#define ZONE_ERRORSDEBUGZONE (15)
```

- Define parameter dpCurSettings, such as:

```
DBGPARAM dpCurSettings = {
    //Usually name of module
    TEXT("MyDriver"),
     { // Names for 16 zones
       TEXT("Init"),TEXT("Actions"),TEXT("Exceptions"),TEXT(""),
       TEXT(""),TEXT(""),TEXT(""),TEXT(""),
       TEXT(""),TEXT(""),TEXT(""),TEXT(""),
       TEXT(""),TEXT(""),TEXT("Warnings"), TEXT("Errors")
     },
    // Zones enabled by default
    ZONEMASK_ERRORS| ZONEMASK_EXCEPTIONS|ZONEMASK_INIT
};
```

- Register debug zones by using appropriate macros, such as:

  - ❑ DEBUGREGISTER() for Debug build. Use NULL as parameter if uses for .exe. Use handle as parameter if uses for .dll.

  - ❑ RETAILREGISTERZONES() for retail and debug build. Use NULL as parameter if uses for .exe. Use handle as parameter if uses for .dll.

- Include appropriate macros in the driver code (see Table 6–10 for details).

- Make appropriate OS build (Debug or Retail).

- Load the image to device.

- Use Platform Builder to configure active debug zones for your module (see Chapter 2 for more information).

TABLE 6–10 Debug zone macros.

Macros	Description
RETAILMSG (<Expression>, <Message>)	Conditionally outputs a printf-style formatted message.
RETAILLED (<Condition>,<Parameters>)	Conditionally outputs WORD value to the LED.
ERRORMSG(<Expression>, <Message>)	Conditionally outputs a printf-style formatted message with ERROR with the file name and line number of the error.
DEBUGMSG(<Expression>, <Message>)	Conditionally outputs a printf-style formatted message.
DEBUGLED(<Condition>,<Parameters>)	Conditionally outputs a WORD value to the LED.
DEBUGCHK(<Expression>)	Asserts an expression and produces a DebugBreak if the expression is FALSE.
DEBUGZONE(<Zone Id>)	Tests the mask bit in the current debug zone settings.
DEBUGREGISTER(<Handle>)	Registers debug zones for your process or module only on Debug builds.
RETAILREGISTERZONES(<Handle>)	Registers debug zones on Debug and Retail builds

Chapter 7
Starting the Operating System

Understanding the processes that take place during the system startup is important for building devices based on Microsoft Windows Embedded CE. As we look at the process of system initialization, the role of each of the components that make up the system kernel, as well as the role of the included code and custom code developed by the Board Support Package (BSP) manufacturer, becomes much clearer.

No boot loader is required in order to load the Windows Embedded CE operating system (OS). The use of a boot loader simplifies development tasks significantly, but its presence is not required for the end device. It implies that the image of the operating system is located in ROM and that during a device startup, a jump is made to the address of the kernel startup function. However, not all platforms support such an option (for example, x86). Using the boot loader makes it possible to perform a preliminary platform preparation, to load the image of the operating system into the correct location in RAM, and only then jump to the kernel startup function.

At first, let us look at how the boot loader performs during the system startup. For more information about the boot loader implementation, see Chapter 5, "Board Support Package (BSP)." Next, we shall take a look at how the Windows Embedded CE kernel is started.

Image Preparation

While building a system image, the following actions are performed to prepare an image for execution:

- Preparing for the execution of the OS image in place (in accordance with the settings of the CONFIG section of the binary image builder (.bib) file).

- Creating a special structure that contains information about the image contents and table of contents (TOC).

- Assigning the pTOC variable in Nk.exe the meaning of a TOC pointer.

This results in an image that is ready to execute in certain addresses of virtual memory that contains a special structure depicting the image contents. In order to launch the system for execution, the boot loader must load the image into correct addresses; it must then verify that by shifting from the start of the image by 0x40, the CECE signature (0x43454345) is present [the ECEC in memory (0x45434543)]. Next to it, there is a pointer to the ROMHDR structure, and after that, there is a pointer to the TOC (pTOC) structure. The boot loader reads the value of the pointer to the TOC structure and validates the entry for NK.EXE. Following that, it jumps to the address of the kernel startup function.

The startup kernel function StartUp() is developed by using assembler language. Implementation can be separated out. It can take place partly in the platform's common code (\PLATFORM\COMMON\SRC\SOC\<*SOC_DIR*>\OAL\STARTUP\ and (\PLATFORM\ COMMON\SRC\<*CPU_FAMILY*>\COMMON\STARTUP\), and partly in BSP code directly (\PLATFORM\<*PLATFORM_ NAME*>\SRC\OAL\OALLIB\). This function's code depends heavily on the platform. The main tasks of the StartUp function are to transfer the processor into a predefined state and to perform an appropriate low-level initialization of the hardware, including initializing the memory controller, disabling interrupts, TLB cache and the Memory Management Unit (MMU) module, and performing initialization of the system-on-chip (SOC). After the processor is initialized, the StartUp function will call the functions KernelStart or KernelInitialize (x86) (\PRIVATE\WINCEOS\ COREOS\NK\LDR\<*CPU_FAMILY*>\). The KernelStart/KernelInitialize function performs the following main actions:

- Copies sections defined in the ROMHDR (through ulCopyEntries, and ulCopyOffset) into RAM by using KernelRelocate(). After this, global variables Nk.exe become accessible for read and write operations.

- Initializes the first-level page table based on OEMAddressTable (ARM and x86).

- Enables the MMU module and cache (ARM and x86).

- Finds the entry point into kernel.dll (FindKernelEntry).

- Calls the kernel entry point by passing a pointer to KdataStruct as a parameter, which also contains a pointer to the OEMInitGlobals and OEMAddressTable functions (x86 and ARM).

In the current implementation, the kernel.dll entry point function is named NKStartup(). Its implementation is located in the \PRIVATE\WINCEOS\COREOS\KERNEL\<*CPU_FAMILY*>\ directory. The kernel entry point function performs the following actions:

- Initializes the NKGLOBALS structure. This structure contains all functions and variables that are exported by the kernel to the OAL and Kernel Independent Transport Layer (KITL) if KITL is implemented as a separate DLL library.

- Calls the OEMInitGlobals function by passing the initialized NKGLOBALS structure to it.

- OEMInitGlobals returns the structure OEMGLOBALS. This structure contains all functions and variables that are exported by the OAL to the kernel and KITL layer if KITL is implemented as a separate DLL library.

- The ARMSetup() function is called for ARM processors, whereas the MIPSSetup() function is called for Microprocessor without Interlocked Pipeline Stages (MIPS) processors.

- If the image has KITL, the kernel attempts to load it and calls the entry point.

- The OEMInitDebugSerial() function is called.

- By using the OEMWriteDebugString() function, the kernel outputs to the debug output a string that contains the information about the kernel starting with "Windows CE Kernel for …".

- The OEMInit() function is called which initializes the hardware platform.

- The KernelFindMemory() is called, (\PRIVATE\WINCEOS\ COREOS\NK\KERNEL\loader.c).

- The KernelInit() function is called (\PRIVATE\WINCEOS\COREOS\ NK\KERNEL\nkinit.c). For ARM, the KernelStart() function is called from (\PRIVATE\WINCEOS\COREOS\NK\ KERNEL\ARM\armtrap.s, which calls KernelInit().

- In some architectures, a forced rescheduling is performed after the exit from KernelInit().

Startup Process

Figure 7–1 shows part of the system startup process: StartUp() – KernelStart()/ KernelInitialize() – NKStartup() (<Kernel Entry>()). The code implemented in the OAL layer is shown in gray. It also shows the main tasks being performed and the functions called.

The OEMInit() function is implemented in the OAL layer, and it is responsible for platform initialization including the interrupt, timer, KITL, and bus.

The KernelInit() calls the following functions:

- APICallInit () configures the system API: \PRIVATE\WINCEOS\ COREOS\NK\KERNEL\ apicall.c.

- HeapInit () initializes the kernel heap: \PRIVATE\WINCEOS\ COREOS\NK\KERNEL\heap.c.

- InitMemoryPool () initializes a physical memory pool: \PRIVATE\WINCEOS\COREOS\NK\ KERNEL\physmem.c.

- PROCInit () initializes infrastructure for support processes: \PRIVATE\ WINCEOS\ COREOS\NK\KERNEL\process.c.

- VMInit () initializes virtual memory for the kernel process: \PRIVATE\WINCEOS\ COREOS\NK\KERNEL\vm.c.

- THRDInit () initializes threads; creates a tread with a working SystemStartupFunc function and launches that thread for execution by using the MakeRun() function: \PRIVATE\ WINCEOS\COREOS\NK\ KERNEL\thread.c.

- MapfileInit () initializes support for memory-mapped files: \PRIVATE\WINCEOS\ COREOS\NK\ MAPFILE\mapfile.c.

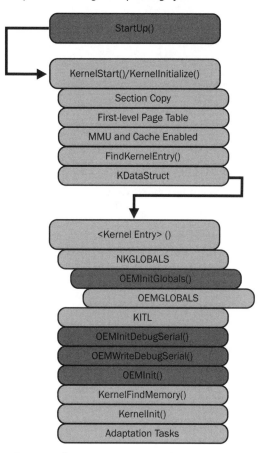

FIGURE 7–1 System startup process StartUp()->＜KernelEntry＞

The SystemStartupFunc() function (\PRIVATE\WINCEOS\COREOS\NK\KERNEL\schedule.c) performs the following actions:

- Calls the KernelInit2() function that completes kernel initialization.

- Calls the LoaderInit() function the initializes the kernel loader for EXE/ DLL – \PRIVATE\WINCEOS\COREOS\NK\KERNEL\loader.c.

- Initializes a cookie that protects the stack: __security_init_ cookie().

- Initializes a page pool: PagePoolInit(), CELog, profiler, etc. - LoggerInit(), system debugger – SysDebugInit().

- Calls IOCTL – IOCTL_HAL_POSTINIT. A developer can use its implementation for additional initialization after kernel initialization.

- Creates two threads that are ready to execute. The first one has a working PowerHandlerGuardThrd function and the second one has a working RunApps function.

The RunApps() function (\PRIVATE\WINCEOS\COREOS\NK\KERNEL\kmisc.c) performs the following actions:

- Loads filesys.dll.

- Creates a thread ready for execution with a working function, which is the entry point of filesys.dll.

- If the image has filesys.dll and the file system, it waits for the file system to be initialized (SYSTEM/FSReady event), then loads MUI and system settings from the registry and informs the file subsystem about completion of required tasks: (* pSignalStarted) (0).

- A thread becomes a thread for cleaning dirty pages in the background.

Figure 7–2 shows part of the process of system startup: KernelInit() – SystemStartupFunc() – RunApps(). It also shows the main tasks performed and the functions called.

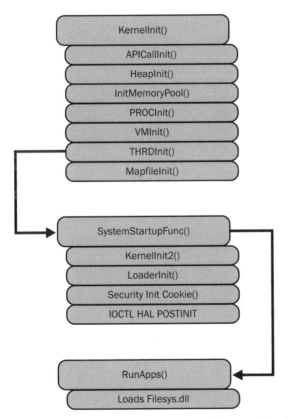

FIGURE 7–2 System startup process KernelInit()->RunApps()

Loading the File System

Let us proceed to the process of loading filesys.dll. As opposed to the previously covered parts of the kernel, the source code of filesys.dll is not provided in Shared Sources, and therefore, the load of filesys.dll can be traced by using the load log by setting certain values in Debug Zones as well as by using the code that interacts in some way with the loading of filesys.dll.

Next, we shall look at the cold boot. During the cold boot, filesys.dll performs the following main actions:

- Initializes the object store memory and maps it for itself.

- Initializes an application programming interface (API) set of the file system and intermediate APIs (databases, point-to-point message queue, event log, and registry).

- Initializes registry data.

  ❑ The initialization procedure will differ depending on the type of registry used (hive–based or RAM–based).

  ❑ During this stage, the Device Manager (device.dll) can be loaded if it is necessary to load the drivers for accessing the media where the hive–based registry is going to be stored.

  ❑ If the Device Manager (device.dll) is loaded during this stage, then after the necessary drivers are loaded, device.dll is suspended while waiting for the initialization of filesys.dll to be finalized.

- Informs the kernel that filesys.dll performed base initialization (sets the SYSTEM/FSReady event) and waits for a signal from the kernel – (* pSignalStarted) (0) to continue initialization (see the RunApps() function above).

- Filesys.dll launches applications specified in the registry key HKEY_LOCAL_MACHINE\Init.

  ❑ If this registry key contains the Device Manager (device. dll) and it's already been loaded, filesys.dll sets the SYSTEM/BootPhase2 event. After this message is received, the Device Manager continues to load the drivers (\PRIVATE\WINCEOS\COREOS\ DEVICE\DEVCORE\devcore.c).

After the initialization of filesys.dll completes, the system is completely operational. Figure 7–3 shows part of the process of starting the system through filesys.dll and the main tasks being performed.

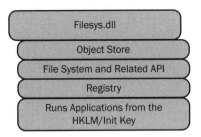

FIGURE 7–3 System startup process through filesys.dll

Loading the Device Manager

The Device Manager (device.dll) loaded during the system startup reads the RootKey value in the registry key HKEY_LOCAL_ MACHINE\Drivers. Next, the Device Manager calls ActivateDeviceEx with the HKEY_LOCAL_MACHINE\<*RootKey*> key, where <*RootKey*> is the value of RootKey. By default, this value is equal to \Drivers\BuiltIn.

HKEY_LOCAL_MACHINE\<*RootKey*> contains the settings for bus enumerator (BusEnum.dll). The bus enumerator driver reads all sub keys in the registry key where it's located, and for each key it calls the ActivateDeviceEx() function. The order in which the drivers are calling ActivateDeviceEx() is determined by their Order value. The drivers with lower Order values are loaded first. Drivers without the Order value being set are loaded after the drivers with an Order value, which are usually in the registry's enumeration order.

If the Device Manager is loaded when the registry is initialized, it first loads the drivers from the registry's boot section that is mounted by filesys.dll (Boot.hv). The load procedure is the same as the one described above.

Let us look at the format of values of the HKEY_LOCAL_MACHINE\Init key for automatically launching applications at the system startup. The Init key may contain two types of values: one with a name of LaunchXX and DependXX type, where XX value can be between 00 and 99.

LaunchXX contains a value of REG_SZ type, which must be the name of the program that needs to be launched, e.g., program.exe, without parameters. The value of XX determines the load order; the lower the XX value, the earlier the application will be launched.

DependXX contains a value of the REG_BINARY type; it also makes it possible to deter-mine the dependencies of applications on other applications during the load by specifying what applications should be loaded before the application specified in the corresponding LaunchXX key. Indexes of XX applications that the specified application is dependent on are indicated as a list of words string (word–2 bytes), with the words' byte order reversed.

The application specified in the Init key must inform the system that it loaded successfully and that dependent applications can be loaded by calling the SignalStarted() function with a parameter that is passed to it by the system as a command line parameter during the load process. This is why it is impossible to specify command line parameters when loading applications from the Init key.

Following is an example of the registry key Init content:

```
[HKEY_LOCAL_MACHINE\Init]
"Launch10" = "shell.exe"
"Launch20" = "device.dll"
"Depend20" = "hex:0a,00"
"Launch30" = "gwes.dll"
"Depend30" = "hex:14,00"
"Launch50" = "explorer.exe"
"Depend50" = "hex:14,00, 1e,00"
```

In this case, the shell.exe application will be launched first; next—the Device Manager (device.dll), which depends (in this example) on shell.exe; next, gwes.dll is loaded, which depends on the Device Manager; finally, explorer.exe is loaded, which depends on the Device Manager (device.dll) and gwes.dll.

Chapter 8
Building Devices

The process of building devices based on Windows Embedded CE can be separated out into several stages:

- Device planning.
    - ❏ Requirements definition.
    - ❏ Selection and/or planning of hardware development.
    - ❏ Selection of a base template for the operating system (OS) design.
    - ❏ Planning of image deployment for production.
- Development of the hardware platform (optional).
- Development and customization of a Board Support Package (BSP) for a selected hardware platform (optional).
    - ❏ Launching Windows Embedded CE on a selected hardware platform.
    - ❏ Driver development.
- Operating system design.
    - ❏ Configuring a run-time image.
    - ❏ Developing applications.
    - ❏ Building and testing intermediate versions of the image.
    - ❏ Creating a Software Development Kit (SDK) to enable third-party developers to build solutions for this device.
- Building the final version of the image for testing and release.
- Final testing of the image.
- Image deployment for production.

The process of building a device starts with a planning phase. This phase is no less important than BSP development or image design. Planning can help ensure that the device is implemented with the fewest resources and in the expected time. A traditional approach to development consists of defining the requirements and the features of the target device. The more complete the requirements, the more possible it is to accurately select a suitable hardware platform for the device. During the planning phase, you can perform testing of the Windows Embedded CE operating system on the available hardware platforms in order to determine more precisely the hardware and software requirements of the device. Often times during the planning phase, developers do not consider how OS images are moved to the device during the production phase. This is a critical factor that may considerably increase the production costs. For instance, in the case of medium and large volumes, if OS images require manual loading to each device, this can substantially increase labor costs.

There are two options in hardware platform selection: use an existing platform or develop a new, independent one. When an existing platform is selected, it is necessary to make sure that the BSP is accessible in the same form as is needed for implementing the device requirements. For instance, if you need to connect additional peripheral devices to the main device and reconfigure the interrupt controller to perform the tasks that will be implemented by the device, then, most likely, it would be necessary that BSP source codes are accessible. If, on the other hand, you need to simply deploy a specialized application over a hardware platform with standard functionality, then, most likely, the BSP source codes would not be necessary.

It is essential to understand the importance of BSP accessibility for a selected platform. The absence of a BSP prolongs the development time considerably, which increases the overall development costs. BSP development is the most labor-intensive part of a device-building process. It requires that the developer know the hardware architecture as well as the operating system architecture. All of the interaction between the operating system and the platform is implemented in the BSP. Therefore, the quality of the BSP determines the resulting quality of the device.

Nevertheless, the implementation of the device requirements may require the creation of a custom device hardware design. In this case, it is necessary to make sure that the source code has a BSP that is sufficiently similar to the hardware platform of the device. The presence of such a BSP may be of considerable help during the development of a custom BSP.

Please note the development tools included with Platform Builder for Windows Embedded CE 6.0 R2 contain several examples of BSP implementation—at least one BSP for each of the following supported processor architectures: ARM, x86, SH4, and Microprocessor without Interlocked Pipeline Stages (MIPS).

The basics of BSP development are covered in Chapter 5, "Board Support Package (BSP)". During BSP development, the components involved include the following:

- Boot loader.
- OAL and Kernel Independent Transport Layer (KITL).
- Drivers.

A boot loader is not required for a BSP, but its presence speeds up the development process considerably. A considerable portion of the boot loader code and OAL code is common. An important function of a BSP is support for KITL over the transport that is accessible on the hardware platform, such as serial port, Ethernet, and Universal Serial Bus (USB). KITL support is practically a mandatory requirement to ensure the efficiency of the development of drivers and for debugging the image of the operating system. KITL can be part of the OAL, or it can be implemented as a separate library. After the main functionality of OAL has been implemented, you can start implementing the drivers for peripheral devices. Note that the mechanism of transforming a hardware interrupt into a system identifier resides in the OAL layer and can be expanded by using installable interrupt service routines when OAL supports this functionality.

For more information about the architecture of the operating system and the drivers, see Chapter 3, "Operating System Architecture," and Chapter 6, "Driver Architecture."

During the planning phase, it is also necessary to determine the type of a device to build. The device type selection determines the standard design template to use as a base when building the device run-time image. Windows Embedded CE 6.0 R2 contains the following device design templates and template versions:

- Consumer media device.
  - Digital media receiver.
  - Set-top box.
  - Custom device.
- Industrial device.
  - Industrial controller.
  - Internet appliance.
  - Gateway.
- PDA device.
  - Mobile handheld.
  - Enterprise Web pad.
- Phone device.
  - IP phone basic.
  - IP phone advanced.
  - Small-footprint device.
- Thin client.
  - Windows Thin Client.
  - Enterprise terminal.
  - Windows network projector.

The main list contains the device design templates. The sub-items contain different versions of the same template. Table 8–1 provides a detailed description of the purpose of each template version.

TABLE 8–1 **Device design templates.**

Design Template	Design Template Version	Description
Consumer Media Device	Digital Media Receiver	Devices that will play and/or store various multi-media resources, including music, video, and images.
Consumer Media Device	Set-Top Box	Devices that will be connected to the TV to access the Internet and to view multimedia resources. By default, it is built with a standard CE shell and a browser that has TV navigation mode enabled.
Custom Device	–	By default, no catalog components are selected. This enables you to select only the required components while going through the OS Design Wizard.
Industrial Device	Industrial Controller	Industrial automation devices such as control panels and programmable controllers.
Industrial Device	Internet Appliance	Devices with a keyboard, monitor, and usually with a browser-based interface.
Industrial Device	Gateway	Devices that function as a network gateway and provide wired and wireless access to Internet connections from a home network.
PDA Device	Mobile Handheld	Mobile devices that support a touch screen and/or a keyboard, such as warehouse terminals for tracking merchandise.
PDA Device	Enterprise Web Pad	A touch screen–based Web Pad with a screen resolution from 640x480 and higher; a standard CE shell and additional applications with their own application–based or browser–based shell.
Phone Device	IP Phone Basic	VoIP phone without a user interface.
Phone Device	IP Phone Advanced	VoIP phone with a user interface, contacts, and a rich and configurable user interface, which may include Windows Messenger and a browser.
Small Footprint Device	–	Devices for which the image size is a significant requirement. It implies that all the required components will be selected directly from the catalog.
Thin Client	Windows Thin Client	Devices with a minimum interface that enables you to obtain access by using the Remote Desktop Protocol (RDP) and, possibly, to use a browser.
Thin Client	Enterprise Terminal	Devices that provide a more familiar thin client interface to a corporate user, such as a self-serve kiosk with its own shell, a cash register, etc.
Thin Client	Windows Network Projector	Devices that map the Remote Desktop of a personal computer running Vista with RDP, such as network projectors.

After the initial design template has been selected, you need to create a base OS design and configure it in accordance with the device requirements. Please note that even if a self-developed BSP is used, it is necessary to clone it prior to creating a base image and use the cloned version from that point on.

The following main settings are available for the OS design:

- Adding/removing components from the catalog into the OS design.
- Setting the parameters in the configuration files. For more information about configuration files, see Chapter 4, "Build System."
    - ❑ Registry (*.reg).
    - ❑ Device memory and image contents (*.bib).
    - ❑ Initialization of the RAM–based file system (*.dat).
    - ❑ Built-in databases (*.db).

    Project settings that are accessible through the Project Properties dialog box. For more information, see Chapter 2, "Operating System and Application Development Tools."
    - ❑ General settings.
    - ❑ Locale settings.
    - ❑ Build settings (configuring the appropriate build variables).
    - ❑ Setting optional build variables directly.
    - ❑ Additional actions during the build process.

The next stage is to create the main application or a set of device applications that provide the main device functionality. This stage can also include the configuration and customization of applications included with Windows Embedded CE 6.0 R2, such as Windows Thin Client or VoIP phone based on the IP phone advanced template. Keep in mind that the code provided with the development tools must be cloned.

During the development process, the OS image builds are preformed regularly for the purpose of driver and application debugging. It is also recommended that the developers create intermediate builds for the testing that must be performed and, if necessary, also create intermediate SDKs for the purpose of developing and/or testing of third-party development for the device. The use of the above-mentioned approach enables the developer to identify the problems, if they appear, prior to final testing of the OS image/device before releasing it to production.

Once these tasks have been completed, you need to build the image for final testing and production.

For production purposes, the release version of the image is built without KITL, debugger, and profiling support, with the Enable Ship Build option set, and usually without CE Control Shell (CESH). It may be necessary to create an image with different settings for testing purposes.

After passing the necessary tests, the final image is ready to be moved to production. If testing has uncovered substantial problems, it is necessary to perform additional customization tasks according to the cycle described above.

Figure 8–1 shows the process for building a device.

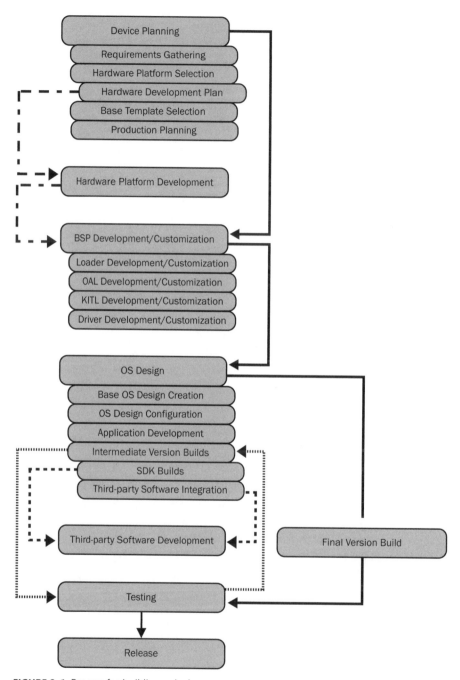

FIGURE 8–1 Process for building a device

Subsequent chapters cover typical tasks that come up during the process of building a device.

BSP Cloning

Any development process should start from cloning a BSP. It is important to understand that any changes made to the BSP during the development will be used in all future OS designs based on that BSP.

BSP cloning is done by using the development tools. To access the tools select Tools, then Platform Builder for CE 6.0, and from the drop-down menu, choose Clone BSP. A Clone Board Support Package window appears, as shown in Figure 8–2.

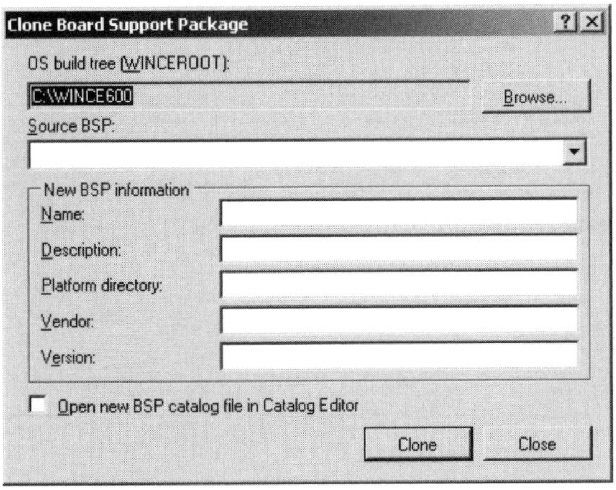

FIGURE 8–2 Cloning a BSP dialog

From the drop-down list, select Source BSP, enter the following information about the new BSP that will be created as a result of cloning:

- **Name** the name of the package the way it will appear in the component catalog.

- **Description** description of the package the way it will appear in the component catalog.

- **Platform directory** the name of the new directory in %_WINCEROOT%\• PLATFORM where the source BSP will cloned into.

- **Vendor** BSP manufacturer's name the way it will appear in the component catalog.

- **Version** BSP version name the way it will appear in the component catalog.

If the Open New BSP Catalog File in Catalog Editor flag is set, then after cloning is completed, the new BSP file will open in the catalog file editor.

Figure 8–3 shows an example of a completed form.

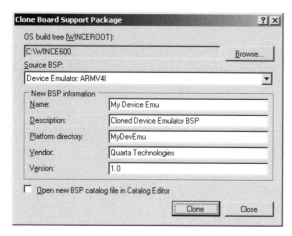

FIGURE 8–3 Completed form example

After the form is filled out, click Clone and wait until cloning completes. This process creates a corresponding BSP directory, as shown in Figure 8–4.

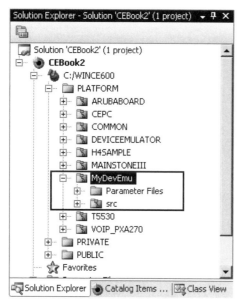

FIGURE 8–4 BSP directory

The BSP is an available selection item from the Third Party section of the catalog, as shown in Figure 8–5.

FIGURE 8-5 BSP selection item

After cloning, it can be used just like any other BSP.

If the Open New BSP Catalog File in Catalog Editor flag was set during the cloning process, the BSP catalog file will open in Catalog Editor. You can perform the necessary editing tasks in that file, as shown in Figure 8–6.

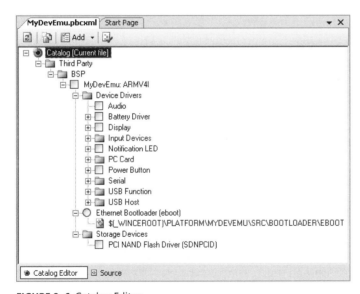

FIGURE 8-6 Catalog Editor

Cloning a Component or a Project

Development tools come with a great deal of source code for drivers, programs, static libraries, and dynamic libraries. Often, the developer needs to modify the source code included with the component's development tools in order to perform a certain task.

Chapter 4, "Build System," includes a detailed discussion of the process of building a Windows Embedded CE operating system and its components. All components are represented by a folder or a folder hierarchy in the file system located in special catalogs (PUBLIC, PRIVATE) on different levels starting from the build tree root %_WINCEROOT%, plus the configuration files that control the build process (Sources, Dirs). Similar to the BSP process, the changes will be made to each of the OS designs that use that particular driver, program, or library. It is important to keep in mind that subsequent upgrades to the development tools may erase those changes. It is for these reasons that it is necessary to clone the part of the code that will keep changing.

Because components are represented by folders and folder trees, cloning is done by simply copying and making the needed corrections in the Sources file. Drivers are cloned into the platform directory; other projects are simply cloned into the operating system design directory.

For the projects that generate .DLL and .EXE files on output, the process of cloning is simplified by using the Sysgen_capture.bat utility, which collects all the necessary settings into the Sources file. Projects that generate .LIB files are usually cloned by simple copying, possibly by taking into account general settings of the Sources file (see Sources.cmn below). Some of the catalog components can be cloned by using built-in development tool options. To do that, right-click the component, and, if the built-in utility can clone this component, the drop-down menu will display the Clone Catalog Item. Click that item to launch the cloning process.

In conclusion, a few recommendations regarding cloning:

- When cloning a project, go up the catalog hierarchy and if you locate the Sources.cmn file—add from that file into the copied Sources file either the entire content or the following variables:
    - ❏ COMMONPUBROOT.
    - ❏ _PROJROOT.
    - ❏ _ISVINCPATH.
    - ❏ _OEMINCPATH.
- After copying is done, it is necessary to set/change the settings of at least the following variables in accordance with the following tasks:
    - ❏ *RELEASETYPE*   specifies where the build results will copied to. For drivers and projects that are related to a specific hardware platform and were cloned into an appropriate BSP directory, the release type is set in PLATFORM. For other projects the type is set depending on the purpose of the project and can be LOCAL, OAK, SDK, DDK, CUSTOM.
    - ❏ *Set WINCEOEM as 1*   This is necessary to ensure that the project can link to system libraries and header files of the projects that are built from the PUBLIC directory.

Please note that these settings are also available in the Project Settings dialog box.

Automatic Application Launch at Startup

When custom built applications are integrated into an OS image, there is often a requirement for them to launch automatically at startup.

The process of starting the operating system is discussed in more detail in Chapter 7, "Starting the Operating System." At startup, the system loads all applications specified in the HKEY_LOCAL_MACHINE\Init registry key with the values of Launch*XX* type, where XX can be between 00 and 99 and represent the sequence that applications are launched. If it is necessary to specify the dependency of a launched application on other automatically launched applications, the Depend*XX* values are used, where XX matches the XX value in the LaunchXX key where dependency is specified.

LaunchXX contains a value of the REG_SZ type which must be the name of the program that needs to be launched, such as program.exe, without the parameters. The XX value determines the load order, so the lower the XX value, the earlier this application launches.

DependXX contains a value of the REG_BINARY type, which enables you to determine the dependency of applications on other applications during the load by specifying which applications must be loaded prior to the application specified in the corresponding LaunchXX key. The indexes of XX applications that a given application is dependent on are specified as a lists of words (a word is 2 bytes) with a reverse byte order.

The application specified in the Init registry key must inform the system that it has loaded successfully and the dependent applications can be loaded by calling the SignalStarted() function with a parameter that it is passed to by the system as a command line parameter during the load. This is precisely the reason why it is not possible to specify the command line parameters from the Init key during the application load.

An example of the Init registry key is shown below:

```
[HKEY_LOCAL_MACHINE\Init]
"Launch10"="shell.exe"
"Launch20"="device.dll"
"Depend20"="hex:0a,00"
"Launch30"="gwes.dll"
"Depend30"="hex:14,00"
"Launch50"="MyShell.exe"
"Depend50"="hex:14,00, 1e,00"
```

In this case, the shell.exe application launches first, then it loads the Device Manager (device.dll), which depends (in the example) on shell.exe, then it loads gwes.dll, which is dependent on the Device Manager, and finally, MyShell.exe, which depends on both the Device Manager (device.dll) and gwes.dll.

In order to launch your own application, you need to specify appropriate values in the OS design registry file (Project.reg) located in the Parameter Files folder of the Solution Explorer window, as shown in Figure 8–7.

FIGURE 8–7 OS design registry file

Double-click the file to open a graphic registry file editor where you can conveniently enter the necessary values into the registry, as shown in Figure 8–8.

project.reg	Start Page			
HKEY_CLASSES_ROOT		Name	Type	Data
HKEY_CURRENT_USER		(Default)	REG_SZ	(value not set)
HKEY_LOCAL_MACHINE				
HKEY_USERS				
RegEdit	Source			

FIGURE 8–8 Registry file editor

Before configuring settings for an automatic startup, it is necessary to make sure that they will not override the general system settings and BSP settings. To view general system settings, open and view the Common.reg file in the file editor, as shown in Figure 8–9.

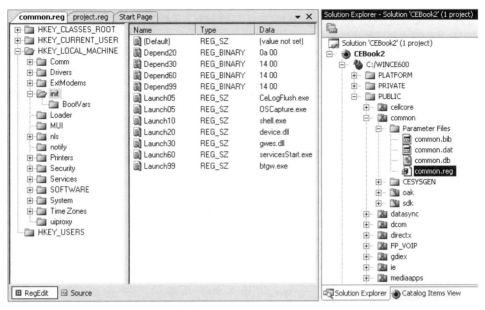

FIGURE 8–9 Editing Common.reg in the file editor

In order to view the BSP settings, it is necessary to open and view the Platform.reg file of the corresponding BSP used in a given design, as shown in Figure 8–10.

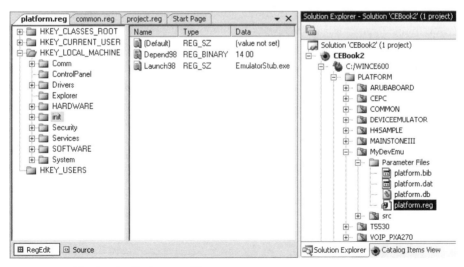

FIGURE 8–10 Viewing the Platform.reg file

Automatic Load of Drivers During the System Startup

When custom built drivers are integrated into a device OS image, it is often required that these drivers be loaded automatically at the system startup.

The process of starting the operating system is discussed in more detail in Chapter 7, "Starting the Operating System." The Device Manager (device.dll) is responsible for loading stream drivers at startup.

The Device Manager (device.dll) loaded at the system startup reads the value with the RootKey name in the HKEY_LOCAL_MACHINE\Drivers registry key. Next, the Device Manager, calls ActivateDeviceEx with the HKEY_LOCAL_MACHINE\<RootKey> key where <RootKey> is the RootKey value. By default, this value is \Drivers\BuiltIn.

The HKEY_LOCAL_MACHINE\<RootKey> contains the settings for loading the bus enumerator (BusEnum.dll). The bus enumerator driver reads all sub-keys of the registry key where it is located, and for each key, it calls the ActivateDeviceEx() function. The order of calling the ActivateDeviceEx() function for the drivers is determined by the settings of their Order value. The drivers with the lesser Order values are loaded first. Drivers without the Order settings are loaded after the drivers with the Order settings in accordance with the registry's numerical sequence.

In order to configure an automatic load of a custom-built stream driver during the system startup, it is necessary to enter appropriate values into the OS design registry file (Project.reg) located in the Parameter Files folder of the Solution Explorer window, as shown in Figure 8–11.

FIGURE 8–11 OS design registry file

Figure 8–12 shows an example of the registry settings for the MyDriver.dll driver whose functions are implemented without a prefix (the Flags value is equal to 8).

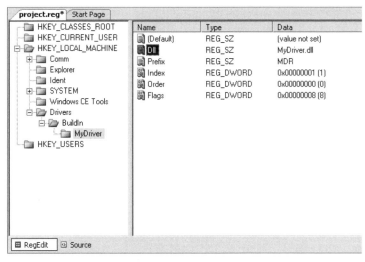

FIGURE 8–12 Registry settings for MyDriver.dll

Device Power Management

Power management is one of the important tasks for the device in general and is critical for mobile devices that are not permanently connected to an AC power source.

Windows Embedded CE includes a base implementation of the power-management subsystem named Power Manager. Power Manager is represented by two catalog items: Power management and Power management minimal.

Power Manager provides applications and drivers of peripheral devices with an infrastructure that enables them to manage power efficiently. This includes requesting that a necessary power state is set for peripheral devices or the system as a whole. The use of the power management mechanism enables you to detach the overall power state of the system from the power state of a specific peripheral device. For example, when the system is switched to a lower power usage state, the GSM/GPRS will continue to receive the power needed for implementing the functionality of receiving calls and transferring data. Power manager is the central point for collecting information regarding the general status of power usage by the system and peripheral devices, as well as the information about power management requirements for devices. Power Manager uses this information to perform itsnecessary actions by utilizing the built-in power management algorithm.

Power Manager interacts with applications and device drivers to ensure that peripheral devices and the system in general operate in a required power state. Applications and drivers are not required to support power management. Power Manager interacts only with those device drivers and applications that inform it about power management support.

In order to interact with Power Manager, an application must use a special application programming interface (API) set. For the Power Manager to be aware that a driver supports power management, the driver must contain an identifier of an appropriate device class in its registry settings (IClass parameter), or during initialization, the driver must call the AdvertiseInterface function with the same class identifier.

A base Power Manager is implemented by using a layered MDD/PDD architecture (see Chapter 6, "Driver Architecture"). The source code is located in the \PUBLIC\COMMON\ OAK\DRIVERS\PM\ folder. The PDD part of the driver determines power management states supported by the system, as well as the logic and the method of switching from one power management state to another. A device manufacturer can rewrite the PDD part of the Power Manager in accordance with its own power management requirements for the target device.

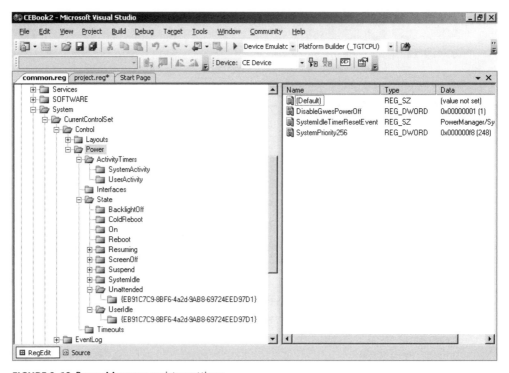

FIGURE 8–13 Power Manager registry settings

Peripheral devices can have four predefined states:

- **Full on**   marked in registry settings as 0.
- **Low on**   marked in registry settings as 1.
- **Standby**   marked in registry settings as 2.
- **Sleep**   marked in registry settings as 3.
- **Off**   marked in registry settings as 4.

Registry settings are used to map the power states of the system to the power states of peripheral devices and other settings of the power management subsystem. Those settings are located in the HKEY_LOCAL_MACHINE\System\CurrentControlSet\Control\Power key of system registry. Figure 8–13 shows an example of the Power Manager registry settings in the Common.reg file that is opened in a graphic registry editor of the development studio.

In the HKEY_LOCAL_MACHINE\System\CurrentControlSet\Control\Power\State sub key, the sub keys represent a listing of system power states. Mapping a default device state and individual devices are specified as values of a corresponding key of the system state, as shown in Figure 8–14.

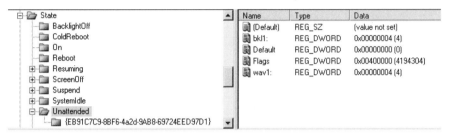

FIGURE 8–14 Mapping of a default device state and individual devices

In Figure 8–14, the Unattended state of the system is mapped into the On (0) state for all devices except for bkl1: (backlight) and wav1: (audio output) – those are Off (4). The globally unique identifier (GUID) of the key, which determines the system's power state, is used by the sub keys to specify the settings for mapping the system's power state to the devices of an appropriate class (in this case, it is CE_DRIVER_POWER_MANAGEABLE_DISPLAY_GUID, a display with a Power Manager support). In our example, the system's power state Unattended is mapped as off (04) for the devices of a display with a Power Manager support class, as shown in Figure 8–15.

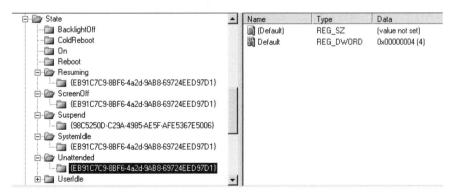

FIGURE 8–15 Mapping system power state for a class of devices

Base implementation of Power Manager is based on activity timers. The registry key HKEY_LOCAL_MACHINE\System\CurrentControlSet\Control\Power\ActivityTimers contains sub keys that determine two activity timers: SystemActivity and UserActivity. The UserActivity timer is activated if the user does not perform interactive actions during a predetermined time. The SystemIdle timer is activated if the system has no active processes during a certain period of time.

When timers are activated, the Power Manager makes a determination to switch to another power state. The switchover does not happen all at once, but with a certain delay (timeout) during which the timer must not reset, i.e. timer activation conditions must be retained, such as no user activity.

The settings for switchover timeouts are kept as values in the HKEY_LOCAL_MACHINE\ System\CurrentControlSet\Control\Power\Timeouts key, as shown in Figure 8–16. A timeout value depends on the device power source type at a given time (alternative current or battery), as well as depending on what power state the system is switching from and to.

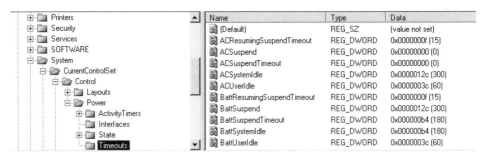

FIGURE 8–16 Switchover timeout registry key

The registry key values determine a timeout in seconds. For example, switching from the On to the UserIdle state results in a 60-second timeout after the UserActivity timer goes off when it is using a battery power source. If the timer is not reset during that time, there will be no user activity.

Figure 8–17 shows Power Manager interaction with applications and drivers.

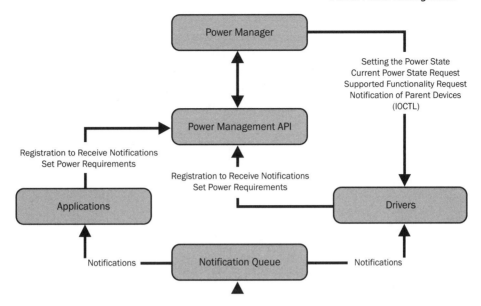

FIGURE 8–17 Power Manager interaction

To ensure support for power management, the peripheral device driver must be a stream interface driver, and it must support the following IOCTL control codes, as shown in Table 8–2.

TABLE 8–2 IOCTL control codes.

Code	Purpose
IOCTL_POWER_CAPABILITIES	This IOCTL queries to determine device-specific capabilities. If a driver fails this IOCTL, the Power Manager assumes the target driver does not handle the remaining IOCTLs and will not send them. All drivers that support the Power Manager interface must handle this IOCTL.
IOCTL_POWER_SET	This IOCTL requests a change from one device power state to another. If the driver does not support the proposed device power state, then it should write its adjusted device power state into pBufOut.
IOCTL_POWER_QUERY	This I/O control checks whether changing power states is feasible. This I/O control is deprecated and is not called by Power Manager.
IOCTL_POWER_GET	This IOCTL gets the current device power state. The Power Manager will only send this IOCTL to drivers that support the power management IOCTLs.
IOCTL_REGISTER_POWER_ RELATIONSHIP	This IOCTL notifies the parent device so the parent device can register all devices it controls. The Power Manager ignores the return values from this IOCTL, which provides an opportunity for a parent device to notify the Power Manager about any active devices that it controls. The Power Manager sends this IOCTL to devices that include the POWER_CAP_PARENT flag in the Flags member of the POWER_ CAPABILITIES structure.

Power Manager controls power states of peripheral devices by sending IOCTL control codes to the drivers that support power management. Applications and drivers can request changes to a power state of the system in general or a peripheral device. A driver should not change its power state by itself; it requires that a request is sent to the Power Manager, which makes a decision whether a power state can be changed. Power Manager may decline the request of a driver or an application, or it may change a power state to a different level than what was requested. For example, a device that is in the On mode (0) is requesting to switch to a sleep mode (3), but the Power Manager, which has complete information about system processes, may decide to switch the device only to the Low On mode (1). On the other hand, a driver may not decline a request from the Power Manager regarding a power change of a peripheral device, and must process this request.

Drivers and applications use the following API, as shown in Table 8–3, to request changes to a power state.

TABLE 8-3 API for requesting changes to a power state.

Function	Purpose
DevicePowerNotify	Sends a request to the Power Manager about changing a power state of a peripheral device.

Drivers and applications can register in order to receive notifications when power changes occur by using the following set of API, as shown in Table 8–4.

TABLE 8-4 API for registering for notifications.

Function	Purpose
RequestPowerNotifications	Registers a message queue to receive power change notifications.
StopPowerNotifications	Stops receiving power change notifications.

Such applications and drivers can request that the Power Manager keep specific peripheral devices in a certain power state by using the following set of API, as shown in Table 8–5.

TABLE 8-5 API for keeping peripheral devices in a specific power state.

Function	Purpose
SetPowerRequirement	Informs the Power Manager about power requirements of a given peripheral device.
ReleasePowerRequirement	Informs Power Manager that it can release previously set power requirements of a given peripheral device.

An application can also request that the Power Manager change the power state of the system as a whole by using the following API, as shown in Table 8–6.

TABLE 8–6 API for changing the power state for the system.

Function	Purpose
SetSystemPowerState	A request sent to the Power Manager about changing a power state of the system as a whole.

Similar to the situation with a request for a power change of a peripheral device, the Power Manager may decline an application's request for a power change of the system.

Device File System

Compared to the desktop Windows operating systems, the Windows Embedded CE file system is implemented with one root catalog "\" for all mounted file systems. File systems are mounted as subdirectories of the root catalog; one file system can be mounted as a root file system. A directory name is determined by the settings of a value with the name Folder, which is located in the key that contains the Storage Manager's profile settings: HKEY_LOCAL_MACHINE\System\StorageManager\Profiles\<*Media_Profile_Name*>.

Figure 8–18 shows storage manager profiles settings from the Common.reg file that is open in the registry's graphical editor of Visual Studio.

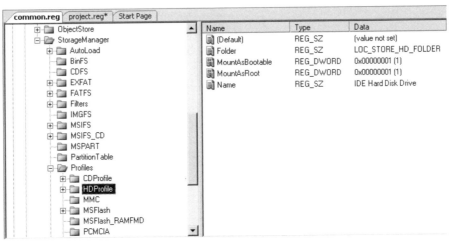

FIGURE 8–18 Storage Manager profiles settings from the Common.reg file

Sub keys of the HKEY_LOCAL_MACHINE\System\StorageManager\Profiles\ key represent various profiles. For the HDProfile representing an IDE hard drive, the folder name is determined by the LOC_STORE_HD_FOLDER macro, which is replaced by a value during the process of localization, such as *Hard Disk*.

The file system types that Windows Embedded CE 6.0 supports are listed in Table 8–7.

TABLE 8–7 Supported file system types.

File System	Brief Description
FAT or FATFS	A standard FAT file system. The maximum file size is 4 GB; it also has a partition size limit. It is simple to implement and is sufficiently reliable. It is supported by many operating systems.
exFAT	A new file system that removes the limitations of the FAT file system. It enables you to create files greater than 4 GB in size as well as large size partitions. It can be extended by the device manufacturer. Supported by Microsoft Windows Vista with Service Pack 1.
TFAT	An exFAT–based file system that supports transactions. It contains two copies of FAT tables: it requires support from a media block driver.
BinFS	File systems that provide the capability for mounting a *.bin file (which is a result of romimage.exe execution) as a file system. It enables you to divide the system image into parts: the part that contains the system kernel and everything else required to get the media driver up and BinFS where the rest of the system image resides as part of the .bin file.
CDFS/UDFS	File systems that provide the capability for working with CD and DVD media devices.
RAM (object store)	A new driver of the object store file system that implements a fully functional file system with directories, files, etc. It removes the restriction that requires that the file system be mounted in the memory as the root system which was mandatory in prior versions of the operating system[1]. Now, just like all other file systems, this file system is managed by FSD Manager[2].
RELFSD	During the development, the file system mounts a release directory of the operating system on the developer's workstation into the \Release directory of the device.

File systems can be loaded by using two methods:

- Automatically by the Storage Manager at system startup.

- By responding to a request while mounting a Storage Manager.

---

[1] It is sufficient to set the PRJ_ENABLE_FSMOUNTASROOT environment variable in order for the file system to be mounted into RAM as \Object Store, instead of the root. It is also necessary to set one of the two variables (PRJ_BOOTDEVICE_ATAPI or PRJ_BOOTDEVICE_MSFLASH) depending on whether the file system of what type of media (disk or flash) is going to be mounted as a root system instead of a RAM file system.

[2] Particularly, this provides the capability to implement the file system's RAM encryption by using the file system's filter.

The settings for automatically loaded file systems are stored as sub keys of the HKEY_LOCAL_
MACHINE\System\StorageManager\AutoLoad key, as shown in Figure 8–19.

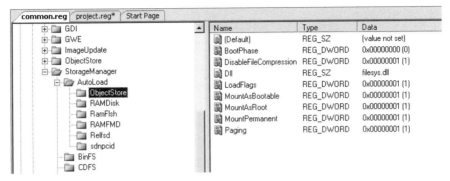

FIGURE 8–19 Sub keys for configuring automatically loaded file systems

The type of a file system that is mounted by request is determined by Partition Manager
according to the type of the mounted partition. The settings for mapping the partition
identifier to the file system are located in the registry key HKEY_LOCAL_MACHINE\System\
StorageManager\PartitionTable, as shown in Figure 8–20.

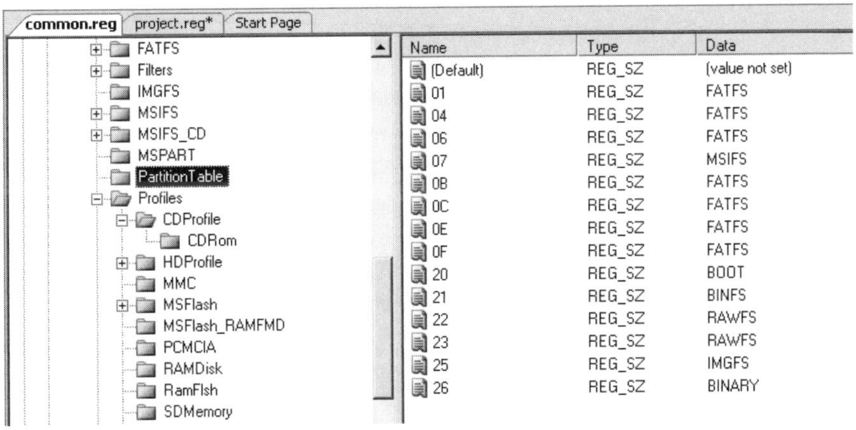

FIGURE 8–20 Settings for mapping the partition identifier to the file system

The default file system settings are located in the registry keys that use the following naming
convention: HKEY_LOCAL_MACHINE\System\StorageManager\<*File_System_Name*>.

These settings can be redefined or added to for a specific media profile in the registry keys that have the following naming convention: HKEY_LOCAL_MACHINE\System\
StorageManager\Profiles\<*Media_Profile_Name*>\<*File_System_Name*>.

Windows Embedded CE 6.0 file systems support filters that are implemented as special libraries that provide a predefined set of functions. A filter can be registered on the file system
level; that way, it will be loaded for any media on which the specified file system will be

mounted. If the filter is registered on the media profile and file system level, the filter will be raised only when the file system is loaded for the media specified in the profile. The filter's operations are transparent to the rest of the system and applications.

Figure 8–21 provides an example of file system filter settings from the Common.reg file that is open in the registry's graphic editor of Visual Studio.

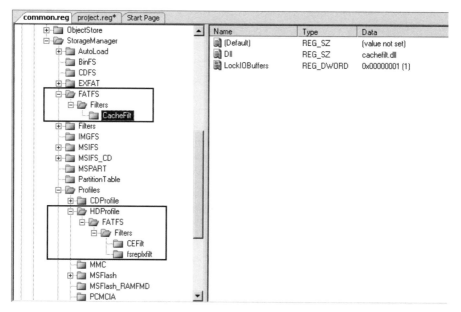

FIGURE 8–21 File system filter settings from the Common.reg file

The upper rectangle shows registration of a filter for the file system (the registration settings are shown on the right-hand side). This filter will be loaded for all media that FATFS file system (classic FAT) will be mounted for. The lower rectangle shows registration of two filters: one for HDProfile and another for the FATFS file system; these filters will be loaded only when the hard disk with a FAT file system will be mounted.

Windows Embedded CE includes several additional services for the file subsystem:

- Caching.
- Encryption.
- Replication.

Windows Embedded CE operating system includes two types of caching services for the file system:

- File caching.
- Disk caching.

File caching is implemented as a file system filter (file system caching manager). It can work with any file system, it does not require changes to the file system implementation, and it caches file data.

Disk caching is implemented as an auxiliary library. To use this service, the file system driver must use this library in its implementation. Disk caching is usually used for caching file system metadata. FATFS, TFAT and exFAT files systems can be configured to use disk caching.

Figure 8–22 provides an example of caching settings for FATFS file system from the Common. reg file that is open in the registry's graphic editor of Visual Studio.

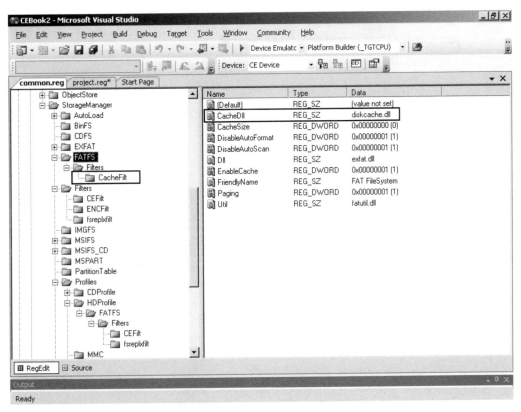

FIGURE 8–22 Caching settings for FATFS file system

The upper rectangle shows the CacheDLL settings of disk caching for the FATFS file system – diskcache.dll. This library is available in Shared Sources and is located in the \PRIVATE\ WINCEOS\COREOS\STORAGE\DISKCACHE\ directory. The lower rectangle shows the registry key that contains the settings for file caching for the FATFS file system implemented as a file system filter cachefilt.dll (see previous figure). This library is available in Shared Sources and is located in the \PRIVATE\WINCEOS\COREOS\FSD\CACHEFILT\ directory.

Windows Embedded CE includes a mechanism for encrypting file system data. This mechanism is implemented as a file system filter named encfilt.dll. This filter is registered to the file system and a media profile the same way as any other file system filter that is shipped as a source code. Its implementation is located in the \PUBLIC\COMMON\OAK\DRIVERS\FSD\ ENCFILT\ directory.

When building a device, the developer must choose one of two options of the internal file system (also see Figure 8–23):

- ROM-only file system.

- RAM and ROM file system.

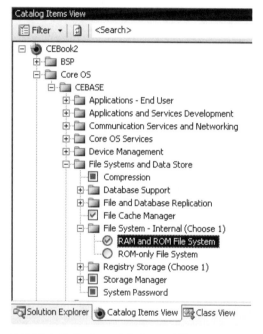

FIGURE 8–23 Options of the internal file system

When choosing the ROM and RAM File System option, the content of ROM is mapped to the \Windows directory, the file system (object store) is initialized in the memory in accordance with the .dat file settings (see Chapter 4, "Build System"). and it is mounted as a root file system.

When choosing the ROM–only File System option, the content of ROM is mapped to the \Windows directory and the file system is not created in the memory, but it still provides the capability to mount the external file system a root file system.

A typical task while building a device is to ensure that the system state is saved between cold boots. It means that you have to save registry files and registry settings that are created and/or modified while working with a device. A solution to this task is to mount an energy-independent storage as a file system root and to use registry hive. In order to mount storage as a root storage containing the registry, it is necessary to configure appropriate registry settings by creating the values MountAsBootable and MountAsRoot of the DWORD type with a value equal to 1 in the registry keys with of the following type: HKEY_LOCAL_MACHINE\System\StorageManager\Profiles\<*Media_Profile_Name*> or HKEY_LOCAL_MACHINE\System\StorageManager\Profiles\<*Media_Profile_Name*>\<*File_System_Name*>. The HKEY_LOCAL_MACHINE\System\StorageManager\Profiles\<*Media_Profile_Name*> key determines the settings for any file systems that will be mounted on the volumes of a specified media profile. The HKEY_LOCAL_MACHINE\System\StorageManager\Profiles\<*Media_Profile_Name*>\<*File_System_Name*> key determines the settings for a specific file system that will be mounted on the volumes of a specified media profile. This key's settings predetermine the value specified in the HKEY_LOCAL_MACHINE\System\StorageManager\Profiles\< *Media_Profile_Name*> key.

The settings required for implementing a hive-based registry is discussed in more detail in the next chapter.

Device Registry

Similar to the desktop version of Windows, Windows Embedded CE saves the settings of the operating system, applications, and drivers in the system registry. The Windows CE registry is organized similar to the desktop operating system registry, and it has the following four root entries:

HKEY_CLASSES_ROOT.

HKEY_LOCAL_MACHINE.

HKEY_CURRENT_USER.

HKEY_USER.

The HKEY_CLASSES_ROOT hive contains the settings related to the processing of file extensions and the COM subsystem. The HKEY_LOCAL_MACHINE hive contains the system settings as well as the settings for the drivers and applications of the system as a whole. The HKEY_CURRENT_USER hive contains the current user settings, which is actually a reference to a corresponding sub key of the HKEY_USER hive. The HKEY_USER contains sub keys that represent settings for all users, including a default user.

In order to work with the registry, you can use an API set similar to the one available with the desktop version. The API functions are listed in Table 8–8.

TABLE 8–8 API functions for working with the registry.

Function	Purpose
ReadGenericData	Reads the system password from the registry.
RegCloseKey	Closes a handle of the registry key.
RegCopyFile	Saves a copy of the current registry in the memory to a specified file.
RegCreateKeyEx	Creates a specified registry key.
RegDeleteKey	Deletes a specified registry key and all of its sub keys.
RegDeleteValue	Deletes a specified value from a given key.
RegEnumKeyEx	Enumerates sub keys of a given registry key. Returns one key for each call. When there are no more keys, it returns ERROR_NO_MORE_ITEMS.
RegEnumValue	Enumerates values of a specified registry key. Returns one key for each call. When there are no more keys, it returns ERROR_NO_MORE_ITEMS.
RegFlushKey	Flushes all changes to a specified key, its sub keys, and values into the registry.
RegOpenKeyEx	Opens a given registry key.
RegQueryInfoKey	Requests information about a specified registry key.
RegQueryValueEx	Requests type and value of a specified registry key.
RegSetValueEx	Sets a given value for a specified registry key.
WriteGenericData	Writes the system password from the registry.

Windows Embedded CE supports two registry types:

- Hive-based.

- RAM-based.

By default, Windows Embedded CE 6.0 uses a hive–based registry. A hive–based registry saves registry data as files (hives) that can be located in any supported file system.

A hived–based registry has the following characteristics:

- It supports a multi-user configuration.

- It provides the capability to save the registry settings between the device cold boots.

- It is divided into three parts.

  - System hive (System.hv, Default.hv).

  - User hive (User.hv).

  - Boot hive (Boot.hv).

The name and location of the system hive is determined by the SystemHive registry value of the HKEY_LOCAL_MACHINE\init\BootVars key. A catalog for defining user directories with user hives is specified in the ProfileDir registry value of the HKEY_LOCAL_MACHINE\init\ BootVars registry key.

Boot.hv is the boot hive that is stored in the ROM. Default.hv is the system hive that is kept in the ROM. The system hive stored on the media saves only the changes related to the registry hive stored in the ROM. The user hive has a similar functionality.

During the first boot, registry hive files are automatically created in the media device. The media–based registry hive files are bound to the registry from the image. When the image is changed, during the first boot, the media–based registry hive files will be created anew and the prior files will be removed.

Figure 8–24 shows the settings for the hive–based registry's location as they appear in the Common.reg file that is open in the Visual Studio graphical registry editor.

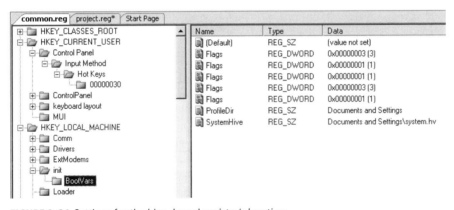

FIGURE 8–24 Settings for the hive–based registry's location

In order to configure a hive–based registry, it is necessary to perform the following actions:

1. Select a catalog item that includes support for a hive–based registry.

2. Select catalog items that include support for the media device and the file system where the registry files are going to be saved (Storage Manager, FAT File System, Device Manager, etc.).

3. Make sure that settings for all drivers that are required for starting the media device with a file system in the registry settings files are enclosed by special markers:

   HIVE BOOT SECTION *<settings for required drivers>*;END HIVE BOOT SECTION.

4. Set the load flag for the first stage of the device launch (0x1000) for all the drivers that are needed to start a media device with a file system on it.

6. Configure the desired settings for the location of the system hive and user hive:
[HKEY_LOCAL_MACHINE\init\BootVars]

"SystemHive" = "*<full_path_to_the_system_hive_file>*"

"ProfileDir" = "*<path_to_the catalog_for_user_directories>*"

7. The paths do not include the name of the directory under which the media device is mounted. Those paths are specified relative to the directory of the mounted media, such as "MyRegistry\system.hv" and "UserProfiles".

8. Configure the load stage of the Storage Manager and the Device Manager by using the following key and the flags shown in Table 8–9:

[HKEY_LOCAL_MACHINE\init\BootVars]

"Flags" = dword:*<flag_value>*.

9. The flags are combined with a logical OR operator. Usually, the '3' value is used by the hive–based registry, which means that the registry will be saved to the mounted media that requires a block driver.

TABLE 8-9 Load stage flags.

Flag Value	Description
0x0001	Storage manager is launched during the first stage of the system start for the hive–based registry.
0x0002	Device Manager is launched during the first stage of the system start for the hive–based registry.
0x0004	Storage manager is launched during the first stage of the system start for the registry in ROM, such as when it is stored in BinFS on an external media device.
0x0008	Device Manager is launched during the first stage of the system start for the registry in ROM, such as when it is stored in BinFS on an external media device.

10. Set the load flag for the corresponding media profile for the selected file system:
[HKEY_LOCAL_MACHINE\System\StorageManager\Profiles*<Media_Profile_Name>*\ *<File_System_Name>*]

"MountAsBoot"=dword:1

The registry settings that have to do with the location of hive registry files and the stages of loading the storage manager and driver manager are usually stored in the Project.reg file. The presence of HIVE BOOT SECTION markers needs to be verified in the Platform.reg and, possibly, Common.reg files.

By default, changes in the registry are written to the media while the device goes to suspend state. If needed, you can call the RegFlushKey function directly in order for the changes to be saved to a registry hive file on the media. You can also set an additional environment build variable PRJ_ENABLE_REGFLUSH_THREAD, which will add a thread to the system—a thread that will periodically flush the registry changes to the media.

Usually, in order to mount a media device, it is necessary to have an appropriate block driver (Promise Controller ATAPI driver, Serial ATA, Intel StrataFlash NOR Driver, etc.) present in the image; the Device Manager is necessary in order to load this driver; the storage manager, the partition driver, and the file system driver are necessary in order to mount the volume and its file system above the block media.

Also, the operating system provides the capability to keep a hive–based registry in the memory. This mechanism is designed for use with energy-independent memory, such as SRAM or similar kinds; however, it can be used with a memory region allocated in the Config.bib file.

A RAM–based registry keeps the registry data in an object store. Therefore, during a cold boot the data is lost. If, in the case of a RAM–based registry, there is a requirement that the registry data is kept during a cold boot, it is necessary to either ensure that RAM has an independent power source, or make sure to save the registry data to an energy-independent media when the device goes off and then restore it after a cold boot. Windows Embedded CE provides a necessary infrastructure for that process.

Device Databases

Often times, a built-in application needs to have a capability to store structured data. In order to do that, it is necessary to have a fast and compact database that is well integrated with the operating system. Windows Embedded CE includes two types of databases:

- CEDB.
- EDB.

CEDB consists of records that have several properties. The properties are determined on the database level. Records are stored in the database; the database, in turn, is stored in a volume that can contain several databases.

CEDB has the following characteristics:

- It is a single-user database.
- Every single operation is atomic.
- Maximum database volume size of 16 MB.
- Maximum record size of 128 KB.
- Does not support named properties.
- No restrictions on the number of properties per database.

■ Does not support password-protection.

EDB database is a new database format for Windows Embedded CE. Just like CEDB database, it has the *<property>-<field>-<database>-<volume>* architecture.

The database is implemented based on a minimal version of the SQL Server Compact engine and provides the following capabilities:

■ Support for multiple users.

■ Support for transactions.

■ Maximum database volume size of 64 MB.

■ Improved productivity.

■ A maximum record size of 8 KB, not counting the thread data.

■ Supports named properties.

■ A maximum number of properties in a database is 1024.

■ Supports password protection.

Support for CEDB is retained for compatibility with prior versions of the operating system. It is recommended that EDB is used with the new projects or, if it doesn't provide enough capabilities, an appropriate version of SQL Server Compact.

The API set for CEDB and EDB does not contain any similarities in the desktop version. You can receive more information in the product documentation[3].

Device Plug and Play Messaging System

Windows Embedded CE has a subsystem that is similar to the PnP messaging system of a desktop operating system. When the drivers are loaded, it can provide the system with the information about the classes supported by the device by using either a registry setting (IClass) or by calling the AdvertiseInterface() function directly. A device class is basically a predefined set of functionality implemented by the device.

For instance, DEVCLASS_STREAM_GUID is a regular stream interface driver and DEVCLASS_CAMERA_GUID is a camera driver.

A messaging subsystem is implemented as part of the Device Manager subsystem. Their interaction is shown in Figure 8–25.

---

[3] Windows Embedded CE Features/File Systems and Storage Management/Databases and Windows Embedded CE Features/File Systems and Storage Management/File Systems and Storage Management Reference/Database Reference

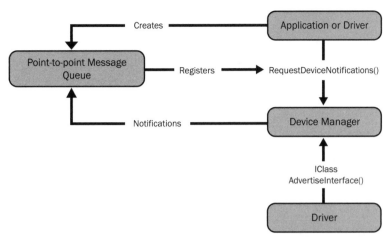

FIGURE 8–25 Plug and Play messaging system

Any driver or an application can be registered to receive a notification about a device that implements a certain class being connected or disconnected. It enables you, among other things, to implement a system that supports an auto-start of applications from external media when they are mounted.

An API set used for working with the notification subsystem is shown in Table 8–10.

TABLE 8–10 API for working with the Plug and Play notification system.

Function	Purpose
RequestDeviceNotifications	Requests a receipt of notifications from the Device Manager related to connecting and disconnecting devices that implement functionality of a certain device class (IClass, AdvertiseInterface).
StopDeviceNotifications	Stops the previously requested Device Manager notifications about devices being connected or disconnected.

Using this system enables you to create drivers and applications that start automatically or that launch a certain procedure when a predefined device type appears in the system. For instance, it applies to automatic scanning of all external mounted file systems by anti-virus software when they are connected or starting a navigation program when connecting a GPS device.

Device System Shell

A typical task that needs to be performed while building a device is to set up one's own application as a system shell. For Windows Embedded CE, replacing the shell only means specifying one's own program in the auto-start registry key HKEY_LOCAL_MACHINE\Init and, if needed, masking or removing the shell auto-start registry key from the files provided in the development tools.

Please note that the standard shell (explorer.exe) provides the system with an additional API (Shell API); if the program uses it, then it can operate only above the standard shell. In that case, a program label (see the section below titled, "Creating File Shortcuts in the Device") can be placed into a standard shell auto-start folder (\Windows\StartUp), and the custom shell's position can be set on top of all windows, which previously hid the task panel.

Keep in mind that the standard shell auto-start folder is not automatically created when the image with an added standard shell is built.

Adding Files to the Device Image

Integration of third-party software, including drivers, is one of the most typical tasks while building a device. In spite of its perceived complexity, this task is relatively straightforward to perform.

In order to include a file into the system image, it is necessary that, prior to the Makeimg stage, the image build in the release directory has a binary image builder (.bib) file, which contains entries that appropriately include the required files in the image.

It can be the Project.bib file or a separate newly-created file. Copying the Project.bib into a release directory will occur automatically. When a separate (one's own) file is used, it is necessary to ensure that it is copied into the release directory before the Makeimg stage. It can be done by using Custom Build Action from the OS design settings. This task can also be performed by first launching the image build without the Makeimg stage, manually copying the required files—including the configuration files—into the release directory as the next step, and then launching the Makeimg stage.

The format of the required entries in the .bib file is shown below:

```
<NameOfFileInTheImage> <FilePathOnDisk>\<FileNameOnDisk> <ROMregion> <FileProperties>
```

Note that these entries should be placed in the appropriate section of .bib file (FILES or MODULES). For example:

```
FILES
File.txt c:\MyFiles\File.txt NK SH
```

This example is not useful because it requires configuration data being passed to someone else, which requires the creation of an additional folder tree for saving the files included in the image.

It would be more useful to find a way to copy all necessary files into the release directory before the MAKEIMG stage of the image build; in which case the .bib file entry in our example will look as follows:

```
FILES
File.txt $(_FLATRELEASEDIR)\File.txt NK SH
```

The most convenient method of copying that enables you to keep the files in the same location and to conveniently share them and their configuration is to create a component or a project that contains all the necessary files including the configuration files. In this case, the copying of files can be done by using standard and accessible mechanisms for copying additional files into the release directory (POSTLINK_PASS_CMD)[4].

Creating File Shortcuts in the Device

When a RAM–based file system is used, the initialized DAT files determine the hierarchy of directories and files. Copying is done when the hierarchy is initialized. Therefore, the same files are located in the \Windows directory where ROM is mapped to and in the memory where they are copied when a file system is initialized in the memory.

The use of file shortcuts instead of copying the actual files enables you to save the memory space when the memory based file system is used. When the end device is created, you can add the necessary shortcuts to the desktop and to the menu ahead of time to make them more accessible for the end user.

For example, in order to automatically launch a program when a standard shell is used, you can place its label into the auto-start folder \Windows\StartUp\.

A label in Windows Embedded CE is represented by an .lnk file of a predefined format.

<NumberOfASCIISymbolsOfACommandAfterAPoundSymbol>#<CommandExecutedWhenYouClickTheLabel>

For example:

```
17#\Windows\calc.exe
33#\Windows\QuartaProg.exe Top Shell
```

Adding the label file into the image is done the same way as for all other files.

---

4   Mike Hall (Microsoft) wrote a useful utility named CEFileWiz that creates all the necessary configuration files for including files into the image. The author provides regular updates to this utility. To download it, visit his blog at: http://blogs.msdn.com/mikehall/ (listed under Interesting Tools in the left-hand side of the page).

Chapter 9
Application Development

This chapter covers the differences between native and managed code, choosing when to create an operating system (OS) design subproject or a separately developed project, how to prepare for application development, making device connections, and application debugging approaches. For detailed information about native code application development for Windows Embedded CE, see Douglas Boling's book, "Programming Windows Embedded CE 6.0 Developer Reference, 4th Edition," and for more information about managed code application development, see the book of Andy Wigley, Daniel Moth, and Peter Foot, "Microsoft Mobile Development Handbook." Alternatively, you can use the MSDN Web site to find documentation, code samples, articles, virtual labs, and Web casts.

You can build applications for Windows Embedded CE by using native code or managed code. Native code applications can be built as subprojects of the OS design, or as individual projects. When building projects by using native code separately from the OS design, the first step is to build an OS design, and later build applications for it. After that, an SDK should be created and installed with the development tools. Managed code applications can be built only as separate applications. However, as opposed to native code applications, managed code applications actually do not require an SDK to be installed with the development tools, and instead require the execution environment of the device.

Native Code and Managed Code

Native (unmanaged) code is code written in C/C++ or ASM and compiled on a development workstation to produce binary code that is native to the device processor. Applications built in native code do not require additional subsystems as part of the device in order to run. However, applications must be built for each supported processor type.

Managed code is code written in C#/VB.NET by using the .NET Compact Framework and compiled on a development workstation to platform-independent Intermediate Language (IL). The .NET Compact Framework Base Class Libraries (BCL) provide an application programming interface (API) for managed applications. The run-time Execution Engine (EE) together with the BCL are called the Common Language Runtime (CLR) and provide execution support for managed applications on a device. Managed code is compiled to binary code that is native to the device processor by CLR on a first call. This process is called Just-In-Time (JIT) compilation. Applications built in managed code require the CLR subsystem as part of the device in order to run. An application can be built once and work for all supported processor types.

Figure 9-1 illustrates native and managed code application architectures on a device.

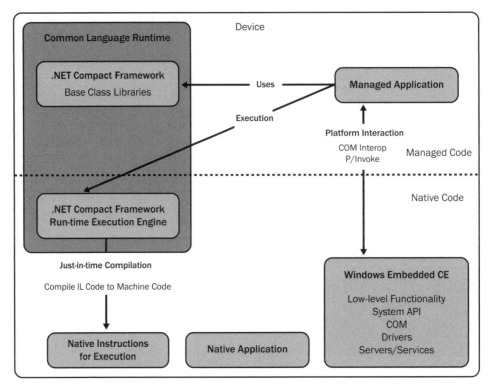

FIGURE 9–1 Native and managed application code architectures on a device

Native code applications have the fullest possible access to the system, but writing native code applications is a more complicated task than writing managed code applications, especially if an application interacts with Web Services, Windows Communication Foundation, and so on. Not all system features that are directly accessible from native code applications are accessible from managed code applications, but this situation has been improving in the .NET Compact Framework with each release. Also, the .NET Compact Framework[1] provides Platform Invoke (P/Invoke) service and COM interoperability (COM Interop). P/Invoke is used to call native code dynamic link libraries (DLLs), and COM Interop is used to interact with COM objects.

Table 9–1 summarizes native and a managed code from a developer's perspective.

---

1   .NET Compact Framework 2.0 and later.

TABLE 9–1 Native and managed code comparison.

Native Code	Managed Code
Compiled to machine code.	Compiled to Intermediate Language code.
At least recompilation is required to support different CPU architectures.	No recompilation required for different supported CPU architectures.
No need for additional infrastructure to run on device.	Needs Common Language Runtime on a device to run.
Maximum possible access to system API and services.	Access to services and API supported by the .NET Compact Framework. P/Invoke to access a platform API and COM Interop to interact with COM objects. Access to system API and services requires additional work or may be impossible.
Full supports of COM and ActiveX development.	Managed components can be exposed as COM components with some limitations.
Can use Microsoft Foundation Classes, Active Template Library, Windows Template Library, and Standard Template Library.	Uses Base Class Libraries. Some third-party libraries are available.
Can develop by using the following tools: Visual Studio 2005 Service Pack 1, Visual Studio 2008.	Can develop by using the following tools: Visual Studio 2005 Service Pack 1 with appropriate .NET Compact Framework update (see Chapter 2) for .NET Compact Framework 2.0, and Visual Studio 2008 for .NET Compact Framework 2.0 and 3.5

A developer should consider using native or development code depending on the required development tasks and keeping in mind the considerations mentioned above.. Note that some system code can't be managed, including OAL, drivers and services.

OS Design Subprojects and Separate Projects

The easiest way to develop a device application is to build it as a subproject along with the OS design. The only suitable toolset for this purpose is Visual Studio 2005 with the Service Pack 1 with Platform Builder for CE 6.0 add-on installed.

When debugging an OS design subproject, you can debug at the system level if you have the Kernel Debugger included in the OS design. An OS design subproject can be automatically included in the produced run-time image. These OS design subprojects are useful for building system services, drivers, or for any kind of system-level development. Note that an OS design subproject can be only native; all managed code development should be done as separate projects.

A separate project can be used for all non-system development, especially when a developer needs to use auxiliary libraries such as Microsoft Foundation Classes, Active Template Library, Windows Template Library, Standard Template Library, and others. It is useful to use separate projects to develop COM, ActiveX, business applications, network applications, and so on.

To build an application using native code separately from the OS design, it is necessary to create an SDK. Then, Visual Studio 2005 with Service Pack 1 and Visual Studio 2008 can be used to develop applications.

Table 9–2 compares OS design projects and separate projects from a developer's perspective.

TABLE 9–2 Comparison of OS design subprojects and separate projects.

OS Design Subproject	Separate projects
Only native code development.	Native and managed code development.
Can debug down to the system level.	Cannot debug the OS.
Even using standard Microsoft auxiliary libraries may require additional work.	Seamless support for auxiliary libraries such as Microsoft Foundation Classes, Active Template Library, Windows Template Library, and Standard Template Library. Note that auxiliary libraries should be included manually into an OS run-time image if necessary.
Seamless drivers and services development.	Practically impossible to develop drivers.
Can automatically be included in an OS run-time image.	Should be included into an OS run-time image manually.
Can develop by using the following tools: Visual Studio 2005 Service Pack 1 with Platform Builder for Windows Embedded CE 6.0 Service Pack 1.	Can develop by using the following tools: Visual Studio 2005 Service Pack 1 and Visual Studio 2008.

A developer should consider creating OS design subprojects or separate projects keeping in mind the differences discussed above. Some application types cannot be developed separately, such as drivers and other hardware-assisted services. These application types are always OS design subprojects. On the other hand, managed applications cannot be OS design subprojects.

Building Applications as OS Design Subprojects

To add a subproject to an existing OS design, complete the following steps.

1. From the main menu in Visual Studio, select Project, and then Add New Subproject. Alternatively, in the menu of the Subprojects node in Solution Explorer, select Add New Subproject.

2. An Add New Subproject Wizard dialog box appears, as shown in Figure 9–2.

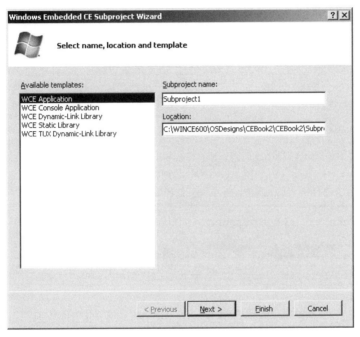

FIGURE 9–2 Add New Subproject Wizard dialog box—start screen

3. Select a subproject type, name, and location. Click Next.

4. A screen appears prompting you to select the desired application type. Select the application type to create and click Finish, as shown in Figure 9–3.

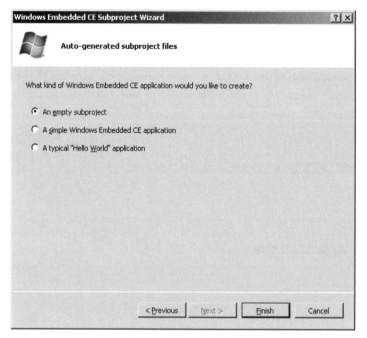

FIGURE 9–3 Add New Subproject Wizard—application type selection

5. This creates a new OS design subproject, as shown in Figure 9–4.

FIGURE 9–4 Operating system design subproject

You can debug a subproject by using standard Visual Studio and Platform Builder capabilities (see Chapter 2 for more details). For OS design subprojects, you can debug down to the system level if you include Kernel Debugger in the OS design, whereas it is impossible to debug at the system level for projects that are developed separately.

Building Applications as Separate Projects

Environment Preparation for Building Native Code Applications

To build a native code application as a separate project, a developer needs to create an SDK and install it in the appropriate development tools. In order to create an SDK, it is necessary to first build the OS image without support for kernel debugging and KITL. To create a new SDK, follow these steps:

1. From the main menu in Visual Studio, select Project, and then select Add New SDK. Or, in the menu of the SDK node in Solution Explorer, select Add New SDK.

2. An Add New SDK Wizard dialog box appears.

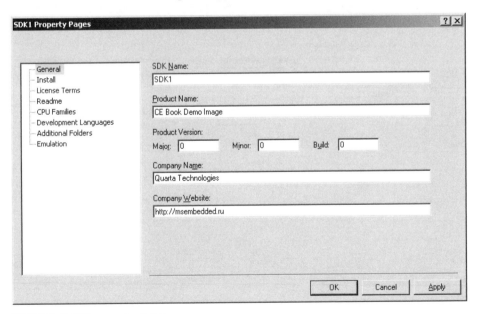

FIGURE 9–5 SDK property dialog

The left side of the dialog box shows SDK property groups, as shown in Figure 9-5. By selecting each group, one by one, you can configure the required settings. When you are done configuring the SDK settings, click Finish.

This creates a new OS design SDK with corresponding parameters, as shown in Figure 9–6.

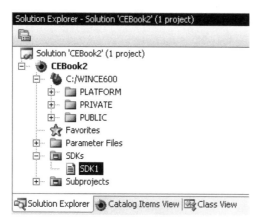

FIGURE 9–6 New SDK of an OS design

If the system image is built for the emulator, and if the emulator is going to be used for building applications, it is necessary to configure the settings for the Emulation group. These settings include RAM and screen resolution, as shown in Figure 9–7.

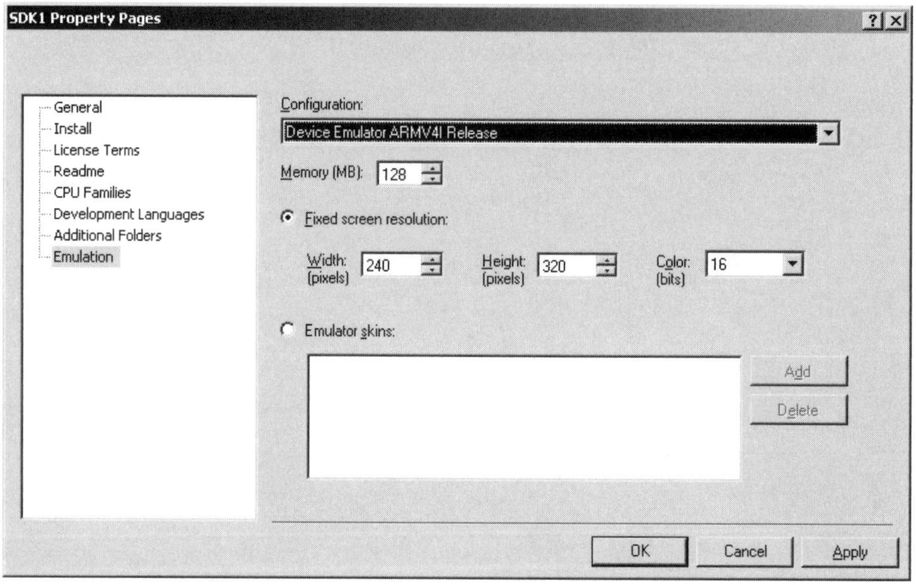

FIGURE 9–7 SDK parameters

Visual Studio 2005 with Service Pack 1 and Visual Studio 2008 ship with exactly the emulator version that includes a BSP with Platform Builder for CE 6.0 image development tools.

After an SDK has been created and configured, it needs to be built. To launch an SDK build process, select a required SDK in the SDK node of Solution Explorer, and in the context menu (right-click SDK) select Build. A build process will be launched. When it is finished, an installation file *<SDK_Name>*.msi will be created in a directory specified earlier in the SDK settings. This MSI installation file needs to be installed on the development computer that has Visual Studio 2005 with Service Pack 1 or Visual Studio 2008 installed, and on which you are planning to build applications for a designated device.

After an SDK has been installed, in the target devices of the development tools, there will be an option to select a device named *<SDK_Name>* as a target when building a new project in native code.

Note that the previous version of the operating system contained a Microsoft Foundation Classes (MFC) component to be included in the OS design. The new version does not include such a component, and therefore MFC support should be added manually by including distributable libraries shipped with Visual Studio 2005/2008.

Environment Preparation for Building Managed Code Applications

As opposed to native code applications, managed code applications do not require the SDK to be installed to develop an application for a device. Managed-code applications require an appropriate execution environment on the target device. For Windows Embedded CE 6.0 it could be .NET Compact Framework 2.0 or .NET Compact Framework 3.5.

To develop managed code applications, a developer can use Visual Studio 2005 with Service Pack 1 and Visual Studio 2008. Visual Studio 2005 with Service Pack 1 enables a developer to develop for .NET Compact Framework 2.0, and Visual Studio 2008—for .NET Compact Framework 2.0 and .NET Compact Framework 3.5.

Although there is no need to create an SDK in order to develop and debug applications that use managed code, when a device emulator is used, it is more practical to create and install an SDK that supports development using managed code. In this case, the emulator launches automatically when a developer starts debugging or deploying from Visual Studio. It is not necessary to configure additional settings in order to connect to it and perform debugging; all that is needed for deployment and debugging is to select a device named *<SDK_Name>* Emulator.

When a new application project is created using managed code, in Visual Studio 2005 you need to select Windows CE 5.0, and in Visual Studio 2008 you need to select Windows CE.

Connecting to the Device to Deploy and Debug Applications

Before a developer can start deploying and debugging applications on a device, a connection between development tools (Visual Studio) and a device should be established.

When using an emulator as a target device and installing the appropriate SDK, there is no need to configure additional connectivity settings for debugging. As mentioned above, the emulator launches automatically when a developer starts debugging or deploying from Visual Studio.

In the case of an actual physical device, additional steps may be required to connect to a device. There are two possible scenarios that may require additional steps: either the device includes ActiveSync support, or it does not. By using ActiveSync, you can establish a connection to the target device through a cradle, USB, Bluetooth, or infrared. ActiveSync performs most of the work automatically. A developer only needs to provide additional settings depending on the connection type. You should have ActiveSync installed on a development workstation to establish a connection to a device with ActiveSync support.

Determining the Device IP Address

If a device does not have ActiveSync, a developer can debug applications over a TCP/IP connection to the target device. To connect to a device by using a TCP/IP connection, perform the following steps.

1. Copy files from Program Files\Common Files\Microsoft Shared\CoreCon\1.0\Target\ wce400\<*Processor_Type*> directory to the \Windows directory of the device, using any available means. The simplest way to have the files on a device is to include those files in the device's run-time image (see Chapter 4 for more details). Copy the following files: ConmanClient2.exe, CMaccept.exe, DbgTL.dll, and TcpConnectionA.dll.

   a. Launch ConmanClient2.exe on the device.

   b. Launch CMaccept.exe on the device.

   c. The device will be available to connect to for three minutes.

2. Determine the device IP address through any available means. Open the Device Properties dialog box and specify the IP address in the TCP Connect Transport settings.

   a. On the Visual Studio Tools menu, click Options, then click Device Tools, and then click Devices.

   b. Select Windows CE Device, and then click Properties.

   c. To the right of the Transport box, click Configure.

   d. In the Configure TCP/IP Transport dialog box, select Use specific IP address, and then type the device IP address.

   e. Close the dialog boxes.

If a developer has a device with a user interface (UI) and standard shell, then the Control Panel can be used to set the appropriates static IP address on the device. If a device does not have a UI and standard shell, then a developer can include cmd.exe (Console Window catalog item) and ipconfig.exe (Network Utilities (IpConfig, Ping, Route) catalog item) into the device run-time image, and then use those utilities to obtain the device IP address by running **ipconfig** at the command prompt. Note that cmd.exe I/O may be redirected to a serial port, so even if a device does not have a UI, the IP address can be received. If none of the described methods are applicable, then a developer can write an application as an OS design subproject that returns the IP address of the device to the developer.

Debugging applications for Windows Embedded CE is practically the same as for desktop applications. The only difference is that a developer should establish a connection to a device before starting debugging. For more information about available debugging options, see Chapter 2.

Chapter 10
Testing Operating System Images

Testing operating system (OS) images is an integral part of building devices. A careful and regular testing of a device during the development stage reduces the overall costs of maintaining a device during its lifecycle and makes it possible to identify potential problems and resolve them early.

Microsoft provides a wide selection of extensible testing tools included in Windows Embedded CE Test Kit (CETK).

Windows Embedded CE Test Kit

The CETK includes a collection of tests for a standard set of drivers and OAL, with the possibility to expand it by using special libraries. Additionally, the CETK includes utilities that enable you to trap errors in the application code, capture screens of a launched device, perform stress-testing, and so on.

There are two scenarios for launching a test.

- By using the client-server architecture.
- Locally on the device.

A client-server testing scheme provides a convenient interface for selecting, configuring and launching tests, as well as for viewing test results. This architecture provides additional advantages when it is necessary to test several devices. Local testing on the device is used when a server is not available, when a connection to the server cannot be established, or when overhead connection costs may significantly distort test results. In order to launch a test process on a device, it is necessary to have all modules required for testing available.

The first method of testing requires the presence of the server side and the client side components. The server-side process is launched on the workstation and is responsible for managing test launches and logging their results. The client side process is launched on the target device. It performs all necessary tests and sends the test results to the server side.

Figure 10–1 provides a general overview of CETK architecture.

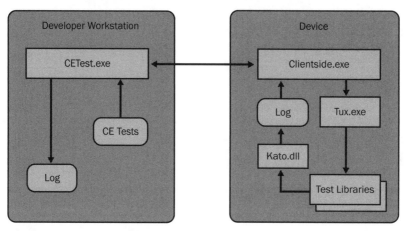

FIGURE 10–1 CETK architecture

A server-side program (CETest.exe) is launched on a workstation or another machine that has the CETK installed. It then connects to the client-side program (Clientside.exe), which was previously launched on the target device if using TCP/IP. The process of selecting and configuring tests is done by using the CETest.exe graphic interface. When a test is launched, all the necessary information is sent to the client. The client, on the other hand, launches the Tux utility by specifying appropriate parameters for running a test. Test results are logged to a file by using a mechanism implemented in Kato.dll.

Please note that to ensure that the client-server solution works, it is necessary to ensure that the Clientside.exe module has been moved to and executed on the target device. If either Kernel Independent Transport Layer (KITL) or ActiveSync are present in the image of the target system, with the appropriate server-side settings, this should happen automatically. Otherwise, the Clientside.exe module needs to be manually copied to the device and launched by specifying connection parameters to the server in the command line or the server-side connection configuration file.

When testing is launched directly on the device, the Clientside.exe module is not used. Testing is done by launching the Tux utility by specifying testing parameters in the command line. When testing is launched directly on the device, the Tux utility and the Tux libraries, which contain all the required tests, need to be copied to the device.

Testing the Image with Support for KITL Enabled

Let us review the process of testing the image with support for KITL in a client-server so-lution. In order to launch the server part, from the Start menu, select Programs, select Windows Embedded CE 6.0, and then select Windows Embedded CE 6.0 Test Kit. It is necessary to ensure that connection settings have been specified before testing can begin. You can configure connections settings in the Device Connection dialog window, as shown in Figure 10–2. This dialog window can be opened by selecting Connection, and then selecting Start Client in the main menu of the server-side window.

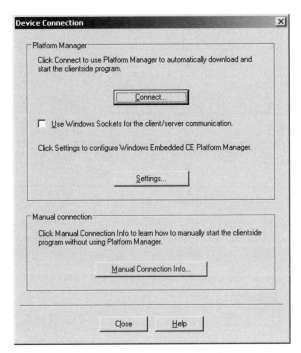

FIGURE 10–2 Device Connection dialog window

You can connect to the device by clicking the Connect button. The Connection Settings dialog box is accessible by clicking Settings. All settings are configured similar to remote utility settings. While the connection is established, the client program, Clientside.exe, is copied to the device and launches on it, as shown in Figure 10–3.

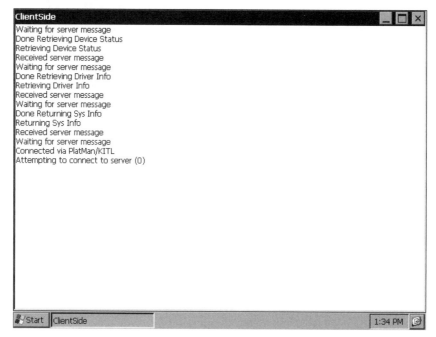

FIGURE 10–3 CETK client-side program

After a connection to the device has been established successfully and the image functionality has been determined in the Windows Embedded CE Test Kit window, a sub item appears in the Windows Embedded CE Test Kit Server folder. This sub-item corresponds to the connected device and has a list of available tests, as shown in Figure 10–4.

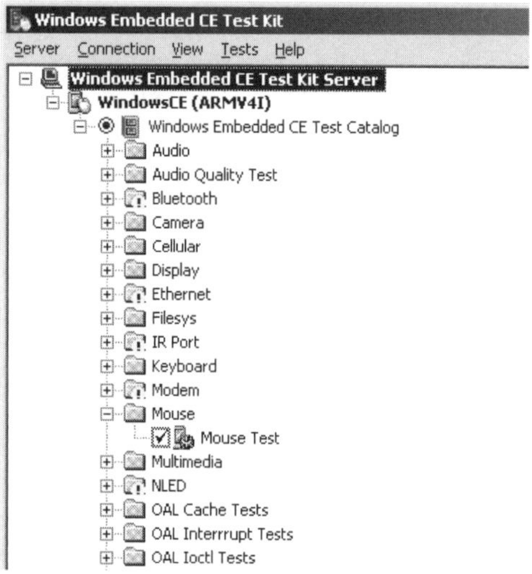

FIGURE 10–4 Available tests

Tests are grouped by a category folder, such as Audio, Display, Keyboard, and so on. The folders marked with an exclamation icon (!) denote that the image does not have this functionality available for testing, or was not automatically detected on the device. In order to select an individual test, open the folder group and check the tests that are required. To modify testing parameters, right-click the test item and in the drop-down menu select Edit. By using testing parameters, you can specify options such as the test length, content, and so on.

After the test content and parameters have been established, you can launch a test by selecting the Tests menu item, selecting Start/Stop tests, and then choosing the device on which the tests will be launched, as shown in Figure 10–5.

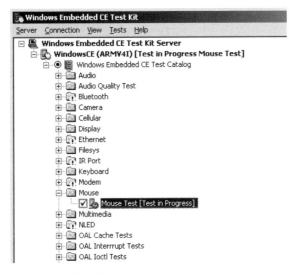

FIGURE 10–5 Specific test selection

The process of test execution is shown in the Windows Embedded CE Test Kit dialog box, located next to the device item and each of the selected tests. Some tests, such as the keyboard and mouse tests, require user interaction. You can stop a test by using the same menu item as the one used for launching a test: Start/Stop tests.

To view test results, from the main menu, select Tests, View results, and then select the target device. In order to view all test results, select View All Results. To view the results of a particular test, select the menu item with the appropriate name, as shown in Figure 10–6.

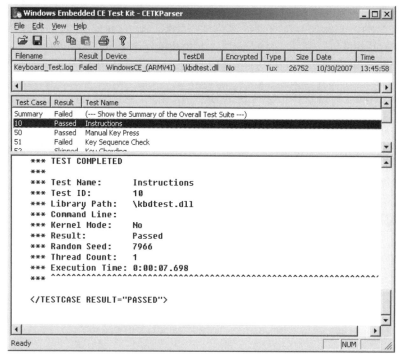

FIGURE 10–6 Viewing specific test cases

The Test Result window is divided into three panels. The upper panel contains a list of completed tests. For each individual test there is a corresponding log file. The files containing the results of testing are stored in the directory \Program Files\Microsoft Platform Builder\6.00\ CEPB\WCETK\results. The central panel shows the results of individual sub-tests that are included in the test item selected in the upper panel. Sub-tests may have following results:

- Passed.
- Failed.
- Skipped.
- Aborted.

The lower panel contains detailed information about each sub-test. This information can be used to diagnose errors during test execution.

The Tux utility is responsible for test execution on the device. This utility can be launched by the client module, Clientside.exe, or started manually for running tests without a server. The tests shown in the server-side window of CETK contain the command-line parameters for launching the Tux utility. The test configuration, logging parameters, and other necessary information are passed to the Tux utility as command-line parameters that are listed in Table 10–1.

TABLE 10-1 Tux utility parameters.

Parameter	Description
-b	Suspends execution after the Tux library is loaded. Used in debugging of test libraries for setting breakpoints.
-e	Disables exceptions processing.
-s *<file-name>*	Performs a number of tests whose configuration settings are stored in the file that is being passed.
-d *<DLL library>*	Loads a specified Tux library to perform testing. This parameter can be reused for loading several libraries.
-c*<parameters>*	Passes specified parameters to a test Tux library. The parameters are passed to the last library that was specified earlier by using the −d parameter.
-r*<number>*	Sets the initial value for the random number generator. This parameter is passed to the last library that was specified earlier by using the −d parameter, which enables you to use different initial values of the random number generator for different libraries.
-x*<range>*	Specifies what tests need to be run. For instance, x10, 12, and 15-20. The parameter can be reused for different libraries. The parameter applies to the last library that was specified earlier.
-l	Outputs a list of all available tests for the libraries specified in the −d parameter.
-lv	This parameter is similar to −l, except that it outputs more detailed information.
-t *<address>*	Specifies the name or IP address of the computer on which the server-side CETK was launched. Using this switch with an empty IP address specifies the workstation as the server. If the parameter is not specified, then tests are performed locally without connecting to the server.
-n	Launches tests in the kernel mode by using KTux.dll.
-h	Outputs a list of parameters of the Tux.exe command line.
Parameters available while using Kato.dll logging.	
-k *<address>*	Specifies the name or the IP address of the computer that the test results will be sent to. The use of this key with an empty address denotes that the workstation is acting as a server. In addition, the log can be sent to the debugger (-o) or entered into a file (-f).
-m	Performs logging in Extensible Markup Language (XML) format.
-o	Outputs the results through the debugger.
-f *<filename>*	Saves results to a file. By default, the results file is overwritten.
-a	Adds results to an earlier created file specified in the <−f > parameter.
Parameters available while using Toolhelp.dll.	
-z *<delay>*	Stops execution of the Tux library after a specified number of seconds.

The CETK architecture provides developers with an opportunity to create their own tests. To create your own test libraries, you can use a template located in \Program Files\Microsoft Platform Builder\6.00\cepb\ wcetk\Tux\Tuxskel or, you can create a subproject of the OS design, such as WCE Tux dynamic-link library. Examples of Tux library implementations are located in the PRIVATE\TEST folder in the root of the build tree if you have installed the private sources during Platform Builder installation.

CETK Utilities

By default, the utilities and auxiliary modules launched on the workstation are located in the \Program Files\Microsoft Platform Builder\6.00\cepb\wcetk\ddtk\desktop\directory. The default location of the utilities and libraries launched on the device being tested is the \Program Files\Microsoft Platform Builder\6.00\ cepb\wcetk\ddtk\<*CPU_FAMILY*>\ folder.

Application Verifier

The Application Verifier utility is used for testing the stability of applications and for detecting typical development errors. It enables you to detect and identify memory leaks, unclosed descriptors, GDI object, as well as unclosed descriptors and GDI-objects, as well as to detect some versions of heap corruption. This utility enables you to receive information that may be difficult to obtain by using other methods. For instance, you may be able to examine a module during the load process when a standard debugger may not be usable.

The Application Verifier utility uses specialized Shim libraries to collect information. The principle of Application Verifier's operation via Shim libraries is shown in Figure 10–7.

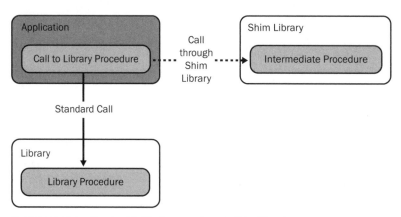

FIGURE 10–7 Application Verifier's operation via Shim libraries

The Application Verifier utility enables two scenarios for its usage: remotely through CETK and locally.

Let us look at the scenario of launching Application Verifier through CETK. After CETest.exe has been launched and a device connection has been established, as we described earlier, in the server-side dialog box, right-click the node corresponding to the device, and in the drop-down menu that appears, select Tools, and then select Application Verifier.

To ensure that this utility is working correctly, it is necessary to add, as a minimum, one module to validate that it is connected to the device. Therefore, in the dialog box that appears, it is necessary to click Close without connecting to the device, as shown in Figure 10–8.

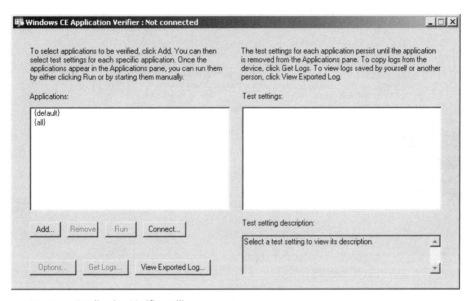

FIGURE 10–8 Application Verifier utility

Then add the module by clicking the Add button and specifying the module's file name.

After the test module has been added to the Applications list, connect to the device by clicking the Connect button. Before testing begins, you can choose what errors the module will be tested for. The software package is shipped with three Shim libraries, as follows:

- **Heap Verifier**   checks for memory leaks and heap corruption.

- **Handle Leak Tracker**   checks for unclosed file descriptors, synchronization objects, and so on.

- **Shell Verifier**   determines unreleased GDI objects.

The module is checked each time it is launched regardless of whether it was launched from the development and debugging tools or directly from the system's image.

After the test module has finished its operation, a log file is created in the device file system root. The log file can be loaded to the test station by clicking Get Logs. The utility is shipped with a convenient log file viewer that can be accessed by clicking View Exported Log, as shown in Figure 10–9.

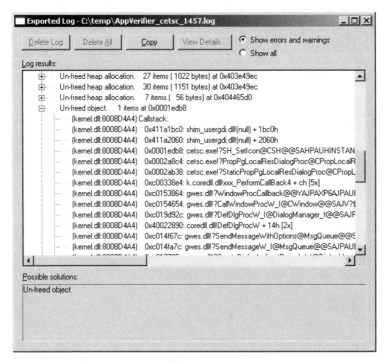

FIGURE 10–9 Viewing an exported log

To launch the Application Verifier utility directly on the device, it is necessary to copy the following files to the device:

- AppVerif.exe.
- Shim_heap.dll.
- Shim_verifier.dll.
- Shim_hleak.dll.
- Shim_usergdi.dll.
- Verifhlp.dll.

Then launch the executable file AppVerif.exe. When the utility is launched directly on the device, the same options are available as when it is launched by using the server-side CETK. The Application Verifier utility is extensible. The ShimGenUI.exe utility is used to create custom Shim libraries, as shown in Figure 10–10.

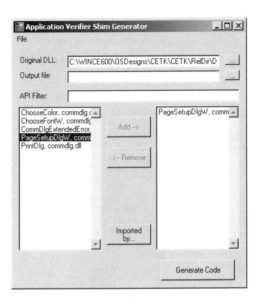

FIGURE 10–10 Shim library generator

After the utility is launched, specify the initial library in the Original DLL field; its function will be redirected to a Shim library. Next, from the list of all available functions of the library shown on the left pane, select the functions you need into the right pane. Clicking the Generate Code button will create initial template files. All that is left for the developer to do is to develop the selected functions and to build a Shim library.

CPU Monitor

The CPU Monitor utility is used to view the processor load and the use of memory on the device, as shown in Figure 10–11. It is launched from the server-side window of the CETK.

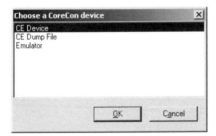

FIGURE 10–11 CPU Monitor utility

After CETest.exe has been launched and a device connection has been established, as described earlier, in the server-side dialog box, right-click the node corresponding to the device, and in the drop-down menu that appears, select Tools, and then select CPU Monitor. A dialog window appears where you will need to select a device and click OK.

Figure 10–12 shows what the CPU Monitor utility dialog window looks like after a connection to the device has been made. The information collected with the help of the CPU Monitor utility can be saved as a .TXT or an .XML file through the main utility's menu by selecting File, and then Save.

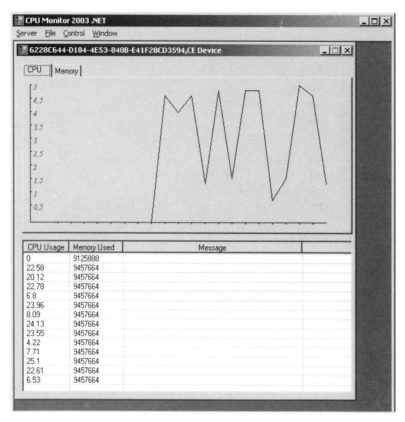

FIGURE 10–12 CPU Monitor utility dialog window

PerfToCsv

The PerfToCsv utility from the CETK test kit enables you to convert the log files of test results into comma-separated values (.csv) files so they can be viewed easily in a spreadsheet application, such as Microsoft Excel.

By default, this utility is located in the \Program Files\Microsoft Platform Builder\6.00\cepb\ wcetk\ddtk\desktop folder and is launched from the command-line prompt by using the following syntax:

```
PerfToCsv.exe <initial_log_file> <converted_file>.csv
```

Print Screen

The Print Screen utility is used to capture screen shots of the target CE device. The screen shots are saved as .bmp files. As opposed to the Remote Zoom utility, Print Screen enables you to do a screen capture without using a workstation.

In order to launch this utility, it needs to be manually copied to the device. Its executable file is called prt_scrn.exe which is located in the \Program Files\Microsoft Platform Builder\6.00\ cepb\wcetk\ddtk*<CPU_FAMILY>* folder.

The Print Screen utility is launched on the device from the command-line prompt by using the following syntax:

```
Prt_scrn [-d <number>] [-s <number1> <number2>] [-e <number1> <number2>] <screenshot_file_name>
```

Table 10–2 lists the parameters available with the Print Screen utility.

TABLE 10–2 Parameters available with the Print Screen utility.

Parameter	Description
-d *<number>*	Determines in what period of time in seconds after the utility is launched, a screen capture needs to be made.
-s *<number1> <number2>*	Sets horizontal and vertical coordinates of the upper left angle of a rectangular screen section for taking a screen capture. A default value is 0 0.
-e *< number1> <number2>*	Sets the position of the lower right angle of a rectangular screen section for taking a screen capture. A default value is the screen resolution (horizontal and vertical, respectively) minus 1.

Windows Embedded CE Stress Tool

To perform device stress-testing, the CETK provides the Windows CE Stress Tool utility that enables you to check the system's stability when it experiences pressure on certain functional blocks and when the system has insufficient resources.

The stress-testing utility utilizes the client-server architecture. This type of testing consists of randomly launching modules from a test kit during a certain period of time. Each module loads a certain functional block of the system. The utility supports the launch of its own test modules that implement a given interface. Figure 10–13 shows the Windows Embedded CE Stress Tool architecture.

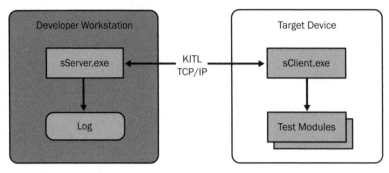

FIGURE 10–13 Windows Embedded CE Stress Tool architecture

When stress testing is performed without the use of CETK, it is necessary to copy the client-side files to the device manually. After that, you can launch the client-side and the server-side programs by using the switches appropriate for the connection type. A connection between a client and a server can be established through KITL or Transmission Control Protocol/Internet Protocol (TCP/IP) by using the required command-line switches for the appropriate connection type, as listed in Table 10–3.

TABLE 10–3 Command-line parameters to start stress-testing utilities.

Connection Type Settings	KITL	TCP/IP
Clientside – sClient.exe	AppKitl	tcp *<name or IP address of the server>*:0
Server-side – sServer.exe	-dev cetk	-dev cetk –prot TCP

The server-side interface is shown in Figure 10–14.

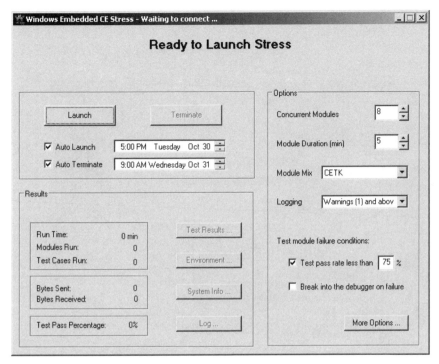

FIGURE 10–14 Server-side interface

The stress-testing parameters listed in Table 10–4 are set in the Windows Embedded CE Stress dialog window.

TABLE 10–4 Stress-testing parameters.

Parameter	Description
Auto Launch	Automatic launching of stress testing.
Auto Terminate	Automatic termination of stress testing.
Concurrent Modules	The number of concurrently launched modules.
Module Duration	The duration of each module's execution in minutes.
Module Mix	A set of modules launched during the process of stress testing. If CETK is selected, the program will launch all modules supported by the image.
Logging	Logging parameters.
Test module failure condition	Conditions that determine a test failure.
More Options	Additional settings for stress testing.

You can launch a stress test by clicking Launch. To terminate a stress test, click Terminate. The server-side program waits for launched tests to end. On the device screen, the testing process appears, as shown in Figure 10–15.

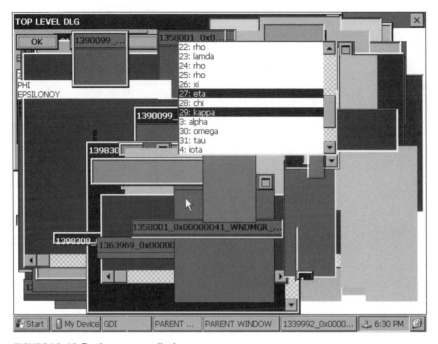

FIGURE 10–15 Testing process display

The results and configuration settings of a completed stress test are saved to an XML file in the \Program Files\Microsoft Platform Builder\6.00\cepb\wcetk\ddtk\desktop\Windows CE Stress\ directory.

Glossary

The glossary includes important terms used in the book and their definitions.

Access checking A check to verify that the caller process has permissions to access the buffer.

Application Logically grouped executable code.

Board Support Package (BSP) A BSP is the common name for all board hardware-specific code. It typically consists of the boot loader, the OEM adaptation layer (OAL), and board-specific device drivers.

Catalog A container of components that presents a selectable feature for an OS design to the user.

Component Smallest OS functional component that can be added to an OS design.

Device Manager Part of the system kernel responsible for working with stream interface drivers.

Embedded pointer Pointer that passes to an API function in a data structure or buffer.

Interrupt service routine (ISR) A small subroutine that resides in the OEM adaptation layer (OAL). The ISR executes in kernel mode and has direct access to the hardware registers. Its sole job is to determine what interrupt identifier to return to the interrupt support handler. Essentially, ISRs map physical interrupts onto logical interrupts.

Interrupt service thread (IST) A thread created by a device driver to wait on an event.

IRQ (Interrupt Request) IRQ values are associated in hardware with interrupts. Each IRQ value can be associated with one or more Interrupt Service Routines (ISRs) that the system will run to process the associated interrupt when it is triggered.

Kernel Debugger The kernel debugger integrates functionality required to configure a connection to a target device and download a run-time image to the target device. It allows the debugging of the Operating System, drivers, and applications.

Kernel Independent Transport Layer (KITL) The KITL is designed to provide an easy way to support debugging services.

Kernel-Mode Driver A driver that runs in the kernel's memory space.

Layered device driver A sample device driver that comes with the Platform Builder. It contains two layers: a model device driver (MDD) layer and a platform-dependent driver (PDD) layer.

Managed code Code written in C# or VB.NET for.NET Compact Framework.

Marshaling A process to check the access rights and validity of data for different processes.

Model device driver (MDD) The platform-neutral layer of a native device driver supplied by Microsoft.

Module A subset of the Windows CE operating system. Windows CE is structured as a collection of modules. Each module is a self-contained subset of the Windows CE operating system that can be used to construct a customized operating system for a particular device.

Native code Code written in ASM/C/C++ that uses the Win32 API.

OEM adaptation layer (OAL) An OAL is a layer of code that logically resides between the Windows Embedded CE kernel and the hardware of your target device. Physically, the OAL is linked with the kernel libraries to create the kernel executable file.

OS design A Platform Builder for Windows Embedded CE6 R2 project that generates a customized binary runtime image of the Windows Embedded CE6 R2 operating system

Platform Dependent Driver (PDD) The PDD layer of a layered driver is the part that interfaces directly with hardware and performs any hardware-specific processing.

Pointer parameter Pointer that is passed to an API function as a parameter.

Process A running application that consists of a private virtual address space, code, data, and other operating-system resources, such as files, pipes, and synchronization objects that are visible to the process. A process also contains one or more threads that run in the context of the process.

Production Quality OAL (PQOAL) The PQOAL is a standardized OAL structure that simplifies and shortens the process of developing an OAL. It provides you with an improved level of OAL

componentization through code libraries, directory structures that support code reuse, centralized configuration files, and a consistent architecture across processor families and hardware platforms.

Reflector service The service that enables user-mode drivers to access the kernel and hardware by performing requests on their behalf.

Run-time image The binary file that will be deployed on a hardware device . It also contains the complete operating system required files for applications and drivers.

Secure copy Local copy of a data buffer.

Stream interface driver A stream interface driver is any driver that exposes the stream interface functions, regardless of the type of device controlled by the driver. All drivers other than the native drivers managed by GWES export a stream interface.

Synchronization primitive/object An object that enables completion of synchronization tasks in a multithreaded environment.

Synchronous access Access to the buffer at the time of an API call.

Thread The smallest software unit that the scheduler can manage on the Operating System. There can be multiple threads in a single driver or application.

User-mode drivers Drivers loaded in user mode and all applications run in user memory space. When they are in this mode, drivers and applications do not have direct access to hardware memory and have restricted access to certain APIs and the kernel.

References

Building Solutions Using Windows Embedded CE 6.0 course

Course 2540N: *Building Embedded Solutions Using Windows CE 5.0*

Windows Embedded CE blog, http://blogs.msdn.com/ce_base/

Boling, Douglas. *Programming Windows Embedded CE 6.0 Developer Reference.* 4th Edition. Microsoft Press, 2007.

Wilson, Y. James, Aspi Havewala. *Building Powerful Platforms with Windows CE.* Addison-Wesley Professional, 2001.

Murray, John. *Inside Microsoft Windows CE* Microsoft Press, 1998.

Resources

Forums

- Russian-speaking forum dedicated to Microsoft embedded operating systems: http://www.msembedded.ru/forum

Blogs

- Windows Embedded CE team blog: http://blogs.msdn.com/ce_base

- .NET Compact Framework team blog: http://blogs.msdn.com/netcfteam

- HopperX blog, dedicated to device issues: http://blogs.msdn.com/hopperx/

- Mike Hall blog, dedicated to Microsoft embedded operating systems: http://blogs.msdn.com/mikehall/

- SQL Server Compact Edition team blog: http://blogs.msdn.com/sqlservercompact/

Newsgroups

- microsoft.public.windowsce.platbuilder

- microsoft.public.windowsce

- microsoft.public.pocketpc.developer

- microsoft.public.windowsce.embedded

Books

- Boling, Douglas. *Programming Windows Embedded 6.0 Developer Reference*. 4th Edition. Microsoft Press, 2007.

- Wilson Y., James and Aspi Havewala. *Building Powerful Platforms with Windows CE*. Addison-Wesley Professional, 2001.

- Murray, John. *Inside Microsoft Windows CE*. Microsoft Press, 1998.

Index

Symbol

N

O

P

Additional Resources for Developers: Advanced Topics and Best Practices

Published and Forthcoming Titles from Microsoft Press

Code Complete, Second Edition
Steve McConnell • ISBN 0-7356-1967-0

For more than a decade, Steve McConnell, one of the premier authors and voices in the software community, has helped change the way developers write code—and produce better software. Now his classic book, *Code Complete*, has been fully updated and revised with best practices in the art and science of constructing software. Topics include design, applying good techniques to construction, eliminating errors, planning, managing construction activities, and relating personal character to superior software. This new edition features fully updated information on programming techniques, including the emergence of Web-style programming, and integrated coverage of object-oriented design. You'll also find new code examples—both good and bad—in C++, Microsoft® Visual Basic®, C#, and Java, although the focus is squarely on techniques and practices.

More About Software Requirements: Thorny Issues and Practical Advice
Karl E. Wiegers • ISBN 0-7356-2267-1

Have you ever delivered software that satisfied all of the project specifications, but failed to meet any of the customers expectations? Without formal, verifiable requirements—and a system for managing them—the result is often a gap between what developers think they're supposed to build and what customers think they're going to get. Too often, lessons about software requirements engineering processes are formal or academic, and not of value to real-world, professional development teams. In this follow-up guide to *Software Requirements*, Second Edition, you will discover even more practical techniques for gathering and managing software requirements that help you deliver software that meets project and customer specifications. Succinct and immediately useful, this book is a must-have for developers and architects.

Software Estimation: Demystifying the Black Art
Steve McConnell • ISBN 0-7356-0535-1

Often referred to as the "black art" because of its complexity and uncertainty, software estimation is not as hard or mysterious as people think. However, the art of how to create effective cost and schedule estimates has not been very well publicized. *Software Estimation* provides a proven set of procedures and heuristics that software developers, technical leads, and project managers can apply to their projects. Instead of arcane treatises and rigid modeling techniques, award-winning author Steve McConnell gives practical guidance to help organizations achieve basic estimation proficiency and lay the groundwork to continue improving project cost estimates. This book does not avoid the more complex mathematical estimation approaches, but the non-mathematical reader will find plenty of useful guidelines without getting bogged down in complex formulas.

Debugging, Tuning, and Testing Microsoft .NET 2.0 Applications
John Robbins • ISBN 0-7356-2202-7

Making an application the best it can be has long been a time-consuming task best accomplished with specialized and costly tools. With Microsoft Visual Studio® 2005, developers have available a new range of built-in functionality that enables them to debug their code quickly and efficiently, tune it to optimum performance, and test applications to ensure compatibility and trouble-free operation. In this accessible and hands-on book, debugging expert John Robbins shows developers how to use the tools and functions in Visual Studio to their full advantage to ensure high-quality applications.

The Security Development Lifecycle
Michael Howard and Steve Lipner • ISBN 0-7356-2214-0

Adapted from Microsoft's standard development process, the Security Development Lifecycle (SDL) is a methodology that helps reduce the number of security defects in code at every stage of the development process, from design to release. This book details each stage of the SDL methodology and discusses its implementation across a range of Microsoft software, including Microsoft Windows Server™ 2003, Microsoft SQL Server™ 2000 Service Pack 3, and Microsoft Exchange Server 2003 Service Pack 1, to help measurably improve security features. You get direct access to insights from Microsoft's security team and lessons that are applicable to software development processes worldwide, whether on a small-scale or a large-scale. This book includes a CD featuring videos of developer training classes.

Software Requirements, Second Edition
Karl E. Wiegers • ISBN 0-7356-1879-8

Writing Secure Code, Second Edition
Michael Howard and David LeBlanc • ISBN 0-7356-1722-8

CLR via C#, Second Edition
Jeffrey Richter • ISBN 0-7356-2163-2

For more information about Microsoft Press® books and other learning products,
visit: **www.microsoft.com/mspress** *and* **www.microsoft.com/learning**

Microsoft®
Press

Additional Resources for Web Developers

Published and Forthcoming Titles from Microsoft Press

Microsoft® Visual Web Developer™ 2005 Express Edition: Build a Web Site Now!
Jim Buyens • ISBN 0-7356-2212-4

With this lively, eye-opening, and hands-on book, all you need is a computer and the desire to learn how to create Web pages now using Visual Web Developer Express Edition! Featuring a full working edition of the software, this fun and highly visual guide walks you through a complete Web page project from set-up to launch. You'll get an introduction to the Microsoft Visual Studio® environment and learn how to put the light-weight, easy-to-use tools in Visual Web Developer Express to work right away—building your first, dynamic Web pages with Microsoft ASP.NET 2.0. You'll get expert tips, coaching, and visual examples at each step of the way, along with pointers to additional learning resources.

Microsoft ASP.NET 2.0 Programming
Step by Step
George Shepherd • ISBN 0-7356-2201-9

With dramatic improvements in performance, productivity, and security features, Visual Studio 2005 and ASP.NET 2.0 deliver a simplified, high-performance, and powerful Web development experience. ASP.NET 2.0 features a new set of controls and infrastructure that simplify Web-based data access and include functionality that facilitates code reuse, visual consistency, and aesthetic appeal. Now you can teach yourself the essentials of working with ASP.NET 2.0 in the Visual Studio environment—one step at a time. With *Step by Step*, you work at your own pace through hands-on, learn-by-doing exercises. Whether you're a beginning programmer or new to this version of the technology, you'll understand the core capabilities and fundamental techniques for ASP.NET 2.0. Each chapter puts you to work, showing you how, when, and why to use specific features of the ASP.NET 2.0 rapid application development environment and guiding you as you create actual components and working applications for the Web, including advanced features such as personalization.

Programming Microsoft ASP.NET 2.0
Core Reference
Dino Esposito • ISBN 0-7356-2176-4

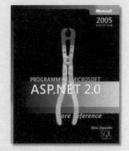

Delve into the core topics for ASP.NET 2.0 programming, mastering the essential skills and capabilities needed to build high-performance Web applications successfully. Well-known ASP.NET author Dino Esposito deftly builds your expertise with Web forms, Visual Studio, core controls, master pages, data access, data binding, state management, security services, and other must-know topics—combining defini-tive reference with practical, hands-on programming instruc-tion. Packed with expert guidance and pragmatic examples, this *Core Reference* delivers the key resources that you need to develop professional-level Web programming skills.

Programming Microsoft ASP.NET 2.0
Applications: *Advanced Topics*
Dino Esposito • ISBN 0-7356-2177-2

Master advanced topics in ASP.NET 2.0 programming—gaining the essential insights and in-depth understanding that you need to build sophisticated, highly func-tional Web applications success-fully. Topics include Web forms, Visual Studio 2005, core controls, master pages, data access, data binding, state management, and security considerations. Developers often discover that the more they use ASP.NET, the more they need to know. With expert guidance from ASP.NET authority Dino Esposito, you get the in-depth, comprehensive information that leads to full mastery of the technology.

Programming Microsoft Windows® Forms
Charles Petzold • ISBN 0-7356-2153-5

Programming Microsoft Web Forms
Douglas J. Reilly • ISBN 0-7356-2179-9

CLR via C++
Jeffrey Richter with Stanley B. Lippman
ISBN 0-7356-2248-5

Debugging, Tuning, and Testing Microsoft .NET 2.0 Applications
John Robbins • ISBN 0-7356-2202-7

CLR via C#, Second Edition
Jeffrey Richter • ISBN 0-7356-2163-2

For more information about Microsoft Press® books and other learning products,
visit: **www.microsoft.com/books** *and* **www.microsoft.com/learning**

Security Books for Developers
Published and Forthcoming Titles

The Security Development Lifecycle: Demonstrably More-Secure Software
Michael Howard and Steve Lipner
ISBN 9780735622142

Your software customers demand—and deserve—better security and privacy. This book is the first to detail a rigorous, proven methodology that measurably minimizes security bugs: the Security Development Lifecycle (SDL). Two experts from the Microsoft® Security Engineering Team guide you through each stage and offer best practices for implementing SDL in any size organization.

Developing More-Secure Microsoft ASP.NET 2.0 Applications
Dominick Baier
ISBN 9780735623316

Advance your security-programming expertise for ASP.NET 2.0. A leading security expert shares best practices, pragmatic instruction, and code samples in Microsoft Visual C#® to help you develop Web applications that are more robust, more reliable, and more resistant to attack. Includes code samples on the Web.

Writing Secure Code for Windows Vista™
Michael Howard and David LeBlanc
ISBN 9780735623934

Written as a complement to the award-winning book *Writing Secure Code*, this new reference focuses on the security enhancements in Windows Vista. Get first-hand insights into design decisions, and practical approaches to real-world security challenges. Covers ACLs, BitLocker™, firewalls, authentication, and other essential topics, and includes C# code samples on the Web.

Hunting Security Bugs
Tom Gallagher, Bryan Jeffries, Lawrence Landauer
ISBN 9780735621879

Learn to think like an attacker—with insights from three security testing experts. This book offers practical guidance and code samples to help find, classify, and assess security bugs *before* your software is released. Discover how to test clients and servers, detect spoofing issues, identify where attackers can directly manipulate memory, and more.

Writing Secure Code, Second Edition
Michael Howard and David LeBlanc
ISBN 9780735617223

Discover how to padlock applications throughout the entire development process—from designing applications and writing robust code to testing for security flaws. The authors—two battle-scarred veterans who have solved some of the industry's toughest security problems—share proven principles, strategies, and techniques, with code samples in several languages.

The Practical Guide to Defect Prevention
Marc McDonald, Robert Musson, Ross Smith
ISBN 9780735622531

Microsoft® Windows® Presentation Foundation Developer Workbook
Billy Hollis
ISBN 9780735624184

Developing Drivers with the Microsoft Windows Driver Foundation
Microsoft Windows Hardware Platform Evangelism Team
ISBN 9780735623743

Embedded Programming with the Microsoft .NET Micro Framework
Donald Thompson and Rob S. Miles
ISBN 9780735623651

See more resources at **microsoft.com/mspress**
and **microsoft.com/learning**

Microsoft®
Press

What do you think of this book?

We want to hear from you!

Do you have a few minutes to participate in a brief online survey?

Microsoft is interested in hearing your feedback so we can continually improve our books and learning resources for you.

To participate in our survey, please visit:

www.microsoft.com/learning/booksurvey/

...and enter this book's ISBN-10 or ISBN-13 number (located above barcode on back cover*). As a thank-you to survey participants in the United States and Canada, each month we'll randomly select five respondents to win one of five $100 gift certificates from a leading online merchant. At the conclusion of the survey, you can enter the drawing by providing your e-mail address, which will be used for prize notification only.

Thanks in advance for your input. Your opinion counts!

*Where to find the ISBN on back cover

ISBN-13: 000-0-0000-0000-0
ISBN-10: 0-0000-0000-0

Example only. Each book has unique ISBN.

Microsoft Press